PRINCIPLES OF GUIDANCE

GUIDANCE, COUNSELING, AND STUDENT PERSONNEL
IN EDUCATION

Walter F. Johnson, *Consulting Editor*

Arbuckle, *Counseling and Psychotherapy: An Overview*
Bailard and Strang, *Parent-Teacher Conferences*
Bennett, *Guidance and Counseling in Groups*
Berdie, *Testing in Guidance and Counseling*
Bernhardt, *Discipline and Child Guidance*
Detjen and Detjen, *Elementary School Guidance*
Downing, *Guidance and Counseling Services: An Introduction*
Hoppock, *Occupational Information*
Johnson, Stefflre, and Edelfelt, *Pupil Personnel and Guidance Services*
Jones, Stefflre, and Stewart, *Principles of Guidance*
Stefflre, *Theories of Counseling*
Warters, *Techniques of Counseling*
Williamson, *Vocational Counseling*

McGRAW-HILL SERIES IN EDUCATION

The Late Harold Benjamin   *Consulting Editor-in-Chief*

Arno A. Bellack   *Teachers College, Columbia Univesity*
Consulting Editor, Supervision, Curriculum, and Methods in Education
The Late Harold Benjamin   *Emeritus Professor of Education*
George Peabody College for Teachers
Consulting Editor, Foundations in Education
Walter F. Johnson   *Michigan State University*
Consulting Editor, Guidance, Counseling,
and Student Personnel in Education

PRINCIPLES OF GUIDANCE

Sixth Edition

ARTHUR J. JONES

Revised and updated by

BUFORD STEFFLRE
Professor of Education
Michigan State University

NORMAN R. STEWART
Associate Professor of Education
Michigan State University

McGRAW-HILL BOOK COMPANY
New York, St. Louis, San Francisco
London, Sydney, Toronto, Mexico, Panama

PRINCIPLES OF GUIDANCE

Library of Congress Catalog Card Number 77-75168
32999
1 2 3 4 5 6 7 8 9 0   MAMM   7 6 5 4 3 2 1 0 6 9

PREFACE

The junior authors have attempted to make this revision retain the point of view so long associated with Arthur J. Jones, while at the same time taking account of recent changes in the field of guidance. We hope this book remains one reflecting the character and insight of a great pioneer in guidance. It is still *his* book, and we are not presumptuous enough to lay claim to it. The chapter "Guidance in the Elementary School," which was written by Anna R. Meeks for the fifth edition, has been revised for this edition.

Arthur J. Jones (1871–1963) must be counted among those few who long ago saw the need for guidance and unerringly set its direction. After receiving his A.B. in 1893 from Grinnell College, where he was a member of Phi Beta Kappa, he remained there as an instructor until 1895. He then worked as a teacher, coach, and administrator in the public schools of Minnesota before going to Columbia University, where he received his Ph.D. in 1907. In that same year he joined the staff of the Rhode Island Normal School, where he remained until 1911. At that time he transferred to the University of Maine, where he taught for the next four years. In 1915 he joined the faculty of the University of Pennsylvania and remained there until 1941. During these twenty-six years he gained national fame as a spokesman for the new movement of guidance.

His book, *Principles of Guidance*, published in 1930, did much to give the emerging guidance movement shape and force. The many editions of the book indicate that his early views were sound and remained so.

He was president of the National Vocational Guidance Association in 1935–1936 and had much influence on that organization. Among his many honors were citations from the American Personnel and Guidance Association, the National Vocational Guidance Association, the B'nai B'rith, and a doctor of laws degree from Grinnell College, which was awarded in 1963.

This eminent guidance pioneer in 1962 wrote in his preface to the fifth edition to this book:

> When I reread the preface to the first edition to this book, published in 1930, I found myself in a world nearly as strange and primitive as that which saw the founding of the National Vocational Guidance Association in 1913. It seems almost impossible that so many changes have been made in these last thirty years. The tests used then would now be called unreliable and their validity questioned. Such terms as "counselor-centered" and "client-centered" were not in our professional vocabularies. Even the term "counseling" itself had but one brief mention, and then there was no discussion of training and certification. In spite of the differences between that time and this, it is comforting to remember that the basic concept of guidance has not changed. Then, as now, guidance implied a concern for *all* personal problems, not just those involved in a selection of a vocation.
>
> It is always inspiring to recall my old friends and coworkers, few of whom are now left. I remember especially Meyer Broomfield, John Brewer, Jesse Davis, Fred Smith, W. Carson Ryan, William Proctor, Edward Rynearson, F. J. Allen, Harry Kitson, George Myers, along with scores of others. Often we agreed, but sometimes we disagreed violently, although we always remained friends in spite of this.
>
> My only hope is that this edition will receive the same warm welcome that has been given to its predecessors.

That warm welcome was forthcoming and has led to this sixth edition, which attempts to perpetuate Jones's view of the basic principles of guidance and to apply them to areas of current concern. We hope we have interpreted his principles correctly and have accurately pointed out their relevance for contemporary problems.

Buford Stefflre

Norman R. Stewart

CONTENTS

FIVE   EMERGING GUIDANCE AREAS

PART ONE

Point of View

1

The Meaning and Function
of Guidance

Principles of guidance of necessity grow out of answers to such questions as "What is guidance?" "How does it help students?" and "What is its relationship to the other activities of the school?" Let us begin with the first question —"What is guidance?"

Guidance is the assistance given to individuals in making intelligent choices and adjustments. It is based on the democratic principle that it is the duty and the right of every individual to choose his own way in life insofar as his choice does not interfere with the rights of others. The ability to make such choices is not innate but, like other abilities, must be developed. One of the functions of education is to provide opportunities for the development of such abilities. Guidance is an integral part of education and is centered directly upon this function. Guidance does not make choices for individuals; it helps them make their own choices in such a way as to promote or stimulate the gradual development of the ability to make decisions independently without assistance from others.

The Meaning of Guidance

In its beginnings guidance was centered on problems related to vocations. It was largely concerned with getting jobs for young people. One of the reasons for this was to reduce juvenile delinquency. Teen-age boys and girls, many of them not in school, had nothing to do; they had time on their hands. Such a situation breeds delinquency.

Even in its beginning, however, the purpose of guidance was more than just finding jobs for youth. Much attention was given to a "wise" choice, that is, one that was suited to the abilities and needs of the individual. Although the vocational aspect has always been stressed, guidance has gone far beyond this; it is now concerned with the entire individual, in all aspects

3

of his life, and with the interrelation between the individual and society. It helps youth to attain a life that is individually satisfying and socially effective.

The Guidance Needs of Youth

Some individuals need guidance throughout their entire lives; others need help only during their youth or in unusually critical situations. The chief guidance responsibility of society is toward children and youth and those who, because of congenital defects, disease, accident, or political-social handicaps, do not have equal opportunities for activities that will satisfy their individual and social needs. Situations that call for guidance are varied and numerous. Guidance functions whenever choices are to be made and where help is needed in making intelligent decisions. Even when there is no choice possible, guidance may help the individual understand and accept the situation; that is, it may enable him to "cooperate with the inevitable." Guidance may also operate when the individual is not conscious that a choice is possible by pointing out the avenues that are open to him. In still other circumstances the time may not be favorable for making a choice because of fatigue, emotional strain, or influences that will make an intelligent decision unlikely. In such situations the best help may well be to suggest that only those decisions be made which are mandatory, leaving open as many as possible until a later, more favorable, time.

However, guidance is needed not just in crisis situations but should be available to normal youngsters coping with normal developmental problems. Developmental guidance is based on the premise that the aim of guidance is not merely the amelioration of trauma or the prevention of mistakes but rather the maximum development of the individual.

Choices are often made on the basis of a person's own past experience or that of others. A person may call to mind some choice that he or one of his friends made in a situation that seems similar to the present one. If what was done before was satisfactory, he might choose to make the same choice again; if the result was unsatisfactory, he might decide to do something else. Such a decision may result in a good choice or in a poor one. The two situations, although similar in some respects, may be very different in others. The choice may have been a good one once, but with the passage of time and with changed conditions, it may be quite unsatisfactory now. Guidance may help here by assisting the individual to examine the two situations carefully to see in what ways they are alike and in what ways they are different and by helping him to get a broader view of the possible choices.

It is often possible, even while still in high school, to get some preliminary experience in an occupation that is being considered. Jobs held after school, on Saturdays, holidays, and especially in the long summer vacations, provide helpful experience. Such jobs may be available in stores, in offices, on the farm, or elsewhere. The guidance value of such experience varies greatly and is dependent upon the attitude of the youth, the supervision given, and the physical and social environment of the job.

When youth attempt to use their own experiences as a basis for choice, they are handicapped by the fact that their experiences are neither extensive nor of great scope or variety. Choices made on such a basis are not likely to be good ones, but very often they do not see this danger. With youthful enthusiasm and undue confidence in their ability, they often make hasty and unwise decisions. Other avenues of lifework may begin to make a strong appeal to them in later years. They may realize too late that these avenues might well have offered success and satisfaction. The necessary training cannot now be secured without great financial sacrifice that would jeopardize the comfort and welfare of the family. Although they may realize that their early choices were unfortunate, they can do nothing about it now. Wise guidance could have been of great value by making them realize that their experience was too limited to give them proper perspective. It could have helped them review carefully the wide range of occupations within their interest and capabilities.

ADVICE AS GUIDANCE

Another very valuable source of help which is frequently used is the experience of others expressed through advice. The value of this source of guidance is clearly seen in the history of mankind. Man's superiority over the lower animals is due, in large measure, to his ability to profit not only from his own experience but from that of others; without this ability there would have been little progress. Such experience may be utilized either directly, through advice given by others, or indirectly, through a knowledge and understanding of history.

Although advice is an old and widely used method of guidance, some guidance authorities condemn it in any form, maintaining that it is harmful. They even go so far as to say that the only time it is safe to give advice to others is when you know they will not use it. This statement grossly exaggerates the dangers of advice and is plainly untrue. Industrial firms spend millions every year on advice, and it pays. Older men who have had years of experience either in the industry that employs them or in similar industries are used as consultants or advisers. The value of their services is evident in the large salaries given to such men. Throughout history sages have been singled out for great honor and reverence. The advice given by a person who has traveled the same way before may be very valuable; however, it can neither be rejected merely because it is old nor accepted just because it is old. The old Chinese dynasties stagnated because of the national credo "Walk in the trodden way," but some of the most valuable sources of help are found in the recorded thoughts and experiences of men and women of the past.

All aspects of the past—social, industrial, economic, scientific, artistic, and religious—have much to teach us. Such sources of understanding are too little used in our present programs of guidance. To be of any use the lessons of history must be read and interpreted not only in terms of the past but also in terms of the present. Teachers of English, history, science, art, and music can open up these sources of help and interpret them as well. The lessons of the past that are of the greatest value are those that state fundamental values of life and general principles of conduct. These lessons will help in many different situations because they usually do not indicate exactly what one should do but leave it to the individual to determine what definite action will be best. This is in accord with the principle that the purpose of guidance is the development in the individual of the ability to solve problems without the help of others. Conditions may have changed so much that the present problem is quite unlike the old one, and what was once a desirable solution may no longer be satisfactory.

Such changed conditions are especially likely to appear in affairs involving youth. The changed attitude of parents and teachers toward youth, the greater freedom given to youth, the new emphasis on self-determination, and the relaxing of discipline have profoundly altered the nature of the problems of young people. Today youth are far better informed on scientific, economic, and social conditions and developments than their parents were when they were of the same age. This development greatly increases the complexity and difficulty of the problems of youth and those of their parents who are trying to help them. In boy-girl relations the restrictions that were once thought desirable have in large part been removed, and some conduct which was once frowned upon is now considered acceptable. When the problem relates to the use by teen-agers of our modern high-powered and complex cars, advice based on the days of the horse and buggy or the Model T is entirely inappropriate. These changed conditions make skillful and well-organized guidance imperative. Guidance now calls for wide experience, deep wisdom, and infinite patience on the part of the one who counsels.

Advice is usually received best and carries more weight when the one who seeks it comes voluntarily to the counselor because he feels the need for help. Gratuitous advice is usually of little value because most people regard such proffered help as an intrusion on what they consider to be their own affair. Such advice is also often given without knowledge or consideration of the needs of the person advised.

In summary, one's own experience as well as that of others may be very valuable in guidance, but it may not be a safe guide in itself. To be of real value, experience must be interpreted in relation to the particular problem that is at hand. Is this problem the same as the one previously faced? Is the solution that was made in the past as satisfactory now as it was then? There may be differences, even though slight ones, in the present situation that may be very significant, thus making the solution that was once satisfactory quite unsatisfactory now. For example, action taken fifty years ago based on a certain religious belief may have been useful then, but it may be quite useless or even undesirable now. Even now two persons may have the same beliefs regarding the worth of the individual and his relation to God and yet be on opposite sides of a social problem. The previous family and social experience and the background of each person have a powerful influence on the belief which is held. Guidance must help young people to develop techniques of utilizing their own past experience and that of others for the solution of the problems facing them in making their adjustments in life.

DEFINITION OF GUIDANCE

Guidance is the help given by one person to another in making choices and adjustments and in solving problems. Guidance aims at aiding the recipient to grow in his independence and ability to be responsible for himself. It is a service that is universal—not confined to the school or the family. It is found in all phases of life—in the home, in business and industry, in government, in social life, in hospitals, and in prisons; indeed it is present wherever there are people who *need* help and wherever there are people who *can* help.

Guidance: Its Relation to Education

Very early in the guidance movement Brewer,[1] a consistent advocate of vocational guidance, recognized the close relationship between guidance and education. Throughout the years the nature of this relationship has been a source of much concern and controversy. The different points of view are largely owing to differences in the meaning of the term "education." "Education" may be used to mean (1) the process of changes that take place within the individual, (2) instruction, or (3) the conscious effort of society to guide the individual so that he will be able to live a life that will be socially effective and individually satisfying. To make clear the relationship

[1] John M. Brewer, *Education as Guidance*, The Macmillan Company, New York, 1955.

between guidance and education each of these meanings needs to be examined more closely.

EDUCATION IS THE PROCESS BY WHICH THE INDIVIDUAL CHANGES

From this point of view education is essentially a process; it is something that takes place *in individuals*; it is the process by which changes are made in the individual or, better, by which the individual makes changes in himself. At birth human beings are the most helpless of all animals. They are absolutely dependent upon others for their very existence. For long years they must be fed, cared for, and protected in order to preserve life and to ensure normal growth and development. Man is much less adjusted by nature to his physical environment than any other animal. He must learn to walk, to eat, to make those adjustments that are necessary to cope with physical nature. Habits must be formed, skills developed, and facts learned before it is safe for him to go out into the world alone. Since he is not naturally suited to his physical environment, changes must be made in him before he can be adjusted.

If this is true of his physical environment, it is much more so of his social environment. Man's physical nature and equipment have remained practically unchanged for centuries. His stature, his features, his brain are essentially the same now as they were when the great pyramids were built. Although man essentially has not changed, the structure of society has become tremendously complex. Social demands have so far outstripped man's physical nature that the gap between the social plane of the infant and that of the adult is very wide—impossible to cross, in fact, without assistance. As civilization advances, the gap is ever widening. The method by which the infant is enabled to bridge this gap, to raise himself from the social plane of childhood to that of manhood, is education. This is accomplished by certain changes that are made by the individual so that he acts in appropriate and desirable ways to situations that confront him. The number of changes and their quality are such as to require long years and special techniques for their development. Education is, then, the process by which the individual makes these necessary changes.

From this point of view education is essentially and wholly an *individual* process. It is some change that takes place in the individual as a result of something that *he* does. It is "the upbuilding of a world in feeling or consciousness."

Each individual builds for himself the world in which he lives. His images, his memories, his thoughts and feelings, his ideals are formed from his own experience—what he himself does. They are his own, and no one can share them; nor can anyone take them away against his will. When we view education from this standpoint, there can be no guidance, for guidance implies assistance given by someone to the one who is educating himself. Insofar as the individual is really self-educated, there is no guidance; however, if we think of education as resulting only from what the individual himself does—if he is the active agent—what is the relation of instruction to this process?

EDUCATION IS INSTRUCTION

The teacher knows the ends to be accomplished; in this he is merely the agent of society. He also knows the best ways by which these ends may be attained, that is, by which effective learning may be achieved by the pupil. His role in the older conception of teaching was comparatively clear and simple.

1. He had to have definitely in mind what was to be learned, but it was relatively unimportant for the pupil to know this.
2. He had to have, in the form of textbooks, materials, outlines, problems, etc., stimuli that were calculated to result in the desired responses by the pupil.
3. He had to see that the pupil made the responses desired. If the pupil made responses other than the desirable ones, he was compelled by punishment or other means to make the "correct" ones.
4. He had to test for product, skill, habit, attitude, etc., and see that the end had actually been attained.

All this made the teacher the active and to a large extent the determining factor in learning. Much teaching is still of this kind; it is directed mainly at forcing the child to learn. Still too frequently the learner is considered inert or even stubborn and not actively interested in or concerned with learning.

But even this more or less mechanical teacher-controlled process is not so simple as it may seem. The child is, even here, a very important and an extremely variable factor. Situations in the classroom are not simple. They are composed of many different stimuli; some of these are the selected stimuli provided by the teacher, but others are supplied by many factors in the immediate environment of the pupil, including the pupil himself. The child can and often does choose from among the stimuli that make up the situation the one to which he responds. He may single out the teacher's prominent nose, her gaudy dress, the wasp in the window, or any one of a dozen things to which he gives attention and to which he responds, rather than the words of the teacher or the material in his textbook.

Efficient education requires not only that a person respond to a stimulus but that he select the desirable groups of stimuli to which he responds—desirable, that is, from the standpoint of society. Again, even though he singles out the desired stimulus, he may respond to it in many different ways. Suppose he is studying the products of South America. He reads the words in his book describing them; these words are the stimuli. What responses does he make? He may go off into a daydream of voyaging on the high seas, of pirates and Spanish galleons; or he may plan a hiking trip on which he will take along some of the products mentioned. There are many ways of responding that may seem much more desirable to him than the responses that the teacher wishes and that are demanded if he is to learn what the products of South America are.

To the teacher trained in the older method these variable responses are extremely annoying; they must be eliminated if possible. The methods used in eliminating them constitute what some regard as guidance, since, in a sense, these rewards and punishments direct the learner. But they are in fact entirely teacher-directed and teacher-controlled; the individual himself has no part in the planning; he is passive; there is no choice. It is, therefore, not guidance as we here consider the process.

Happily, this method is rapidly giving way to one that is not only fundamentally more sound but more effective as well. In the new method, teaching is thought of as helping the child to learn. The child is the active agent in the process. As before, the teacher still determines for the most part the ends to be achieved, although even here there may be pupil cooperation; but he also assists the pupil to understand the ends and to accept them as his own. Assistance, so directed, is guidance. If the pupil is able to select his aims, if, after understanding and accepting the ends, the pupil is able to see by himself what he must do to accomplish the ends, the teacher steps aside; no teaching and no guidance are necessary. Whenever, in the learning process, the teacher *assists the learner to choose*, guidance is present.

There is also another way in which guidance enters into the process of education. The teacher, as an agent of society, sets up ends to be accomplished by the pupil, but the method by which different pupils reach the ends may vary. Reaching the ends is important; the method by which the ends are reached is relatively unimportant, except that it should be the method best suited to the individual pupil. Choices in method are often, if not always, possible. The efficient teacher is continually trying to help the pupil find the one that is best suited to him. When the teacher selects the method, there is teaching but no guidance; when he assists the learner to choose a method, guidance is present.

Whenever, in the process of accomplishing the ends (that is, in learning), the pupil needs help, it is the teacher's function to give it. This help is usually stimuli in the form of outlines, references, suggestions, leading questions, expressions of approval and disapproval, incentives, and anything else that may help the pupil to learn. This is teaching or instruction; it may or may not be guidance. Teaching conceived of as assisting the learner to *choose* ends or methods is guidance.

EDUCATION AS SOCIALIZATION

Society makes a conscious effort to guide and direct the physical, mental, emotional, and moral growth of the individual in order that he will be able to live a life that will be socially effective and individually satisfying. In this broader concept of education, guidance and education are closely related.

This statement does not satisfy the ultraprogressive educator who reacts strongly against any form of control of individual development by society and who contends that the only object of education is the development of the individual. This development is to be determined not by what society wants but by some inward force or law or principle which, if followed, will result in the maximum or optimum development of each individual. Nor will it satisfy the ultraconservative who emphasizes the need for social efficiency as opposed to mere individual development. Each of these elements must, of course, be present, but they should be complementary, not antagonistic. This concept of education might seem to make guidance and education synonymous both when we stress the development of the individual for himself as an end and when we emphasize the needs of society, for education is thought of as the conscious effort of society to assist the individual.

It should be noted, however, that the important words in this sentence are not "the conscious effort of society," but "assist the individual," and the role of society in the education of individuals may not be "assistance" in the real sense. When society merely determines what shall be taught and does nothing to assist the individual—when the individual is thought of as passive —guidance is not present except in a very indirect and remote way. In a sense the entire conscious effort of society to see that the individual reaches certain goals set up by society is assistance. The physical and social environment which is selected and organized by society for the purpose of making sure that the child will develop properly, the curriculum, the textbooks, library, and laboratories, the organized life of the school, all are instrumental in making sure that the pupil develops in certain ways. The habits and skills developed, the interests and attitudes formed, all are powerful factors. This is, at best, a very mechanical and deterministic kind of assistance. In one sense it is not really assistance at all, for assistance implies more or less independent action on the part of the individual, that is, the enlistment of the individual in the enterprise. In the same sense we could say that we assist the plant to grow by watering it; we assist the post to stand upright by digging a hole and placing the post in it; we assist the boy to be clean by washing his face. This is a misinterpretation of the term "assistance." This mechanical assistance, even though it helps to determine the development of the individual and may materially affect his choices, can hardly be guidance, for it leaves out the all-important part that the individual himself plays in the process.

This broader concept of education includes guidance only when the modern, progressive viewpoint of the place and function of the individual is accepted. When only the goals of society are considered, we may have education but not guidance, for guidance implies assistance in making choices. These choices are individual ones and imply a compromise between, or a synthesis of, the needs of society and the needs of the individual. There are certain situations in education where the element of choice by the individual is prominent, and there are others in which it is not.

GUIDANCE AND PURPOSIVE LIVING

If one views the life of the individual as a whole, guidance may be said to have as its purpose helping the individual to discover his needs, to assess his potentialities, gradually to develop life goals that are individually satisfying and socially desirable, to formulate plans of action in the service of these goals, and to proceed to their realization.

This statement clearly identifies the purpose of guidance with that of education. It places major emphasis upon the development of the whole individual who is now functioning and who will function in the future in a social environment. It is a useful concept because it stresses the unity of one's life and shows the impossibility of separating one aspect of life from another. It is based upon the belief that each of us builds up, step by step, a life purpose or goal which serves or should serve as a center of integration for our desires and ambitions and as a guide for our plans. One of the most vital elements in our efforts to educate individuals is the assistance we give in connection with choosing and developing these life purposes or goals. From this point of view guidance and education are seen to share the same purpose and sometimes the same methods.

EDUCATION IS DISTINGUISHED FROM GUIDANCE

There are still a few people who regard education and guidance as separate and distinct, but their number is rapidly diminishing. Such a complete separation is impossible; it violates the essential nature of both elements. The differences of opinion now are chiefly between those who would make guidance and education synonymous terms and those who regard guidance as an aspect and an essential element in education. The reason for this controversy is found partly in the different meanings attached to the term "education" and partly in the failure to distinguish between the parts played by the teacher and by the learner in the process of education.

The position taken by the authors is that guidance is found in that area of educational endeavor which involves assistance given by agencies or persons to the individual in making choices and in helping him choose a line of action, a method of procedure, a goal. It is not choosing *for* him or directing his choice; it is helping him to make the choice.

Education deals with the entire scope of human development. From one standpoint it is the conscious effort of society to change and develop the individual so that he may conform to society, take his place in it, improve it, and in doing this secure his own optimum development. From another standpoint it is the conscious effort of the individual to adjust himself to his physical and social environment, to improve it, and so to secure his own highest development.

Here are two forces, the individual and society, working for the same ends. When society merely determines what will be learned and how it will be learned and does nothing to secure the cooperation of the individual in the choice of things to be learned or methods to be used, guidance is not present, for there is no choice by the individual. Society in general and the teacher in particular may need to influence or direct the growth of the individual since wise choices in later life are dependent to a large extent upon habits and attitudes formed in early years. This might be considered good education, but it is not guidance. On the other hand the individual may consciously attempt to establish a goal without help. When he does this, guidance is not present. Although education may, and often does, take place through the effort and initiation of the individual alone, the same thing is true as above: this is education but not guidance. It is only when the cooperation of the individual is secured and assistance given him in choosing his goals or his methods that guidance is present. All guidance is education, but some aspects of education are not guidance; their objectives are the same—the development of the individual—but the methods used in education are by no means the same as those used in guidance.

Guidance: Its Relation to Discipline

A peculiar phobia appears in some guidance leaders when they consider the relation of guidance to discipline. Apparently they fear that any contact with discipline will interfere with the success of guidance workers. This fear is quite unwarranted and arises largely from misunderstandings. Guidance functions in all sorts of problem situations, past, present, or future.

It is help given or received by all personnel in the school system—super-intendent, supervisor, specialist, teacher, custodial worker, student. It is found wherever there are problems to be solved in teaching, in supervision, in discipline. In fact discipline offers one of the most useful and rewarding areas for guidance.

The confusion of these leaders is best resolved by examining the meanings which may be attached to the term "discipline." Discipline has two different but related meanings. First, discipline is a planned series of activities or exercises considered necessary for the attainment of a certain goal. An example is the training of an athlete for a race or for some other athletic contest. This meaning would include the development of regular exercise, eating, and sleeping habits as well as certain restrictions. Another example of this meaning is the college curriculum leading to a degree. In this first sense discipline also means a set of rules or laws affecting conduct such as the discipline of the church, the law, or medicine. This meaning may be called "positive" discipline.

Second, discipline means punishment for conduct that is considered undesirable. Failure to achieve a required standard in school, for example, may result in punishment, or discipline. The punishment may also be the natural result of undesirable conduct such as the "morning after" a "binge" or failure in a contest because of breaking training. This meaning may be called "negative" discipline. Its purpose is to prevent conduct that is undesirable. It is intended to help the individual understand what is necessary to attain the goal and to motivate him to keep to the exercises and the rules that have been set up.

It will be seen that the two meanings of discipline are closely related and that guidance has a unique function in both of them. Guidance helps set the goal and develop a program of activities leading to it. It also encourages and motivates the individual to keep at the activities and exercises that are essential in attaining the desired end.

GUIDANCE AS PUNISHMENT

When discipline means punishment by some authority for unacceptable behavior, guidance may help the student to understand why the behavior is unacceptable. Elementary school is not too early to help students to understand the function of punishment as seen in the history of human society and to comprehend what their community would be without laws leading to the punishment of offenders.

The responsibility for assistance to students in cases of discipline, in both its positive and its negative meanings, may rest upon any school personnel. Teachers have responsibility in this area because they deal directly with that part of the curriculum which is allotted to them. They are responsible for helping the pupils in their classes or subject areas to understand the educational content, to do the exercises required, to attain the desired goals. They must provide the motivation necessary for the attainment of the objectives and administer such punishments as may be necessary for failure to study or to achieve academically. In addition each teacher is responsible for the behavior of the children in his class and to a large extent for their attendance and health. Without a doubt the chief responsibility for all these guidance services rests upon the teacher.

PREVENTIVE GUIDANCE

By far the most effective discipline is that which operates before the crisis occurs and helps the student to understand and accept the type of behavior that is demanded by the school. In most cases discipline of this kind helps the student to realize what is required and therefore makes punishment unnecessary. Here the teacher is the most important factor, but the counselor may also be of real assistance. This type of discipline is not always possible, however, because one cannot always foresee the approaching crisis. Furthermore, not every crisis can be prevented. When a crisis does come, the student is in dire need of help, and the counselor has a clear responsibility to give him help.

ROLE OF THE COUNSELOR IN DISCIPLINE

Authorities in the field of guidance agree that the counselor should not be charged with the responsibility for the administration of punishment because by so doing, he may make it difficult to establish and maintain the rapport that is so essential for counseling and guidance. Experience amply confirms this opinion, but this does not mean that the counselor never has any responsibility in the field of discipline. In fact, discipline offers one of the richest and most rewarding areas for guidance.

Just as the counselor should not be involved in the actual punishment of the student, neither should he be the "lawyer for the defense" and seek to free him from punishment. If he has established rapport with the student, however, he may be able to find out why the misdemeanor was committed. He may discover what the student wished to accomplish by the act and help him to understand why his purpose was undesirable and what the effect of such behavior would be on other students and on the school.

The counselor can often help the guilty student to realize and frankly confess that his act was undesirable and to accept his punishment as well deserved. Thus it can be seen that the counselor may have a definite responsibility in cases of discipline and may be able to make a real contribution to the student and to the school by helping the student to understand and modify his antisocial behavior. In summary, guidance and discipline are closely related, and the counselor's role, even though it does not involve the administering of punishment, is both clear and unique.

Guidance: Its Relation to Other Educational Specialties

One of the most important developments in the field of education during the past century has been the increased specialization in educational services. Among the first specialties to emerge were the four large areas of teaching, counseling, administration, and supervision. More recently the specialized services of the physician, the psychologist, the psychiatrist, the dentist, the social worker, and the health educator have been recognized as important to education.

Additionally, we now see the subject-matter supervisor, the curriculum coordinator, and the remedial expert coming into our schools and performing useful functions needed in a complex educational setting. Each specialty has a distinct title and often requires a definite course of training leading to a certificate issued by the state or by some professional organization of high standing; each one also has a fairly definite core of work and responsibility. Each employs some techniques that are especially characteristic of the specialty. These characteristics and requirements have given a clear and definite professional status to the many educational specialties. Such specialization has some disadvantages and dangers, but there can be no doubt that it has greatly increased the effectiveness of the entire educational system.

Although each of these areas has a definite responsibility for certain services and uses characteristic techniques and thus makes its own contribution to the overall program of education, the lines separating one area of service from another are not entirely clear and distinct. There is considerable overlapping in objectives, in content, and in the techniques used.

The interrelation and overlapping in objectives and techniques may be seen by a brief discussion of the four large areas of service previously mentioned. Teaching is concerned with helping students to learn. Counseling deals with helping students to develop the ability to solve their own problems. Supervision is responsible for providing leadership in improving instruction. Administration is concerned with the control, direction, and management of the school, that is, the provision of conditions favorable for learning.

COMMON OBJECTIVES

It is clear that the basic services of the school are found in teaching and counseling since both deal directly with the individual student, his problems, and his needs. The function of administration and supervision is to promote the effectiveness of teaching and counseling. All four areas are bound together by the same objectives. Each should supplement, assist, and increase the effectiveness of the other areas in helping students to develop those habits, skills, attitudes, and ideals that will enable them to adjust to modern democratic society and attain a life that will be worthwhile.

COMMON TECHNIQUES

Although there are techniques that are characteristic of each area, they may be used in other areas as well. For example, each of the four areas is concerned with help in learning, and the techniques of teaching are available to all educational specialists and are used by them. Every member of the school staff faces situations that involve face-to-face counseling, and therefore all should use the special techniques of counseling. Many principals and superintendents fail in their dealings with teachers and parents because they do not know the techniques of counseling, and many teachers fail in their relations with students for the same reason.

Some define teaching as helping the child to learn and say that it is fundamentally guidance, since guidance is assistance to individuals in meeting new situations, in solving problems, and in making adjustments. Some of these problems are related to occupations, others to social relations, and still others to the mastery of school subjects. Some of the most important problems of children are connected with learning to read and write, to understand arithmetic skills, to comprehend and appreciate literature. A paraphrase of the standard definition of vocational guidance might be as follows: "Instructional guidance is the assistance given to individuals in understanding and accepting responsibility for the development of skills, in providing situations favorable for learning, in developing the desire to learn, and in making progress in learning."

Some of the best guidance and the most effective counseling is given by skilled teachers to pupils in their classes. At one time or another every teacher has pupils come to him with problems relating to out-of-school, family, or religious difficulties. It is quite natural for students to seek help on such problems; the teacher has, or should have, close contact with students, for he meets them much more frequently than the counselor. He knows, or should know, about previous difficulties, home conditions, financial problems, and other matters that have troubled them. Whether the teacher is able to give the needed help or not, he cannot refuse to confer with a pupil; if he is a real teacher, he must be interested in him and in his problem. Every teacher should know what general methods to employ in finding out what the real problem is, and he should make the pupils feel that he cares. He should be able and willing to recognize his own limitations and, when necessary, to refer the student to the counselor or someone else who may be better qualified to help him. He should know the best ways of making such referrals because they are among the most important elements in guidance. He should prepare the student for the referral conference by pointing out that the counselor is able and willing to help him. At the same time he should retain his own interest in the student and make him feel that he will always be ready to confer with him.

Because even the most skilled teacher is not able to give adequate assistance to all pupils for whom he is responsible or to deal successfully with all types of problems, there is now, and always will be, a definite need for well-trained and competent counselors in the elementary and secondary schools. These counselors should be consultants to teachers and parents, helping them to deal with more difficult cases. They should also be resource personnel, assuming responsibility for more difficult problems and for special cases. In the teamwork method which will be described later, the counselor might well be the chairman or leader of the group.

NECESSARY TEAMWORK

There are still some authorities who seem to believe that such overlapping in objectives and techniques is very undesirable. In their efforts to develop and maintain a special professional status for the counselor, they contend that counseling is the sole prerogative of the counselor and that teaching is the prerogative of the teacher. They believe that, when a teacher attempts to counsel a student, he steps out of his role as a teacher and becomes a counselor and that, when a counselor teaches, he becomes a teacher and is no longer a counselor. This idea is the result of the unfortunate confusion in the use of the two terms. The word "counseling" is used both for a technique and for an area of service (that of the counselor); "teaching" is also used to indicate a technique and a position (that of the teacher). The counselor often employs the technique of teaching in addition to others, and the teacher uses many techniques, one of which is counseling. But the teacher does not become a counselor because of this. He does not have the training or the assigned role of a counselor. When a mother uses first aid for her child, she uses one of the techniques of a physician; but this does not make her one. Neither teaching techniques nor counseling techniques are the sole property of any one area of educational service.

The fact that every service in the school involves the techniques of teaching, counseling, and other educational skills is of extreme importance. It should serve to emphasize the pressing need for planned cooperation among all school services. It also means that in the preparation of administrators, supervisors, teachers, and counselors there should be sufficient emphasis both on teaching techniques, so that all can teach well, and on counseling techniques, so that all can give effective guidance.

Guidance as an Organized Function

GUIDANCE INHERENT IN THE ENTIRE SCHOOL

It is apparent that guidance is inherent in every part of the school which is concerned with assisting the pupil to make choices, adjustments, and interpretations. Any attempt to confine it to a given area of assistance or to restrict its function to a particular group of the school staff is certain to fail. Such an attempt to simplify the situation by an arbitrary division of the complex whole into separate parts inevitably sacrifices the unity of the process and results in greater confusion. Guidance involves all types of choices and must include within its scope the curriculum, teaching, supervision, and all other activities of the school. The classroom teacher can no more be divorced from guidance than can the counselor; in many ways he is fundamentally more important. On the other hand, to identify all guidance with the teacher would be equally fatal. Adequate guidance requires the cooperation of the whole school staff—administrators, teachers, personnel workers, and specialists.

AREAS OF CHOICE NOT PROVIDED FOR BY THE SCHOOL

Must we, then, spread the work of guidance throughout the school with no attempt to coordinate it or to provide specialized services? Is there no place for a department of guidance more or less separate from the work of the classroom teacher and the principal but coordinated with them? To the latter question we must emphatically answer that there is such a place. There are various categories of problems, choices, and adjustments that should be adequately provided for in schools. Some of the most important of these arise at crucial places in the educational progress of the pupil, such as (1) the end of the compulsory attendance age; (2) the completion of elementary school; (3) the beginning of junior high school; (4) the completion of junior high school; (5) the entrance to senior high school; (6) the completion of senior high school; (7) the entrance to college; (8) the leaving of school at any time; (9) the taking up of an occupation.

The choices and adjustments at these times are of extreme importance and call for special forms of assistance. Many facts necessary for an intelligent choice can be provided in the ordinary school; many habits, attitudes, and ideals needed can be taught. In proportion as the school is organized with these needs in view, to that extent will the special work of guidance in providing for information, habits, attitudes, and interests be reduced. If properly planned, any type of organization should allow ample opportunity to give special attention to ways in which needed information can be made available and assistance given.

SPECIAL CRISES REQUIRING REORGANIZATION OF MATERIAL

Many choices and problems of adjustment to school and work require a reorganization of information already obtained from classroom activities as well as a selection from among the facts at hand. Such reorganization and selection are often very difficult and, without assistance, beyond the power of the individual. They sometimes involve factors other than the individual himself. Difficulties that arise in school or occupation or home not infrequently are due to clash of personalities or to a complexity of conditions. Adjustment involves not only the individual himself but other people and other factors as well; it is not something that he can work out by himself alone. It can be accomplished only by cooperative effort, and this cannot be left to haphazard activity. Such cooperation must be planned.

PROBLEM CASES

The aim of guidance is to develop individuals so that they will be able to solve their own problems as far as this is possible. But even the best efforts of the school will not result in the entire elimination of problem cases. There will always be occasions when every student will need special assistance, and it is probable that some students will continually need help. Special facilities must be provided for meeting these needs.

SCOPE OF AN ORGANIZED GUIDANCE PROGRAM

Some superintendents and principals believe that no specialized personnel is necessary for guidance, that the classroom teacher can provide all the assistance needed, and that it is the function of the principal to provide for coordination of effort. This attitude is due in part to the very real danger that the provision of a separate guidance department may result in the teachers' feeling that *all* guidance functions will and should be performed by the counselors and that they themselves have no guidance responsibilities. In some cases this attitude is due to the failure of the principal or superintendent to understand fully what the function of guidance is. Some of this confusion could be avoided if we called the specialized department "personnel work" instead of "guidance." Guidance is a function of the entire school; the function of the department of personnel work is to coordinate the guidance activities of the school and to supplement these activities by specialized work. This department would also have the responsibility of keeping constantly before the rest of the staff the need for assistance in areas that are likely to be neglected and of stimulating all to more effective action. In some schools and colleges this department is called "student services" and is coordinate with administration and instruction. The scope and function of any specially organized department of guidance or pupil personnel in the school system will depend upon the effectiveness with which the system as a whole is organized and administered from the guidance point of view.

We are still in a developmental stage of guidance and do not always know just what problems can be most advantageously handled by specially organized guidance departments. As the curricular and supervisory personnel of the school become conscious of the purpose of guidance and are reorganized in accordance with it, more and more of the actual guidance work may be successfully left to these agencies. We cannot accurately forecast exactly when this will be, nor can we determine completely what activities, if any, should always be performed by the special guidance bureau. It may be found, for example, that much of the work, especially that concerned with securing information and developing the habits, ideals, interests, and techniques necessary to intelligent choice, can be done better if organized as a regular part of classroom procedure and not left to the organized guidance department. On the other hand, it will undoubtedly be found that certain kinds of assistance can be most efficiently and economically given by the department of guidance itself.

At present, organized departments of guidance or pupil personnel are concerned chiefly with certain crises, certain areas of problems, certain very important adjustments that the ordinary work of the school either does not provide for at all or does so very inadequately.

Summary

Guidance is the assistance given to individuals in making intelligent choices and adjustments in their lives. The ability to make wise choices is not innate; it must be developed. The fundamental purpose of guidance is to develop in each individual, up to the limit of his capacity, the ability to solve his own problems and to make his own adjustments. Experiences of the individual himself and that of others may be very helpful in making choices, but they may also lead to choices that are unwise and harmful. In order to make experience valuable the individual must learn to analyze the past experiences to see whether the previous problem is like the present one and whether the solution arrived at before was a good one or whether a better one can now be found.

Guidance is not confined to any one type of situation. It can involve all types of life situations—personal, social, religious, occupational.

Guidance is an integral part of the educational process. Although it is most needed and most effective in childhood, adolescence, and early adulthood, for some people it may be a lifelong requirement. The chief responsibility for guidance rests upon the home and the school. In the school every member of the staff is concerned with the guidance of the students entrusted to him. Trained counselors are essential to assist parents and other members of the staff in their guidance responsibilities and to deal directly with special problems of youth.

Exercises

1. The National Vocational Guidance Association adopted the following statement: "The purpose of vocational guidance is to assist individuals to choose, prepare for, enter upon, and make progress in an occupation." Make a list of ten important problems of youth which are not included in this statement and which you feel should be the responsibility of the guidance department of the secondary school.

2. Find the meanings of the following: to assist, to lead, to advise, to counsel, to guide, to regulate. Compare the definitions of these words and be prepared to discuss the distinctive meaning of guidance.

3. Evaluate the following statements:
   a. We have no need for a counselor because in our school every teacher is a guidance worker.
   b. Our counselor has absolutely nothing to do with discipline.
   c. There is nothing new about guidance; after all, guidance is just good teaching.

References

Johnson, Walter F., Buford Stefflre, and Roy A. Edelfelt: *Pupil Personnel and Guidance Services*, McGraw-Hill Book Company, New York, 1961.

Miller, Carroll H.: *Guidance Services: An Introduction*, Harper & Row, Publishers, Incorporated, New York, 1965.

Ohlsen, Merle M.: *Guidance Services in the Modern School*, Harcourt, Brace & World, Inc., New York, 1964.

Shertzer, Bruce, and Shelley C. Stone: *Fundamentals of Guidance*, Houghton Mifflin Company, Boston, 1966.

Traxler, Arthur E., and Robert D. North: *Techniques of Guidance*, Harper & Row, Publishers, Incorporated, New York, 1966.

PART TWO

Learning about the Individual

2

Understanding the Individual

Guidance, like teaching, is a service given by one person to another. We often say the teacher is "teaching a class," but what he is really doing is teaching *each one* in the class—helping each pupil to learn. The counselor often meets pupils in a group, but his purpose is to help each individual in the group. This help cannot be effective unless the teacher or counselor knows the problems faced by each pupil and his characteristics, his abilities, and his desires. On the other hand, if the help offered is to be accepted by the individual, he must know himself, his limitations, and his strengths. Successful guidance, like successful teaching, is predicated on the student's being understood by the counselor and by himself.

Human behavior can be observed from two frames of reference. The *external* or *objective* frame of reference, as described in this chapter, implies that behavior is examined from an outside observer's point of view. The teacher who observes that Joan is tired, the mother who believes that Rick is carefree, and the counselor who comments that Melinda lacks purpose have all made their observations based upon their previous work with these and other children. Their observations may or may not be correct. A second frame of reference, termed the *phenomenological* approach, seeks to understand the behavior of the individual from *his own* point of view. This is discussed in Chapter 3.

Importance of Understanding

It would seem to be self-evident that effective counseling toward specific goals is impossible without a clear understanding of the individual by the counselor, the teacher, and the parent, and that guidance should not be attempted unless such understanding is present. But life is full of tragedies in home and in school because of the lack of such understanding. Many parents try to determine the future of their children, especially that of their

25

sons. If the family tradition for generations has been that the firstborn son becomes a physician, lawyer, or minister, then an attempt may be made to fit a boy into the tradition regardless of his abilities or interests. There are certain values in such traditions—common memories, common experiences, common friends that bind families together. However, these decisions are based on the desires of the parents and not on the needs of their children. Such family-centered vocational and educational decisions indicate a lack of appreciation of the importance of understanding the individual.

Students in high school tend to prefer occupations that are of a higher social status than that of their parents. This preference is especially marked in children whose fathers are in unskilled or semiskilled occupations. To understand the meaning of such a preference we need to take account of the desires of the parents which may be finding expression through the vocational selections of the children.

Choices of curriculum in high school are too often made on the basis of the "standing" of the curriculum and not on the needs of the student. The high salaries now paid to subprofessional workers have changed to some extent the relative social status of high-school curriculums, but teachers, as well as parents, are still too inclined to influence the better students to take certain courses because of the prestige involved without sufficient consideration or understanding of the needs, abilities, and interests of the student himself.

It is often said that what the student does, what courses he takes in school or college, what occupation he chooses, should be based on the needs that he, himself, feels. There is no doubt that these are important, but the needs that one feels at any given time may not be based on a clear self-understanding. We often feel a variety of needs at any given time, but some are quite superficial and relatively unimportant. We may feel a "need" for a Cadillac, to "keep up with the Joneses," but an understanding of ourselves and our financial status may make us willing to settle for a used Volkswagen. Assistance in making choices should be based on as thorough an understanding as is possible of the individual, of his basic needs, and of the real circumstances surrounding his decisions.

Major Life Areas Needing to Be Understood

Understanding an individual is dependent upon knowledge of how he acts in different situations. This understanding may come from observations by those who know him in school, at home, or in the community. These observations need to be combined and judgments made regarding the motives and reasons behind the observed acts. This is by no means an easy thing to accomplish. It calls for sympathetic insight into the desires and needs of students and the unusual ability to put aside any preconceived ideas of what the individual may be.

THE INDIVIDUAL IN HIS SCHOOL

Students do not exist in isolation but in institutional contexts. One of the most important of such contexts is that provided by the school. Schools have characteristic "climates" which do much to influence the behavior of their students. In some schools, academic achievement is highly valued and study and hard work are methods of pleasing not only the teachers but one's peers. In other schools, athletic skills may have a higher priority and there is much pressure on students to excel in sports. Still other schools give much attention to personal popularity, which may be based on such matters as personality, social skills, and clothes. Whatever the prevailing ethos of the school, it will have a marked influence on the behavior of the student. The peer group is always an important influence on the child, and if we want to understand his behavior, we need to understand what his peers think is important.

THE INDIVIDUAL IN HIS HOME

A second life area that is important in our attempts to understand an individual is his home. Research on social class has suggested that varying social economic levels may have varying child-rearing practices and inculcate different values. Certainly we should not stereotype the child and say that because he is lower class he will do thus and so, while a child who is middle class will behave differently. The research is not that clear-cut in its findings. But there do seem to be some generalizations which are possible about a home which would relate the student's behavior to the status of his parents. A principle of child development has long suggested that the child's interaction with his parents is an important determinant of his total behavior. A teacher or counselor might want to consider the kinds of activities that the child engages in at home, the emotional climate of the home as characterized by acceptance or rejection, the nature of the association among the children, and the skills taught or ignored in a home all of which may be of importance in the child's total adjustment and particularly influence his behavior in school.

When the school and the home stand for the same values, the child may learn them readily. When there is a discrepancy between what the home thinks is important and what the school thinks is important we may well expect some conflict in the child. In such a case the counselor may be an important bridge between the school and the home and thus help both the parent and the teacher to know and understand the student more completely.

THE INDIVIDUAL IN HIS COMMUNITY

Community conditions are of great importance in securing an understanding of individual students and in developing effective self-concepts. Such conditions are fully as significant as those in the home or in the school. Differences in the social status of families in a community often are reflected in the attitudes of different groups of high-school students toward one another. Differences in dress, in habits of speech, in social manner, in points of view, and in values are often seen. In some schools, rivalries and clannish customs often appear and cause feelings of hostility between groups. Neighborhood gangs and ethnic subcultures may be important and divisive influences affecting the student's comfort in the school as well as the extent of his learning. In spite of efforts made by the school staff to overcome these unfavorable conditions, they often continue. In the school itself, students in the college preparatory course are likely to look down on those taking other courses. Such differences often show themselves in school elections and in committee selections. Even though the school faculty does not approve of such practices, they cannot ignore them if they wish to understand the students. Unpopular students do not understand why they are not dated or elected to office and are bewildered or deeply hurt. A knowledge of community and home conditions and sensitivity to such rivalries in and out of the school are the keys to a real understanding of the student.

It is important to keep in mind that understanding an individual involves much more than an assembly of facts about him and his behavior. Facts themselves are often misleading, and they must be interpreted by reference to other facts and to the circumstances in which they are found. Understanding cannot come merely from observation of what a person does, how he acts, and how he seems to feel. It is important to know the influences that were responsible for his behavior, "how he got that way," what his purpose was in doing what he did. Many times he himself does not understand why he acted as he did.

Psychological Barriers to Understanding

A meaningful understanding of the individual is not always easy to secure. Certain psychological barriers may impede our progress toward understanding. Young people especially are reluctant to reveal themselves as they really are. Because of the intensely personal nature of our lives, it is difficult—perhaps impossible—to have complete empathy for another person, that is, to feel what it would be like to be in his position. Finally, because individuals change, we can never be sure that our understanding is up to date—the student in May is not the same student that he was in September.

RELUCTANCE TO REVEAL ONE'S REAL SELF

Young people in particular are very hesitant to reveal their "true self" to others, especially to adults. This difficulty is described by James Whitcomb Riley in *A Child's World*:

> The child heart is so strange a little thing,
> So mild, so timorously shy and small,
> When grownup hearts throb, it goes scampering
> Behind the wall, nor dares peer out at all
>   It is the veriest mouse
>   That hides in any house
> So wild a little thing is the child heart!
>   Child heart, mild heart
>   Ho, my little wild heart
> Come up here to me out o' the dark
>   Or let me come to you.

Adolescents often go to great lengths to keep another person from knowing what they really are. They are cruel to keep others from knowing that they are really tenderhearted; they pretend to dislike someone in order to conceal their inner feelings of respect and liking. Many persons, old and young, feel that it is indecent to "bare one's soul and dare the day." It is almost as bad as being a nudist! They also feel that "it is none of your business." This attitude, in itself, reveals something about the individual. A wise and sympathetic counselor or teacher, who has not forgotten his own youth, can look behind this bravado and learn much about the student.

DIFFICULTY IN UNDERSTANDING ANOTHER PERSON

It is difficult for adults to understand the behavior of adolescents; we so easily forget what we thought and did when we were "young and gay." A common danger is that we may read our own present motives, feelings, and aspirations into the expressions and activities of the student. Another serious difficulty is that, although we can secure some information about the individual, what we get sometimes interferes with our understanding of him. "We cannot see the forest for the trees." The human being is a complex organic unit. He is "more than the sum of all his parts." We can gather together all the facts that can be obtained about him—his background, his surroundings, his experiences, his many characteristics—and still not understand him. There is real danger in half-truths and in unrelated information. No one type of information can stand alone; it must be considered in relation to all the other data. Real understanding of another person involves an unusual ability to put oneself sympathetically and intelligently in his place. At the same time one must stand apart and be impersonal. The privacy of the individual must be respected; we must not delve too deeply nor be in a hurry to see what the student is not ready to disclose.

INDIVIDUALS CHANGE

One difficulty in dealing with the adolescent is that he is constantly changing, even from day to day. As a consequence, by the time data are obtained and recorded, he has changed, and the data are important only as they show a developmental picture of the student. Such a picture is important, but it does not tell us what he is now. A current picture is very difficult to attain. Cumulative records have great value in showing the development of the individual from year to year—his scholastic record, his changing interests, his attitudes toward teachers and fellow students, the changes in his personality patterns. But more important is a truly understanding teacher or counselor who can interpret the conflicting behavior of the developing adolescent. Such understanding is absolutely essential. The past must not be confused with the present. Records tell us what was; only the individual himself can tell us what is. We must take care not to confuse marks, scores, and records of incidents with the living individual we are trying to understand and help.

Social Changes Are Barriers to Understanding

Great and rapid changes in our society increase the difficulty of understanding across the generations. Adults and adolescents live in truly different worlds. The meaning of work, the role of the family, religion, and morals, the philosophy of the schools have all undergone considerable transformation during this century. These changes impede the understanding which is so essential for the function of guidance.

THE MEANING OF WORK IS CHANGING

The school counselor or teacher is apt to be someone who is receiving much satisfaction from his work and to whom work is a very central part of his identification. He may sometimes forget then that many people do not get such satisfaction from their work. Such people may work simply because they need to have money in order to live, but may turn elsewhere for their basic pleasures.

With increased urbanization, industrialization, and rationalization of job activities there may be greater alienation between the worker and his job. Few workers now have the total control over their product that the craftsman traditionally did. As a consequence the likelihood of their achieving deep satisfaction through their work is lessened. Some economists even believe that we are approaching a time when work will occupy a less and less important position in the lives of citizens. A guaranteed annual income may be provided for all our citizens apart from whether or not society has a meaningful job for them to do. Such an idea is quite contrary to our traditional "Protestant ethic" with its view that work is good and an end in itself.

The principles to be derived from the changes in our occupational structure are that the meaning of work may be different to the student than it is to the counselor; second, that basic life satisfactions may in the future be achieved in new ways less related to job activities; and finally, that in doing vocational guidance we need to remember that the work roles available to our students in the future are literally unknown to us; therefore we should not spend our energies helping a child select a specific occupation but rather help him become a flexible adult able to cope with inevitable changes.

THE FAMILY CHANGES

In any consideration of the present difficulty in the guidance of youth the changes in the home and community should be kept in mind. In most present-day homes there is no longer the same amount of intimate interrelationship that once was present. The increased tempo of life has too often materially reduced or even eliminated the time or the opportunity for such relationships.

It is difficult to determine all the causes for this change which has been both gradual and complicated. It was not caused by increased time on the job since the "workday" of the majority of workers has decreased until the forty-hour week is now the standard and pressure is being exerted to make it even shorter. Nor can it have been caused by the increased time necessary for household duties, because electrical appliances of all kinds—for cooking, dishwashing, laundry work, housekeeping, refrigeration—have materially reduced the time necessary for such responsibilities. There is actually more time available for home life and for closer relationships. In some homes this "free time" is being utilized to enrich home life and has resulted in closer relationships between parents and children, but this is not always the case.

There seem to be two main factors that are largely responsible for this situation. One of these is the increased participation of fathers and mothers in activities outside the home in social, civic, church, and political affairs. Such activities, for example, those of the parent-teacher association, are often very useful and desirable, but they reduce materially the time spent in the home—evenings, Saturdays, and Sundays. These activities make it difficult or even impossible to have the unhurried personal contacts with children which are so essential for effective understanding and assistance.

The second factor is the increased independence of children which results in a decrease in the feeling of need for help or even for association with parents. The many out-of-class activities in the school—athletic, musical, dramatic, school government, social—provide group satisfactions and reduce both the time and the need for companionship at home. At home the children have the radio, the television, and the record player at their disposal, and they need no assistance from their parents to enjoy these facilities.

These changes have often resulted in doubts on the part of parents that they are capable of setting standards which are valid in a world so different from that of their own childhood.

Another area of great importance in the lives of young people in which there have been far-reaching and significant changes is that of morals and religion. The reasons for these changes are difficult to determine. Developments in our social, economic, and industrial life probably have contributed to the change, as has the interaction of different beliefs, customs, and morals brought to America from all parts of the world. Whatever the cause, we cannot fail to understand the great importance of different moral codes and religious beliefs to the development of young people, even though both these areas are considered to be the private concern of the family, the church, and the individual rather than of the school. But if the school is interested in getting an understanding of the child and in helping him to develop adequate goals, it cannot neglect these areas, for they have a profound and often a determining influence on such goals. An understanding of the changes in these areas is of very great importance both to the home and to the school.

Many people believe that religion has a greater hold on people than it ever has had and point out that the growth in church membership in all denominations has steadily increased and many new churches are being built. Evangelists attract great numbers of people, and hundreds come forward and announce their determination to accept religion. Some believe that the fear of destruction by atomic bombs and the ensuing uncertainties have served to increase the interest in religion. Others feel that, in spite of the growth in churches' membership, the real hold of religion on people has perceptibly decreased, that it is no longer as important a factor in our lives as it once was. They say that, although the organized church is still very important, it no longer occupies the position of leadership that it once had. It is certain that family prayers have practically disappeared, and even grace at meals is unusual.

Of one thing we are certain: religious customs have changed. The great majority of people are far more liberal in their beliefs and more tolerant of those who do not believe as they do than they once were. Young people are increasingly thinking for themselves and refusing to accept religious dogmas merely because they have been recognized for centuries. In this atmosphere of controversy, of changing beliefs, and of lack of belief, it is small wonder that young people are confused and often unable to adjust properly and to distinguish between transient and permanent values. Wise assistance is needed. Much of this help must be given by the home and the church, but the school also has a responsibility here.

Our situation regarding morals contains so much that is undesirable that we may even wonder whether our moral standards are not weakening. Racketeering, graft, and corruption are everywhere apparent, in politics, business, industry, government, and labor unions. Some men become wealthy and powerful not because of their contribution to society but because of trickery, clever dealing, influence, control of the political machine, or even theft, intimidation, or murder. Our legal system is slow, cumbersome, and too often ineffective. Criminals sometimes escape just punishment because they have money or influence or because of the work of lawyers who specialize in helping criminals evade the consequences set up by the law. The old virtues of industry, thrift, and honesty have, in some cases, been the actual cause of poverty and suffering. Men who have worked long and hard and who have been thrifty have sometimes been cheated by the unscrupulous and lost their money. They have found themselves poor and ruined not because they were dishonest or prodigal but because they were thrifty and honest.

Standards of good conduct are continually changing. Some conduct that was once considered acceptable is now unacceptable, and what was unacceptable is now acceptable. No longer do all believe that conscience is an infallible guide in deciding what is right. Right conduct is determined not only by the motives of the actor but also by the consequences of the act. In the complexity of modern life it is often very difficult to determine the real effects of an act, and this makes it hard to make right decisions. We need to know the probable effects of the proposed action on others and on ourselves before we can decide intelligently what is best to be done.

Many youth indicate relatively little concern about problems of morals and religion or of home and family. Two opposite conclusions might be drawn from these findings. We might say that young people are well adjusted in morals and religion and to home and family since they apparently have few problems in these areas. On the other hand, it is possible that young people have little consciousness of morals or moral obligations. It may be that church and religion are not vital forces in their lives and that they have little trouble with parents and home because parents are not important guiding and restraining influences in their lives. In other words, young people may not be conscious of problems in these areas because they have little sense of moral obligation and little restraint imposed on them. The mounting delinquency rate among youth might indicate that the second conclusion is correct.

THE CHANGING EDUCATIONAL PHILOSOPHY

One of the most important social changes in recent years has been that in our philosophy of education as it concerns the place of the child in the teaching-learning process. This change is so intermingled with the changes in the home and in religion and morals that it is difficult to tell whether the changes in the philosophy of education are responsible for the changes in the home and society or the reverse. Formerly, education was the process of passing on to the young the cultural heritage of the past. It was the process of inculcating in the young those habits, skills, ideas, and knowledges that were necessary to enable them to take their place in adult society. The central figure in this process was the teacher. The student was the recipient and, as far as possible, passive and obedient. He was thought to be too young to have any voice in determining what he had to do or to learn. Discipline was the process of preventing behavior that would interfere with this attitude of docility. The curriculum was organized by the school, and methods were developed with the purpose of molding the pupil into the kind of individual who would make a good citizen and an exemplary person. This educational philosophy was the prevailing point of view in the schools of all countries until the beginning of this century.

The new educational philosophy places the child at the center of the educational process and is concerned primarily with his development, that is, with what he is now rather than what he may become or what society may demand of him. His needs for personal development, his own interests and desires, are dominant. His impulses for action are of extreme importance and should not be unduly restricted. He should have a large part in decisions regarding what he should do—even regarding what he should study. The extreme of this position is that he should not be made to do what he does not want to do. Failures are considered undesirable and should be avoided. Because punishments and restraints are negative, they should either not be used at all or at least be minimized. The rule of promotion for all is sometimes adopted.

Even though some of the extreme implications of this philosophy have not been generally accepted, its impact has been very great. Probably its most important implication is the emphasis it places upon the enlarged place of the individual in choosing his own way of life and in selecting his own activities. Even young children are allowed and often encouraged to make important choices for themselves. Many of these choices may be unfortunate; but when the choice seems undesirable, instead of arbitrarily refusing to allow the child to do what he has chosen to do, we try to help him evaluate the wisdom of his choice.

The underlying idea of this educational position emphasizes the fundamental purpose of guidance—helping the individual to make wise choices. The necessity for adequate guidance in the very early years of life in order to develop this ability is emphasized. While this emphasis is certainly desirable, the popularity of this new philosophy has also resulted in much confusion, uncertainty, and even bewilderment among teachers and parents. It has been difficult for them to adjust themselves to it, and they are often at a loss to know what to do.

Parents and teachers who grew up when a different educational philosophy was in vogue often cannot understand the young people of today and are puzzled by their actions. This puzzlement makes them uncertain about the best methods of dealing with today's students. The usual result is that little or nothing is done to change the behavior of the student or to develop his sense of values.

We have as yet failed to solve the problem of dealing with these delinquent youth. We know that the old method of treating them as criminals is not good; we also know that leniency of the courts does not by itself solve the problem. Some more effective guidance is absolutely essential. Many national and local agencies are working hard to solve the problem, and some of the suggested solutions seem to be hopeful. At the root of any successful plan must be some form of intelligent guidance.

In summary, the last few years have seen great changes in our society. Adults trying to understand adolescents must take account of the fact that the world of their own childhood is gone. It is not likely to return. If you wish to understand today's youth, you must first understand his world—however much a stranger you feel in it, however much you may disapprove of some of its elements—for the youth and his world are so much a part of each other that they cannot be known separately.

Aids in Understanding

Many techniques are needed to help us understand youth. Such an understanding cannot be attained merely by watching what they are doing. We must know the reasons and motives that impel them to act as they do. This level of understanding requires close and sympathetic personal relationship over a reasonably long period of time. The problem is made more difficult because youth may not understand themselves and therefore are unable to give much direct help to adults who are striving to learn more about them.

CUMULATIVE RECORDS

A cumulative record is a collection of information about a student and constitutes a picture of his development—physically, academically, and socially. In the past such records were made up of collections of material filed in the counselor's office. Now some schools are putting this material on magnetic tape and storing it in computers. When a counselor wishes to retrieve the information, the computer prints out for him the material which he wants and needs.

These records, which have great value in showing year-to-year development, include, as we have stated earlier, his scholastic record, his changing interests, his attitudes toward teachers and fellow students, and the changes in his personality patterns. Well-organized anecdotal records—objective statements of significant incidents—may be very helpful if carefully made from time to time. Autobiographies often reveal characteristics and attitudes unsuspected even by the student himself. Valuable as they are, such records are quite inadequate to provide a real understanding of the pupil. What is needed most is a sympathetic and understanding teacher or counselor who can interpret the conflicting behavior of the developing adolescent and look behind and beyond the records themselves to see him as he is. This is essential in any attempt to give guidance to the individual.

COOPERATION IN THE SCHOOL

The development of the self, the ego, is a gradual process which may continue throughout life, but for most people the period of childhood and youth is by far the most important time in the formation of the self. Understanding of an individual comes from a knowledge of how he acts in different situations and why. It might be that the person best able to understand the youth would be the one who has the closest relation to him for the longest period. Often this will be a parent, especially the mother. There is no doubt that the mother can be, and often is, a very knowledgeable observer of how her child acts and how he changes in behavior as he grows, but parental love and pride often interfere with judgment and obscure important elements essential for understanding.

Teachers see children six to eight hours a day, five days in the week, for nine or ten months a year and observe their acts and judge their motives. Teachers, however, see the individual in a more or less restricted situation and are not completely qualified to understand him. Fellow students, on the other hand, observe their classmates in many types of situations which are more varied and lifelike than those seen by parents or teachers. Although the counselor is the person who is charged with the responsibility for bringing together all the data in the school records, including the observations and opinions of teachers and peers, he may have comparatively little personal contact with individual students. Often, however, he can judge more objectively than parents and teachers, even though he might not be able to develop a completely accurate understanding of the whole personality by himself.

It must be conceded that there is no way by which the real self of an individual can be accurately determined, but it seems clear that the only way in which the school can approximate such an understanding is by the cooperation of all the individuals and agencies who come in contact with the individual. This means that, since all the institutions in the community have a responsibility for the education and training of children and youth, they must also cooperate in developing an understanding of them.

COOPERATION WITH THE HOME

The school and the family share the greatest responsibility for understanding. They are so closely related that there is every reason and need for cooperation, but effective methods to bring this about have as yet not been developed. The major responsibility for initiating such cooperation rests upon the school system. During the past ten years a number of systems have been experimenting with different types of cooperation, some of which seem to be very promising. Efforts are made to clarify the particular responsibility of the school, the family, and the community as well as to eliminate misunderstandings that have arisen among them and to emphasize the need for cooperation and point out ways in which it can be accomplished.

Close personal relations are developed among teachers, parents, business and professional people so that they are known to each other as individuals. Through social occasions and professional meetings they come to know one another better and to realize the necessity for cooperation among friends in all areas, not only in the schools.

In many schools lay people have been invited to come to the school for a variety of reasons so that they can know and understand it better. Some schools are providing "parent" rooms where there are easy chairs and books and pamphlets on school matters and where desirable conferences with teachers, counselors, and administrators can be arranged.

At present the chief means of cooperation with the home is through reports to the parents on the status and progress of the child, but it is difficult to make such reports meaningful to them. The primary meaning is conveyed by the grades received, promotion or nonpromotion, and comments on the child's behavior. At times conferences are arranged between the teacher and the parents to discuss the status of the pupil. Too often, however, this conference is held only when there is something wrong. If the pupil is getting along well in school, no need for a conference is seen. Likewise, when the teacher visits the home, it is usually because of some problem either in the child's work or in his behavior. The difficulty in providing these conferences is very great; but in the schools where such methods have been adopted, a very definite change has been seen in the relation between teachers and parents not only in their personal contact but also in their friendly cooperation in the solution of problems of pupils and in the improvement of school facilities.

COMMUNITY INFORMATION

Teachers and counselors should know their community if they are to be of maximum help to students. The school needs to know about the community activities of the students. Which ones are active in church work? Which ones are leaders in their neighborhood peer groups? Contacts with service clubs such as Rotary, Kiwanis, and Lions have been found to be very useful in revealing sources of assistance and also in securing information about students who are friends or relations of members of these organizations.

Many schools have found it helpful to initiate some type of community survey, which reveals the resources of the community, such as men and women who are leaders in business or industry and who are willing to talk with students about opportunities and qualities essential to success in life. Such contacts will help students to understand social and economic conditions and to realize how they may prepare themselves for lines of work for which they are especially fitted.

With the expansion of poverty programs there is a new area of community information which needs to be understood by the counselor. Such programs as those undertaken by the Neighborhood Youth Corps, the Job Corps, and VISTA may be important sources of referral and important forces for community change. The counselor who is unaware of these community activities is unaware of the environment in which his students live. Although the complexity of and the continuing changes in such programs make it difficult to be up to date with regard to them, the counselor who is going to continue to do an adequate job will in the future be required to spend more time and energy relating what he does to programs that emanate from municipal, state, and federal sources. The rise of such programs, incidentally, reflects a deeper commitment on the part of America to be useful to its young citizens. These may also reflect a skepticism on the part of the larger society with regard to the worthwhileness of the educational and guidance activities that have traditionally characterized our schools.

Summary

Effective guidance of youth depends on a sympathetic understanding of the individual. Securing this understanding is a difficult and time-consuming task. It demands close cooperation with the individual, the family, the school, and the community. It demands a vicarious entry into the individual's problems, his failures, and his successes. It attempts to discover what he is as well as how he got that way.

Four things are imperative to effective guidance: We need a better understanding of children and youth and of their developing problems and needs. We need to have the youth understand himself, his home, his school, and his community. We need to discover, by cooperative effort, effective methods of helping the home, school, and community to adjust themselves to the constant changes in their functions and character and of helping children and youth to learn how to use their extended freedom and wider opportunities. Finally, we need to help youth to develop necessary restraints and to evolve a set of values that will enable them to form self-concepts that are realistic and that will help them in their choice of personal, social, and occupational activities.

Exercises

1. Describe instances where the help offered you by parents, teachers, counselors, or others was ineffective or even harmful because they did not know enough about you. If you do not recall any such experiences, describe some instances that you have observed in the case of others.

2. Do you feel reluctant to give information about yourself to others? If so, what are the causes of such reluctance? Describe the situation and the conditions in which you would feel free to give information about yourself.

3. Usually there are differences between the picture we have of ourselves (our self-concept) and the way we are seen by others (our public image). Discuss these differences in the case of someone well known to you. What accounts for such differences? Do you see ways to lessen these differences?

References

Frank, Lawrence K., and Mary Frank: *Your Adolescent at Home and in School,* The Viking Press, Inc., New York, 1956.

Friedenberg, Edgar Z.: *Coming of Age in America,* Random House, Inc., New York, 1963.

Gottlieb, David, Jon Reeves, and Warren D. Ten Houten: *The Emergence of Youth Societies,* The Free Press of Glencoe, New York, 1966.

Havighurst, Robert J.: *Human Development and Education,* Longmans, Green and Co., Inc., New York, 1953.

Martin, William E., and C. B. Stendler: *Child Behavior and Development,* Harcourt, Brace & World, Inc., New York, 1959.

3

Self-understanding and Guidance

Scientific observation of most forms of life and all objects is restricted to the external or objective frame of reference. Only with human beings, because of their ability to report hopes, fears, dreams, and ambitions, can we seek to understand the behavior of the individual from *his own* point of view. This is termed the phenomenological approach because it stresses that all behavior, without exception, is completely determined by, and pertinent to, the individual's own field of experience.

A counselor's concerted attempts to understand the student may be frustrated if his observations are not reconciled with the view that the student holds of himself. Only through drawing out this self-understanding can the power and insight that comes from within the individual be released to mobilize his talents and integrate the assistance which the counselor may wish to offer.

There are several terms that are virtually synonymous with self-understanding. Among them are "self-image," the "ego," "self-concept," and "phenomenal self." The concept of self-understanding has gained prominence through the theoretical statements and research of Combs and Snygg, Rogers, Jourard, and Super, among others.

It is an interesting and stimulating approach to guidance. It provides a dynamic center around which to group the factors related to one's individual and group behavior. It involves bringing together into consciousness the characteristics, abilities, aptitudes, potentialities, and ideals of the individual and organizes them in such a way that he understands both the ever-changing nature of contemporary society and the personal flexibility he must exhibit if he is to adapt to its demands.

The individual is at the center of his phenomenological world. That is, we can never completely understand him since we seldom have access to more of his private world than he wishes to share openly. One's self-concept is the resultant force from the collision of his internal and external worlds. An indication of sound mental health is the ability to value both worlds and not be forced to deny or distort that which is inconsistent with either world. To understand human behavior we need to assume that all of us have drives to actualize, maintain, and enhance ourselves. Our actions and words, therefore, constitute an attempt to satisfy our needs in the world as we perceive it. Insight into an individual's self-concept frequently is invaluable in understanding his behavior.

Counselors quite justifiably direct much attention toward assisting the individual to understand himself. A well-formulated self-concept takes into account the realities of the complex world in which he lives, assists the individual to feel secure within his environment, accurately assesses his areas of personal strength and weakness, and makes logical decisions based upon this assessment. In summary, if the individual is to be assisted in understanding himself, the counselor must strive to see the world through his eyes.

The Nature of the Self

Seldom do we ponder that which is within us and known to no other. Most of our mental energies are directed at those things which are overt and measurable. But what of the unheard voice within a person? Moustakos suggests fourteen principles which summarize the basic approach and recognition of the self in true experience and the creation of human understandingness.

"1. The individual knows himself better than anyone else.

2. Only the individual himself can develop his potentialities.

3. The individual's perception of his own feelings, attitudes, and ideas is more valid than any outside diagnosis can be.

4. Behavior can best be understood from the individual's own point of view.

5. The individual responds in such ways as to be consistent with himself.

6. The individual's perception of himself determines how he will behave.

7. Objects have no meaning in themselves. Individuals give meanings and reality to them. These meanings reflect the individual's background.

8. Every individual is logical in the context of his own personal experience. His point of view may seem illogical to others when he is not understood.

9. As long as the individual accepts himself, he will continue to grow and develop his potentialities. When he does not accept himself, much of his energies will be used to defend rather than explore and to actualize himself.

10. Every individual wants to grow toward self-fulfillment. These growth strivings are present at all times.

11. An individual learns significantly only those things which *are* involved in the maintenance of *self*. No one can force the individual to permanent or creative learning. He will learn only if he wills to. Any other type of learning is temporary and inconsistent with the self and and will disappear as soon as threat is removed.

12. Concepts, ideas, symbols, and events can be denied or distorted, but experience is experienced in the unique reality of the individual person and cannot be untrue to itself. If it threatens the maintenance or enhancement of self, the experience will be of little relevance or consequence to the individual though it may temporarily stifle further growth.

13. We cannot teach another person directly, and we cannot facilitate real learning in the sense of making it easier. We can make learning for another person possible by providing information, the setting, atmosphere, materials, resources, and *by being* there. The learning process itself is a unique individualistic experience. It may be a difficult experience for the individual person even if it has significance for the enhancement of self.

14. Under threat the self is less open to spontaneous expression; that is, is more passive and controlled. When free from threat, the self is more open, that is, free to be and to strive for actualization."[1]

The self, as described by Moustakos, cries for creative expression. He urges those who would enhance expression of the self in educational settings to maximize the value given individual uniqueness, minimize the threat to the self of the learner, and free him to explore as directed by his own interests and potentialities. This, certainly, is quite in keeping with the guidance point of view. Because of this, it is especially helpful for those interested in becoming counselors to be aware of the process by which the image one has of himself is developed and some of the characteristics of the unified self-concept and its component parts.

Development of the Self-Concept

The ability to understand oneself is an unfolding process that continues throughout life and is influenced greatly by social interaction. Developmental tasks can be noted at each level that assist one in this process. During infancy the child quickly learns to distinguish his mother from other women. In early childhood he becomes aware of some of his physical abilities and limitations which are amplified and strengthened by new learnings. Preadolescence is a time when strong sex identity is developed. Family influence

[1] Clark E. Moustakos, "True Experience and the Self," in Clark E. Moustakos (ed.), *The Self*, Harper & Row, Publishers, Incorporated, New York, 1956, pp. 9–11.

weakens at this stage and social acceptability becomes an important and more vital aspect of the self. With added learning the self begins to become more unified, his personal identity is clarified, and his social role begins to take shape. The new identity that emerges during this period is the product of the conflicting pulls that the cohesive family unit and tangential peer demands produce.

Consciousness of oneself in some cases emerges suddenly, almost without warning. A boy walking to school suddenly realizes, "I am myself; I am nobody else." A mother of three children exclaims, "All these years I just did what was expected. I never thought of *me*. At thirty-six I found myself." It is a staggering experience and one that is likely to throw the individual off balance for a time. To some it is electrifying and deeply satisfying; to others it is depressing, for it signifies that a person stands alone in the world.

The greatest single determinant of one's self-concept is his family. Through interaction with this primary reference group the individual develops early experiences of adequacy, acceptance, identification, and expectancies of the society into which he is increasingly moving.

From the first days of life the child begins to develop a sense of whether he is being loved, rejected, or rebuffed. This in turn affects his perception of whether he is an adequate or inadequate individual. The degree to which he feels adequate forms the basis upon which he is able to accept or reject others. Individuals who have no doubt about their adequacy possess the capacity for being quite accepting of others.

Earliest identification of the child is with the family. Progressively, identification moves from the immediate family across the spectrum toward the world of adult life. Relatives, neighbors, and classmates become integrated within the self as the individual develops. The family is reflective of the greater culture of which he is to become a part. It is from the family that the child differentiates goals, values, techniques, and ways of behaving acceptable to society. These, then, lead to the values and directions that he will consider as he makes decisions in the future.

CHARACTERISTICS OF SELF-UNDERSTANDING

An individual, at any moment in time, has access to much more than can be physically observed. The understanding which he develops of himself is guided by four characteristics.

First, *the self-concept is always changing.* Admittedly, this means that a student has great difficulty in getting a clear grasp of who he is. It is this fluidity, however, which makes change in behavior possible. Were an individual's self-concept never to change, he would be unable to adjust to the changing environment that surrounds him. Change may be virtually instantaneous. The older child understands that he is uncertain and relatively incapable of competing with his mother in a household task. When mother leaves and the comparison shifts to younger brother, however, the self takes on a new perspective.

Second, *the self-concept has a basic stability.* Despite the momentary manifestations of change, a deeper understanding of self is carried across events. It is this stability which carries the confident man through defeat after defeat and causes the sudden victor to accept triumph with caution.

Third, *the self-concept is influenced by the intensity with which one experiences aspects of his environment.* That is, one's needs vary from moment to moment. His level of awareness, ranging from very vague to sharp, is dependent upon the particular need which he is currently experiencing. One may enter a room many times throughout the day and night. His level of awareness of lamps within the room will be directly related to the need he experiences for lamps. During daylight hours they may go unnoticed. In darkness they become the object of his immediate search as he enters the room.

Fourth, *the self-concept has direction.* At any given moment the overt behavior may seem random, but the self-concept is organized, has purpose, and seeks to satisfy its need in a meaningful fashion. Each of us has experienced the embarrassment of laughing or appearing needlessly gay on the most somber of occasions. This incongruous behavior can only be explained by the need within the self to give expression to something other than that toward which primary attention appeared focused.

Thus far we have talked of the self-concept as a unified whole. To look at this phenomenon more closely it is useful to think of it as an image rather than a concept. A number of principles have been advanced by Anderson[2] which describe the image's origin, parts, and persistence. These are presented with some interpretive comments for the counselor.

1. *Each person has an image or perception of himself that is unique from the perception he holds of others.* Through life's experiences he has developed an identity that is his own. He understands, and usually accepts, differences between himself and others. This perception is developed early in life and maintained vigorously despite environmental influences.

2. *This image can be divided into two parts.* Each person has a physical image and psychological image. The individual is able to carefully discern the difference between them. He may be the shortest boy in the class, fully realize this, and accept it as nothing more than fact. This shortness, on the other hand, may distress his psychological image of himself. He may ascribe much more than size to the fact that he is the shortest boy.

[2] Camilla M. Anderson, "The Self-image: A Theory of the Dynamics of Behavior," *Mental Hygiene,* Vol. 36, pp. 227–244, 1952.

3. *Neither of these images is complete and neither is more than roughly accurate.* Each day's experiences in some way shape the self-image of the individual. When events and experiences are unable to change self-perception, the individual forces his environment to adjust to him rather than he to his environment. The data of perception, being based upon experience and impression, is sometimes erroneous. A person's insistence that she is plain and untalented may be grounded in parental comments made when she was young, and no amount of contrary evidence can disabuse her of these beliefs.

4. *Both the physical and the psychological image comprise many factors, each of which is subconsciously assigned a value.* Just as the heart is more highly prized than the hand, so each factor is given a value which is known only to the self. At times we can observe indications of the value assigned, but the accuracy of our perceptions is not to be trusted. Was "I'd rather be right than President" any indicator of the value assigned? How about, "I may have received a D, but I earned it honestly"?

5. *The psychological self-image is formed early in life as a result of a succession of experiences that the child has had with his environment.* The adjustments made by the infant to survive the interpersonal experiences he confronts leave him with both an image and a set of defense mechanisms upon which he may call. These mechanisms for the most part remain an integral part of him for the remainder of his life.

6. *In the development of the self-image, the first year of life is the most important.* Each year thereafter is of less importance until the image is essentially completed before adolescence. The prime reason that the self-image develops so rapidly during this period is that the child's helplessness and dependency are greatest at this time. The greater the sense of helplessness, the more defensive the individual becomes in order to ensure survival.

7. *The structure of the self-image determines the day-by-day and the moment-by-moment behavior of the individual.* Decisions and reactions are determined, not by what one is, but by what one believes he is and that which will tend to maintain the image intact. The child whose experience has taught him that he is incompetent will tend to live his life and make his most minute decisions in order to maintain that image. If he has come to believe "I am confident," all energies will be devoted to perpetuate this life pattern.

In summary, the self-concept can be described as having basic characteristics. Further, it can be seen as having parts which, in turn, are composed of weighted factors. The self-concept is formulated early in life, and its stability, while capable of change, sustains it largely intact.

THE SELF-CONCEPT AND DECISION MAKING

As the individual develops, he faces an increasing array of decisions. One of the purposes of guidance is to make him aware of the decision-making process and how he might use his talents and interests to his best advantage.

Students frequently are unable to tap the sources of self-understanding and do not make appropriate use of that part of them to which they alone have access. Without the employment of this self-understanding, decisions will be based upon external knowledge alone. The self and the individual's uniqueness will be denied consideration.

From the preceding section we learned that the individual knows himself better than anyone else and he alone can develop his potentialities. The counselor's approach, therefore, is to enlist cooperation and encourage the mobilization of talents within the student rather than to suggest that he model his decisions after those of his peers or external indicators alone. The counselor's efforts are directed at facilitating self-awareness and assisting the student to draw fully upon the knowledge and powers to which only he has access. These, then, can be discussed in the light of environmental conditions and influences in order that decisions reflect awareness of self and surroundings.

INFORMATION AND THE INDIVIDUAL

Controversy has surrounded the collection and use of information for decades. The argument is advanced frequently that some forms of standardized test results, when shared openly with the student, may do more to debilitate than motivate him because of misunderstanding that may never be clarified. Intelligence test scores in the hands of the inept might well have this result.

Information collected to assist the student in better self-understanding frequently is misused, also. Although the expressed purpose in soliciting this information is to increase the individual's awareness, the teacher or counselor may feel unqualified to use it fully, may be threatened by the student's response, or may feel that the student can be helped in other ways and not choose to share an interpretation with the individual. The student's continued willingness to reveal himself is directly dependent upon his having access to the significance of what he reported.

A basic misunderstanding may lie in the way information is used. A literal interpretation is often meaningless to the student. Only when integrated with existing self-understanding will it take on meaning. The counselor or teacher, then, can suggest a literal meaning and encourage the student to consider its significance for him. As each part is interpreted, discussed, and integrated, the individual gains new insight and extends his self-understanding.

A student who is interested in considering his work future, for example, might take an interest inventory. The results may indicate preference toward work that is mechanical, yet involves meeting people. A dentist, TV home repairman, and cab driver are possibilities that immediately might occur to the counselor. But what are the student's interests and ambitions? What can he identify that he would and would not like to do each day? Does he like a regular pattern of living or variety? Would he like to work inside or outside, in one location or travel? The process of pulling out perceptions such as these, examining his values, and assigning priorities to each is a necessary antecedent to considering any specific job alternatives. With increased self-understanding he can then better integrate the specific results of the interest inventory.

Measurement of Self-understanding

Counselors are concerned with knowing something of the student's level of self-understanding for two reasons. First, as the student allows the counselor to view the world through his eyes, the counselor is able to adjust his own perceptions and be better able to assist the individual in changing or learning behavior. Second, and more important, a knowledge of the student's self-understanding will allow the counselor to assist the individual in knowing whether his perceptions of how he is viewed by others are accurate.

Teachers also may assist students in gaining self-understanding. Through a number of means students can reveal something of their thoughts, dreams, fears, and desires. A teacher may assist the student to place these in perspective and to learn from the process of revealing himself. Some of the more promising means of assisting students in this process are described briefly.

AUTOBIOGRAPHY

The autobiography has been mentioned previously as a device for developing realistic self-pictures, but it has further usefulness in that it causes one to be introspective and come to better self-understanding through attempts to communicate something of one's experiences and feelings. Through these life stories the student may relate how he sees himself and how the world looks to him. This instrument, which is discussed at greater length in Chapter 5, has great utility because it can be adapted for nearly any grade level and can be as brief or detailed, as general or specific as seems appropriate. It also lends itself readily to the regular work of the classroom. A piece of autobiographical writing can be discussed by the teacher or counselor with the student. From this material both may assess the extent of the understanding which the student has of himself.

CREATIVE WRITING

A parallel activity is to ask the student to write about a given topic and draw upon his fantasy life. A title or opening paragraph may be used to lend direction, and he is then asked to express himself as openly as he can. "A Dream I Wish Would Come True" might be used. From the writing, teacher and student can have a helpful interchange that may place many of the student's hopes or fears in perspective.

INTERVIEW

Perhaps the most useful means of assisting the individual to disclose something of himself is through the interview. Through the establishment of a "safe," nonthreatening situation, the student can be helped to share some of his innermost thoughts with the counselor. As these thoughts are sifted and clarified, greater insight frequently takes place on the part of the individual. The counselor is able to interpret what the student is thinking in terms of normal behavior. That which seemed so burdensome may appear quite manageable after inspection. Some minor concerns, on the other hand, may seem to need greater attention as the result of meditating upon them.

GROUP INTERACTION

Some people labor under the delusion that they alone are bothered by a particular feeling, guilt, or problem. Persuasion by a counselor is not sufficient to convince them that others share their dilemma. A frank exploration of these concerns in a group counseling situation, however, might well convince them that others feel exactly as they do. Varying forms of group interaction may be organized by counselors to meet this purpose. Chapter 10 discusses this possibility in greater detail.

PUPPET SHOW

Younger students are less able to respond to written material, but may gain considerable insight through use of a puppet show. The show, which can be developed by the teacher, is centered on a theme that uses students, incidents, and concerns that are closely associated with the audience. At critical moments the students are asked by the puppeteer to suggest what will happen next. An ingenious puppeteer can question the basis for the students' suggestions and assist them to understand why they have predicted these happenings.

Another adaptation of the puppet show makes use of a central character such as a ghost or phantom who cannot be harmed. When doors are locked, he slides underneath. When no exit is available, he glides up the chimney. Although students may understand that he cannot be harmed, the puppeteer creates some anxiety-producing predicaments and urges the class to shout words of encouragement to the puppet hero. "Don't be afraid," shouts one. "Don't let them turn the lights out," cries another. The students' close identification with the puppet hero causes them to broadcast their own intense, but ordinarily guarded, feelings. This can lead to a discussion of the fears we have, the purpose they serve, and the way we might best use them.

SCALES AND CHECKLISTS

Many scales and checklists are available for use with groups of students. Their function is to assist the student in revealing some of his thoughts and feelings. Because they stimulate the student to record his thoughts in a systematic fashion, they are a valuable means of increasing his self-understanding. When the teacher or counselor chooses not to share the results with the student, their value is greatly diminished.

Teachers may want to construct their own instruments. A frequently constructed one is based on incomplete sentences. The teacher lists a number of beginnings such as: "My happiest moment is when . . . ," "I feel most useful when I . . . ," "If I had my one wish granted it would be . . . ," "The moment I really dread is. . . ." Lists of adjectives can also be developed and the student asked to check those which are most like and most unlike him or the way he is feeling at the moment. As with their published counterparts these instruments are of greatest value when the results are shared meaningfully with the student.

SELF-REPORTED OBSERVATION

Students working with counselors have sometimes been helped through a structured form of recording their behavior and then discussing its meaning with the counselor. An uncomplicated example would be that of a student who uses a study schedule that requires him to record any deviations from the established routine. Another student might fill out a rating sheet on how he used an hour of study time. A third, with a history of disruptive classroom behavior, might be asked to record how he felt prior to each time he was disruptive. In each case the student and counselor could review the self-reported observations and discuss their significance in an attempt to increase self-awareness.

SPONTANEOUS PLAYACTING

Most students readily respond to the opportunity to play the part of someone else. Spontaneous playacting is an activity that draws upon both reality and fantasy life. The student, therefore, feels comfortable in acting out or releasing feelings that he would not divulge through other means. These may be concerned, for example, with his ability to get along with others, the image he believes others have of him, or his perception of himself. The teacher or counselor, after observing this acting, may be able to assist the student to increase his self-awareness.

VIDEO PLAYBACK

Many possibilities exist for the use of video recorders in order that self-understanding might be enhanced. Recorders may be used to capture students in the act of studying, taking a test, listening to a lecture, or casually visiting in the student lounge. As a student views the playback with a counselor, he may gain genuine insight into his manner of behaving that he could not gain through any comments, however perceptive, on the part of the counselor. We never cease to be amazed at the way we really appear to others. The video recorder gives us access to that view and may increase self-understanding considerably.

The Case of Lisa

To see the value of the self-concept as an aid in assisting students to understand themselves, let us examine the case of Lisa.

LISA'S FAMILY

Members:	Father:	Robert Becker, *age* 40
	Mother:	Alice Becker, *age* 34
	Children:	Lisa, *age* 10
		Holly, *age* 8
		Amy, *age* 6
		Mark, *age* 4

FAMILY BACKGROUND

The family lived in a newly constructed home in a highly desirable residential area of a large Midwestern city. The home was a short distance from the elementary school and a large shopping center, was nestled beneath towering elm trees, and overlooked a private golf course. The house, outside and inside, reflected upper-middle-class income and good taste, and both furniture and furnishings were recently purchased.

The father, a specialist in internal medicine, was extroverted, extremely intelligent, and made a most favorable personal appearance. He was born and raised on a large wheat farm, which his brothers still operate. The only member of his family to have extensive formal education, he had held a wide variety of jobs as he worked his way through high school, college, and medical school.

Lisa's mother, a product of the same rural environment, had completed two years of college and taught in a one-room rural elementary school to help finance her husband's education. Lack of a teaching certificate prevented her from working near the city in which he received medical training. Despite a facade of social skill, she frequently revealed that she was really a most insecure person and often mentioned that her education was restricted to two years at a small teachers college.

A fat, unkempt child, Lisa always seemed bothered by a cold or adenoid trouble. Her hair was typically disheveled and very oily in appearance. Her clothes were poorly matched and poorly fitted. Frequently she seemed fatigued and lacked interest in her environment. She was withdrawn, did not interact with other children, and spent much of her time daydreaming.

The second oldest child, Holly, was outgoing, self-assured, and well-liked by her peers. She and Lisa shared a room. Some indication of the difference in children was revealed by the room's appearance. Holly's side was neatly arranged, but alive with her art work, pictures of her TV heroes, and an array of colorful pennants. The wall on Lisa's side was bare except for a picture her mother had hung, her bed was unmade, her clothes were scattered across the bed and floor, and several rumpled facial tissues were noticed.

Neither of the two younger children, Amy and Mark, had entered school, and no data were available about them other than that Lisa's teacher had seen them in the home and remarked that both were spirited and outgoing.

SCHOOL PERFORMANCE

Lisa began her schooling in the same rural school where her mother had taught and where her grandmother was now teaching. After five years in this setting, she transferred to the newly constructed elementary school near her new home. Standardized tests results indicated that she was of average intelligence for her class, but was achieving within the bottom quarter.

Her family moved from the rural area to the large city during November, and she was assigned to the fifth grade. During the first days that she attended the new school, her teacher attempted to assess her current level of achievement. Reading skills were extremely deficient, and she seemed to have no background to prepare her for the mathematics curriculum which was being used. Her sole interest was creative writing, in which she exhibited superior thought patterns but very limited communication skills. In all subject areas and class activities except creative writing she was extremely unresponsive.

Continual colds plagued her and caused children to avoid her. The ever-running nose and rumpled tissues were constant signals for peers to stay away. The combination of low academic achievement, lack of general interest, and constant illness perpetuated a withdrawal from the class.

CONFLICTS AFFECTING SELF-UNDERSTANDING

During this traumatic period, only a month in length but much longer in terms of its impact upon Lisa, the effects of classroom isolation were evident. Lisa felt unwanted and rejected by peers. Her lack of social skills made attempts at friendship futile. Concurrently, her classmates were rebuffed in their attempts to involve her in their activity. Her complete lack of interest, her constant cold symptoms, and her unkempt physical appearance all caused peers to avoid friendship.

Mrs. Becker identified closely with Lisa's problems, she told the teacher, but was unable to assist Lisa because these problems in her own person had never been resolved. This caused Lisa to feel that her mother did not like her, and she was particularly hurt when she heard her mother making unfavorable comparisons between herself and Holly.

Dr. Becker's heavy professional schedule removed him from the home much of the time, and he did not have constant contact with the problem. He showed interest in Lisa, however, by attending a conference at the request of the teacher and revealed to her that he had not observed Lisa in the context of the problem. He grasped the essence of the problem immediately and was most anxious to take corrective steps. Immediate arrangements were made by Dr. Becker for Lisa to have a thorough physical examination, which led to the removal of her tonsils and adenoids. His ability to communicate with Lisa was evident from comments made by both parents. He promised to talk with her and help her to understand some of the problems confronting her.

Holly's facile manner of adapting to her new environment and making new friends tended to increase Lisa's anxiety. She genuinely wanted to assist Lisa and often helped her with homework assignments even though she was two years younger. For this she received praise from the mother, but Lisa was again somewhat hurt by the obvious difference in competency.

ATTEMPTS TO HELP LISA

In addition to meeting with Lisa's parents, the teacher told the school counselor of her concern and asked that he assist Lisa in her adjustment after her return from the hospital. Tests were administered by the counselor to assess Lisa's academic aptitude and achievement. As reported earlier, she was of average aptitude, but was among the lowest in her class in achievement.

The counselor talked at length with both Lisa and her teacher separately. He learned that there was a considerable discrepancy between what was happening to Lisa and what she thought was happening. Lisa believed that no one was interested in being her friend, that she was unable to do the work assigned and was regarded by peers and her teacher as not being very intelligent. The teacher told why her classmates had been unable to establish friendships with her. She further indicated that Lisa was having difficulty in adjusting to the work of her new school because of deficient basic skills in several areas and not because of any lack of learning ability, much as the test results had indicated.

As he talked with Lisa, the counselor examined the discrepancy between her perceptions and those of her classmates as reported by the teacher. He helped her to understand the difficulties she still faced and developed with her some procedures that could be used to overcome them. They developed some specific areas on which to work initially. These included attempting to become friends with at least two members of the class during the next two weeks, asking for assistance from the teacher when directions or tasks were not understood rather than daydreaming, and making a concerted effort to improve personal appearance and hygiene habits.

The counselor talked with the teacher and general office secretary. Arrangements were made for Lisa to engage in a series of errands that would involve meeting people, taking responsibility, and completing tasks promptly. They would reinforce extroverted behavior, assertiveness, and alertness.

In studying the case of Lisa, one becomes aware of the differences in self-concept that are indicated for Lisa, her sister Holly, her mother, and her father. Consider the impact of the actions of each upon Lisa. Notice how Holly and Dr. Becker, although apparently of somewhat similar personality type, had rather different impacts upon Lisa. Attention is also drawn to the misperceptions Lisa had of herself and others and the insight she gained through increased understanding of herself. Increased self-awareness, as in the case of Lisa, may occur when parents and educators take direct action to assist the individual.

Summary

If we wish to understand a student, we must consider not only how he appears to adults and to others in his environment, but how he appears to himself as well. Every individual lives in a world that is his own, that is different from anyone else's world, and that represents reality to him. The self-concept—the picture that a person has of himself—is the key to understanding his behavior, for we all do things which are consistent with the notions that we have about ourselves.

Our self-concept may be congruent with social reality, or it may be distorted. To assist people in developing their understanding of self, we must help them to (1) identify that which is unique about them, (2) discern their own patterns of behavior from those of others, and (3) learn to make optimal use of their strengths and weaknesses.

A number of techniques are available that assist the student in revealing himself in confidential and nonthreatening circumstances. Through interpretation and discussion of results, the student is able to incorporate those facts and perceptions which have meaning for him. In this process he learns more of what he really is and what he stands for. Also, he sometimes learns that his internal behavior is miscommunicated and misunderstood by others.

The counselor can be most helpful when he uses information gathered to stimulate the student's thought, to increase his insight, and to clarify his misperceptions. Data become a catalyst and not a dictum to self-understanding when used in this manner.

Exercises

1. Ask someone to give ten different answers to the question "Who am I?" Do these answers give you any clues to the way he views himself? What do you see as the values and dangers of such an assignment in helping you to understand a student?

2. In what ways was your self-concept different during your adolescence from what it is now? How do you account for these changes, and what do they suggest regarding the value of the self-concept as an aid in understanding youth?

3. Much research is being done on the self-concept. Read an article dealing with some aspect of this problem and summarize it for class presentation. (Such articles are most apt to be published in *Journal of Counseling Psychology, The Personnel and Guidance Journal, Journal of Personality and Social Psychology,* and *Journal of Consulting Psychology.*)

References

Combs, Arthur W., and Donald Snygg: *Individual Behavior*, Harper & Row, Publishers, Incorporated, New York, 1959.

Hamachek, Don E. (ed.): *The Self in Growth, Teaching, and Learning*, Prentice-Hall, Inc., Englewood Cliffs, N.J., 1965.

Jourard, Sidney M.: *The Transparent Self*, D. Van Nostrand Company, Inc., Princeton, N.J., 1964.

Moustakos, Clark E. (ed.): *The Self*, Harper & Row, Publishers, Incorporated, New York, 1956.

Rogers, Carl R.: *On Becoming a Person*, Houghton Mifflin Company, Boston, 1961.

4

Achievement and Aptitude Tests

Effective guidance is dependent upon accurate and comprehensive information about the individual. Tests are one of the chief sources of such information. A test may be roughly defined as a device for the determination of the presence or absence, quality or quantity of a trait, characteristic, ability, habit, skill, or knowledge. It is a group of carefully selected samples of the work that an individual might be presumed to be able to do more or less effectively in different stages of his development. Tests may be oral or written. They may be observation of an activity or inspection of the product of an activity, such as a problem in mathematics, an essay, a loaf of bread, a painting, a sewing table, or a jump. Tests are used to estimate capacity as well as actual attainment at any given time; they reveal both deficiencies and strengths. They provide efficient ways of securing data on the educational, social, physical, and economic attainments of individuals. They help school personnel to estimate whether an individual is ready for a certain job, for promotion in school, for entrance to college, or for some other type of activity.

Achievement Tests

Achievement tests are used to find what has been learned, that is, what knowledges and skills have been developed after a period of study or exercise. They are valuable as a means of determining to what extent the individual has attained a certain degree of progress toward a desirable goal, whether he is ready to undertake the next step, and how his attainment compares with that of other members of his group.

TEACHER-MADE ACHIEVEMENT TESTS: VALUES
AND LIMITATIONS

There are two general types of tests given in the schools: tests made by teachers and standardized tests; each has its own value. At best, teacher-made tests may be better adapted to the needs of the pupil and the goals of the local school. Too often, however, they are hastily constructed and badly worded and have no really definite purpose. In the same examination there may be questions requiring mere memory or skill and others requiring judgment. This makes it difficult to determine what particular objectives have been attained. The results of such tests cannot be compared with the results of tests given by other teachers. Some mathematics teachers grade tests entirely on the correctness of the answer, while others consider the method and the reasoning of the pupil in reaching the conclusion. Another factor that often causes differences in the mark is the appearance of the paper; a neatly typed paper usually receives a higher mark than one that is slovenly, dirty, or difficult to read. Still another variable is that some teachers tend to read "between the lines" and give a good or well-liked pupil the benefit of the doubt, thus giving him credit for what he "meant but did not say." For these and other reasons teacher-made tests usually lack "reliability." Reliability, when used with regard to tests, refers to the accuracy of the results, that is, the degree of consistency obtained between repeated measurements of the same individual. Such tests may also lack "validity." Validity, in this context, refers to the extent to which tests measure what they purport to measure.

The senior author tried an experiment in a university to determine the reliability of a nonstandardized test scored by five members of the department of mathematics. An algebra examination was mimeographed and a copy given to each member of the department for grading with the instruction not to compare notes beforehand. The results were rather startling. There was little consistency in the marks given. If the student's entrance to college depended on the judgment of one of the instructors, he would have been refused admission; if it depended on another, however, he would have been accepted.

Although most of the tests given by teachers are of the essay type, an increasing number of teachers are constructing and using their own objective tests. The results of such teacher-made objective tests cannot usually be compared with those achieved by students in other classes but may provide a flexibility of content which makes them peculiarly valuable. Well-constructed essay tests may also have merit that cannot be obtained through other testing instruments. Nor can we eliminate from consideration the subjective judgments of capable, well-trained teachers who know their pupils and who can, through this knowledge, interpret their written, and often imperfect, expressions. In addition these judgments often give reliable evidences of the abilities and progress of students.

VALUES OF STANDARDIZED ACHIEVEMENT TESTS

A standardized test is one composed of empirically selected materials which has definite directions for use, adequately determined norms, and data on reliability and validity. The directions, of course, tell precisely how the test is to be scored. In obtaining the norms, the test is first given to a standardization group representative of a population in schools for which the test is intended. Such norms may permit a comparison of students by age, by grade, or by some combination of the two. Teachers and counselors using such an instrument not only will want to consult the standard references, e.g., Buros' *Mental Measurement Yearbook*, but should also examine the test manual which explains the construction of the test, its standardization, and the research study which bears on its reliability and validity.

LIMITATIONS OF STANDARDIZED ACHIEVEMENT TESTS

Several weaknesses and limitations have come to light in the indiscriminate use of the results of standardized achievement tests. One weakness is that they do not measure all the desirable outcomes in any subject. No effective standardized tests have yet been devised for the adequate examination of aesthetic appreciation, power to organize, initiative, leadership, or character. Some tests attempt to measure such factors indirectly and are undoubtedly very helpful, but they are acknowledged to be ineffective instruments on the whole for this purpose.

When pupils are given standardized tests and their achievement scores taken as the measure of success of their work and also of the success of the teacher, undue emphasis may be placed on the particular elements that are tested, to the neglect of other equally important factors which may not lend themselves to testing. There is also great danger that in their teaching, teachers will also place the main emphasis on the formal testable elements because these are the ones stressed in the test and neglect other elements that are often of greater importance. When this happens, the educative process is greatly weakened.

Another danger is that of uniformity. Curriculum builders are tempted to put in the curriculum the subject matter that is included in the tests, and since the same tests are used in all parts of the country, the subject matter tends to be uniform and not sufficiently responsive to the special needs of different localities.

There is also a tendency to use the average as a measure of desirable and undesirable achievement. To be below the average is to fail or to be unsatisfactory; to be at the average is satisfactory; and to be above the average is worthy of praise. But the student who ranks below the average may be doing work that, for him, is excellent; and the one who is above the average may be harming himself physically or developing unsocial habits— or he may be copying his answers from a friend who sits near him. The rank of any individual in a test should be considered in relation to his ability, his health, and his other personal needs. A standardized test can only tell us what a group has done, not what it should have done. Furthermore, it is sometimes forgotten that any average must, by definition, have as many children scoring below it as above it.

USE OF ACHIEVEMENT TESTS IN GUIDANCE

The values of achievement tests for guidance are many. Any accurate instrument by means of which we can compare the achievement of one person with that of others, with the averages of groups in widely different sections of the country, and with his own previous achievement will be of great help in the diagnosis of his weaknesses and strengths. School progress can be measured, the need for remedial measures determined, and the entire program of the school improved. An arithmetic test may help diagnose whether the weakness of a given pupil is in the fundamental operations, in decimals, in the analysis of the problem, or in carelessness. Tests may show that the cause of failure in physics was due to difficulty in understanding the meaning of the question or weakness in arithmetical computation. French tests have shown whether the difficulty was a weakness in knowledge of vocabulary or in grammatical terms. Such tests, if properly used, help in securing definite data by which improvements can be made. Standardized tests enable us to learn the points of weakness and of strength.

Aptitude Tests

Aptitude has been defined as a measure of the probability of the success of an individual, with training, in a certain type of situation—a job, in school, or in such activities as playing the violin or learning a language. Another definition calls aptitude a condition, a quality, or a set of qualities which is indicative of the probable extent to which an individual may be able to acquire, under suitable training, some knowledge, understanding, or skill. In other words, it is a present situation that indicates the potentialities for the future. An aptitude is not an ability, but it helps to predict the probable development of certain abilities. A test of aptitude may reveal abilities as well as skills, but the significance of the test is in revealing *potential* abilities and skills.

An aptitude is not inborn; it is a combination of inborn capacities and developed abilities, skills, etc., that makes the person what he is at any given time and predicts what he may become. The terms "achievement," "ability," and "aptitude" are often used synonymously, but they have differences in meaning which are important to keep in mind in the discussion of types of tests. Achievement looks to the past; it indicates what *has been done*. Ability is concerned with the present; it indicates the combination of skills, habits, and powers which an individual *now has* and which enables him to do something. Aptitude looks to the future and, on the basis of the habits, skills, and abilities that an individual now has, predicts what he, with training, *may become* and what success he may have in a given occupation or position.

RELATIONSHIP TO INTELLIGENCE TESTS

The tests described here as aptitude tests include some that formerly were called "intelligence tests." This term has been largely discarded because the meaning of "intelligence" is often misunderstood and because, even when it is defined as "the ability to solve new problems or to meet successfully new situations," it is very difficult to find problems or situations to include in the test which are equally new to all. An interesting illustration of this dilemma was found in experience with the Army Alpha test that was used with the armed forces in World War I. It was discovered that the scores of women who took this test were, on the average, lower than those of men. This led to the "unfortunate" statement that women were inferior to men in intelligence. But when the problems and situations used in the tests were analyzed, it was found that they had been chosen because they were within the experience of most men but less familiar to women. When this bias was eliminated, the scores of women compared favorably with those of men.

The establishment of the validity of aptitude tests is a difficult task. Ideally we might like to use the tests to predict who will be successful in an activity, but the problem of determining the qualities and characteristics of a "successful" person is not an easy one. Two people considered to be equally successful in the same type of occupation may be very different in character and in types of ability. The problem then is to determine what makes them both successful.

There are two approaches to the solution to this problem. One is based on the belief that successful people in a given occupation have a general ability characteristic of that occupation. Such an approach has led in the past to the construction of tests purporting to measure that global aptitude, for example, tests of academic aptitude, social intelligence, clerical aptitude, musical aptitude, and artistic aptitude. This approach has been largely replaced by a more empirical one. More commonly now successful workers are given a wide range of tests which are then factor-analyzed to determine what elements seem to cluster together. After such factor analysis, more efficient tests are constructed to enable better predictions of success. Such tests are generically known as "multifactor" tests and seem to have a sounder research base than the older tests.

VALUES OF APTITUDE TESTS

An examination of the "aptitude" tests clearly shows that many of them are not tests of aptitude as defined by most authorities. They test for the possession of abilities only and not for readiness to acquire ability or for the various personality and emotional factors that are so important to success on the job. It is very difficult to arrive at any conclusion regarding the accuracy with which prediction may be made on the basis of these tests. Some reasons for this are as follows:

1. Most tests do not measure all factors important for success and do not consider the relationships between factors, that is, the pattern of factors.
2. Those who seek to evaluate the tests differ regarding the criteria used for success on the job. Some consider only the ability to hold the job; others, production rates; and still others, such various factors as interest, effort, personality.
3. The weight attached to various factors in efficiency rating may differ with the investigator.
4. Many tests make no attempt to find the extent to which the factors tested are really crucial on the job.
5. The range of potential ability of groups tested varies greatly.
6. The statistical measures used to express the accuracy of prediction are fairly satisfactory for groups but quite unsatisfactory when applied to individuals.

From the above it seems evident that the study of aptitudes must, in the future, proceed on a more individual and clinical basis than is true at present and employ methods that will reveal the integration of the various factors rather than each factor separately. Aptitude for any task consists of a constellation of factors. An adequate aptitude test would be one that would measure all the factors necessary for success; this goal is practically impossible. The complete determination of aptitude for any job would require tests of specific abilities, personality, general mental ability, observations by skilled observers, and mental and physical records. Emphasis should be given not to weaknesses and to lack of abilities so much as to strengths and to presence of abilities.

The estimates of the accuracy of these tests for purposes of prediction vary greatly with the authority making them. Some claim a very high degree of accuracy, others are more modest and restrained. Taking all the facts into consideration, we are probably safe in saying that the tests are helpful if used with care and in connection with other data. Practically all of them are very useful in group prediction. If registrars or directors of admission of colleges or vocational schools wish to reduce the number of probable failures among those who enter, they would be quite justified in making their selection on the basis of some of these tests; there would most certainly be failures among those admitted, but not so many as with random selection.

Aptitude tests that are reasonably valid for workers on the job may not be valid for guidance into an occupation; aptitudes for work cannot adequately be determined on the basis of success in or aptitude for success in the training program.

There is a great difference of opinion regarding the predictive value of these tests for determining admission to college. Some colleges rate them very high and practically require them for admittance. They also advocate their use in high school for selecting different courses, such as courses for those who plan to major in mathematics or science or in literature or languages. Other authorities, admitting that they are valuable in reducing college risks, feel that they often eliminate many who have such qualities as high potential for leadership and who would be greatly helped by college training but who may lack some of the elements stressed in the tests. The tests emphasize the ability to do the work required in college, but they neglect the even more important elements that indicate the sane and progressive leadership in society which we have a right to expect in college graduates. For this reason many colleges are asking secondary-school principals and counselors to report on evidences of leadership, attitudes, participation in extracurricular activities, and other contributions to school life.

LIMITATIONS OF APTITUDE TESTS

The limitations of aptitude tests are generally well understood by those who construct them but not always by those who attempt to interpret and use them. Great care should be taken in the interpretation of these tests, and no one who is not trained should attempt to explain the results to students.

One obvious limitation of these tests is that the physical, social, and emotional environment when the test is taken is often different from that on the job or in college. The general atmosphere in college or on the job may and often does contain elements so different as to reduce materially the predictive value of the test. Predictions of success in college based on these tests fail because, for example, college students are forced to study in the midst of the noise and interruptions that freshmen usually have when there are two or more housed in the same room. It is often said of a successful housewife that her success is due to her ability to fulfill her many obligations in spite of, or in the midst of, constant interruptions—the incessant ringing of the telephone, the call for help from her small children, the care of the dog or the cat at the time when some important duties demand her attention. It would be an interesting experiment to administer a college admission test in such a way that there would be frequent interruptions instead of ordered silence and see what would happen. A test so given might measure the prospective student's ability to study *in the environment* which he will have.

Another comment on the use of these tests for admission to college is that they are especially useful when dealing with groups but not so useful when dealing with individuals. One can select with great accuracy the group in which most of the good prospects lie; that is, the college can reduce materially the risks of failures by choosing those who are near the top, but one cannot be sure that all these will succeed. It is also probable that there are a few in the lower group who will make good students, although most of them will fail.

We must not forget that an aptitude test gives us a prediction of the probability only; there is never any certainty of prediction when we are dealing with human beings. Some students who are high in the scholastic aptitude tests have failed in college, and some who are below the standards set for admission, but who, for various reasons, were admitted, attained satisfactory standings.

Current studies aim to construct instruments capable of measuring a college's psychological and social environment, which is a part of its "culture." Colleges differ in the nature of their culture, and these differences may be important elements in the success of the student. Because the culture and social character of the home and community from which the student comes is also different, the culture of one college may be better suited to one student than to another. The nature of the relationship between college and home culture and its effect on success is not now known, but in the selection of a college a comparison of these two cultures would seem to be helpful.

The Use of Achievement and Aptitude Test Data in Guidance: The Case of Henry

This fourteen-year-old boy is in the eighth grade of Hoover Junior High, where, at the end of the first semester, he has come to the attention of the counselor because he had many low marks on his report card: English—F, history—F, science—D, industrial arts—C, physical education—C, music—D.

Henry came to this school in the fall from the village of Clarien, 200 miles away. His personal data blank indicates that he has one brother Joe, who is twenty, living in Clarien. His sister Mary is sixteen; another sister is two. Both live at home. His father is an auto salesman, and his mother does not work outside of the home.

One week after Henry entered Hoover Junior High School, he disappeared from home and went to Clarien where his brother Joe lives. Joe, who is an unmarried auto mechanic, allowed Henry to stay with him three days before he returned him to his home. Recently Henry told his parents that he hated school and that he intended to run away again and join his brother. This prompted his mother to call the principal and report the incident. She said, "Henry agreed to stay in school through the semester, but he insists that he doesn't like it. I hope you can find some way of helping him." (At this point what hypotheses do you have regarding Henry's poor marks?)

Henry missed three days just before Christmas vacation. When the nurse called at his home, she reported: "Henry was at home when I called. He had a slight head cold but no fever nor other signs of illness. He seemed to be in a depressed mood and obviously not very enthusiastic about school. It was difficult to get him to explain his attitude." His mother, who was home with Henry, did not appear much concerned over the situation. She dismissed the matter by stating that he would feel better after Christmas vacation and would probably be eager to get back to school.

Henry is quite careless about his appearance. His red hair is slightly curly and he always seems to need a haircut.

It appeared that Henry needed someone to help him, and an appointment was arranged with the counselor. Some of the notes which the counselor made during his first interview with Henry are as follows:

> Likes to read about the care and protection of animals. Often wishes he could equip a chemical laboratory of his own at home. Remarked: "I'd like to go into animal husbandry if I could get the training."
>
> Stops occasionally at city library on way home from school and reads *Popular Mechanics* and books on wildlife and on the breeding of fine horses. Wants to travel, "just anywhere, but mainly to South America." Wants to go simply because "it would be educational." "School just doesn't get me anywhere. I'd criticize it, but I don't know what to put in its place."
>
> On social interests: Claims to prefer a few close friends but likes "most people." Finds it difficult to make friends in a new school; worries somewhat because "the boys I like seem to be getting girl crazy. I don't think I understand girls."
>
> On recreation: As in earlier report, he mentions hiking and taking pictures as main choices. He has "a very ordinary camera," but hopes to buy a good one soon if he can "earn some money at odd jobs."

Concerning siblings: Enjoys being with his older brother. Gets along well with his sisters except that "Margaret would be happier if I learned to dance and if I were more polite in front of others. It worries me some."

Regarding his parents: "Everything is fine, only I guess Mother isn't pleased with my schoolwork. Dad treats me fine—about like any boy's dad would treat him."

Preferences in school activities: Science experiments and geography. Wants to know more about nature study.

After explaining to Henry about the desirability of securing more information about him, the counselor arranged with the boy to take some tests. Here are some of the results:

Differential Aptitude Test	*Percentile*
Verbal Reasoning	50
Numerical Ability	85
Abstract Reasoning	93
Space Relations	80
Mechanical Reasoning	72
Clerical—speed and accuracy	15
Language Usage:	
Spelling	4
Sentence	8

The counselor next gave Henry an achievement test:

Iowa Every-pupil Tests of Basic Skills	*Percentile*
Silent Reading Comprehension—total	5
Reading Comprehension	2
Vocabulary	10
Work Study Skills—total	20
Map reading	60
Use of references	5
Use of index	3
Use of dictionary	3
Graphing	80
Basic Language Skills—total	5
Punctuation	3
Capitalization	5
Usage	10
Spelling	3
Basic Arithmetic Skills—total	60
Fundamental knowledge	75
Fundamental operations	50
Problems	65

With this information available, the counselor arranged for remedial work in reading and language for Henry in an effort to make school a more meaningful experience for him.

Summary

The construction of standardized tests in achievement and aptitude and their wide use in schools and colleges as well as in industry have inaugurated a new era in guidance. They have been of great service in the improvement of teaching as well as in occupational choice and adjustment to the job.

Standardized tests are not intended to replace teacher-made tests since both have unique values. Standardized tests permit comparisons from one class to another, from one place to another, and from one time to another. If we wish to study a student's development, we will find the results of standardized tests most useful.

Achievement tests tell us what a student knows. Aptitude tests tell us his potential for learning more. While we separate these two kinds of tests for the purpose of discussion, they actually have much in common. A student's achievement may tell us about his aptitude, and his aptitude is usually indicative of his achievement. One way of describing the relationship between these types of test is to remember that achievement tests are apt to be concerned with a narrow—often school-centered—aspect of learning while aptitude tests are more apt to deal with a broader—life-centered— aspect of learning.

While the values of these tests have been demonstrated, they do have limitations which should be kept in mind by all users.

Exercises

1. We do not have all the facts in the case of Henry, but we do know some things. You are asked, therefore, to indicate what you think of the following assumptions by putting the appropriate letter after each of the statements listed below.

Put a W if you consider an assumption to be definitely warranted by the data.

Put a T if you think an assumption seems tentatively supported; the evidence is not conclusive, but it does, nevertheless, point in the direction of the assumption.

Put an I if you consider that there is insufficient evidence to justify an opinion one way or the other.

Put a C if you think that an assumption is contradicted by the evidence.

a. Home life unhappy

b. Friction between parents and children

c. Feeling of inferiority when compared with his older sister
d. Feels lost in new school
e. Concerned because he thinks his mother does not understand him
f. Worried over his own health
g. Is rejected by other boys of his age
h. Desires more attention from girls of his age
i. Physical immaturity interferes with his satisfactory social adjustment
j. Requires more help in adjusting socially to his new school environment
k. Lacks ability to do average eighth-grade work
l. Is lazy
m. Present school work is not "geared" to his main interests
n. Has more mental ability than is required to do the work of his present grade in school
o. Emotional instability is basic to his trouble
2. Study the case of Henry and comment on the tests that were given him. Are they adequate or inadequate for effective guidance? Could you suggest other types that would be helpful? What additional information about Henry would be helpful?
3. Secure a copy of an achievement test in your teaching field. Examine the items, and, by reference to your own beliefs regarding what should be taught in your subject area, discuss the validity of the test.

References

Anastasi, Anne: *Psychological Testing*, The Macmillan Company, New York, 1961.

Buros, Oscar Krisen: *The Sixth Mental Measurement Yearbook*, Gryphon Press, Hyland Park, N.J., 1965.

Ebel, Robert L.: *Measuring Educational Achievement*, Prentice-Hall, Inc., Englewood Cliffs, N.J., 1965.

Goldman, Leo: *Using Tests in Counseling*, Appleton-Century-Crofts, Inc., New York, 1961.

Tyler, Leona E.: *Tests and Measurements*, Prentice-Hall, Inc., Englewood Cliffs, N.J., 1963.

5

Personality Estimates and
Interest Inventories

Although there are many difficulties in assessing achievement and aptitude, assessing personality and interest is an even more complex task because of the indefiniteness of the concepts of "personality" and "interest."

Estimates of the probability of success in any line of work must take into consideration factors other than the specific ability to perform the various kinds of operations required by the job. Skills and abilities will always be important, but other factors profoundly affect success in occupational life, in school, in social life, and in the performance of our obligations to society. Personal qualities and interests are fully as important as intelligence and technical skills.

Meaning of Personality

Psychologists have not been able to agree on what constitutes personality. There are at least three somewhat different meanings in common use: (1) Personality is the combination of the physical and mental qualities, ideals, aspirations, ambitions, aptitudes, and interests that characterize a person. (2) Personality is the structure and pattern of the total behavior of the individual. (3) Personality is the social and psychological impact one makes on others.

PERSONALITY MEANS THE INNER SOURCES OF BEHAVIOR

From the first point of view personality is something that an individual has within himself that causes him to act in certain ways. It is the "inner" sources of his behavior, the causes of his conduct. From this point of view motives, ideals, purposes, and goals are of supreme importance as sources of actual behavior. Such a definition leaves personality necessarily hidden and unknowable. While this concept may be useful to those desiring abstract theoretical explanations of behavior, it makes any real measurements impossible.

PERSONALITY MEANS CHARACTERISTIC BEHAVIOR

From the second point of view inner sources are not personality but important factors in determining future personality. They might be called "personality aptitudes." Personality is how one *behaves*. This is the popular meaning of personality. We say that the glamorous actress *has* personality; the ineffective teacher *lacks* personality. We also say that someone does not always *show* his personality to others, but, rather his *true* personality is revealed only when conditions are favorable. He may seem to his business associates in the office to be cross, crabbed, and miserly, but when he leaves the office and gets home in the evening with his loved ones, he becomes genial, sympathetic, and generous. The advocates of this meaning are more and more including in "behavior" elements that are not visible to others, such as thoughts, plans, purposes, and even emotions. When these elements are included, there is little difference between this meaning and the first one.

PERSONALITY MEANS THE SOCIAL CONSEQUENCE OF BEHAVIOR

From the third point of view personality is thought of as one's effect on others. This definition has some merit, but, strictly speaking, how another person reacts to you indicates his personality, as well as yours. It is, however, dangerous for anyone to infer his personality from the way another reacts unless he knows the kind of person the reactor is and unless it is the customary reaction of many people. It is easily possible that ten people might react in ten different ways to exactly the same thing that one says or does.

Estimating Personality

Whether personality is considered to be "characteristic behavior" or the inner sources of such behavior, the only means of estimating it is by observing how the individual behaves in different situations, what he says, what he does, how he acts, that is, by his behavior. The instruments used for the appraisal of personality may be roughly divided into two classes, although some are quite interesting mixtures. One uses the "atomistic" method, and the other the "global" method. The atomistic method assumes that bits—atoms—of behavior may be added together to construct a total picture of personality. The global method assumes that bits of behavior have no meaning in themselves and that only the totality should be examined.

The atomistic method seeks to get descriptions of an individual's behavior in all sorts of situations. Records of his behavior may be made by the individual himself or by others, such as his playmates, his fellow students, fellow workers, or by parents, teachers, or guidance specialists. The behavior reported may be in social occasions or in situations organized especially for the purpose of discovering significant traits and characteristics. Autobiographies and anecdotal records are often helpful in revealing behavior and sometimes indicate aspirations, attitudes, and beliefs unsuspected by others. Choices of leaders for homeroom, class, or school, for captains and managers of athletic teams are also helpful. It is now common practice for teachers to report characteristic behavior of students. Such estimates are required in the application for admission to college and to other types of educational institutions.

The global method seeks, often through projective devices, to assess the total personality. In this the individual is stimulated to project his personality into the test exercises which attempt to arouse responses that are a projection of the "inner self," of motives and personality traits that are usually hidden, often unsuspected by the individual himself. This global assessment may then be used to explain and predict behavior. Psychologists subscribing to this point of view are more interested in the dynamics of the meaning of behavior than in the overt acts themselves.

SCALES ARE USED IN ESTIMATING PERSONALITY

The use of scales in this regard is based on the belief that those who know a student well—teachers, peers, parents—may be able to contribute valuable information about his personality if they are helped to focus and systematize their observations and judgments. The forms used to guide observers who are estimating personality range from words or descriptions indicating desirable or undesirable traits to definite weighted scales for various items. They vary from small cards with short lists of traits to long, involved lists covering several pages and requiring extensive observation of the individual. Typical of forms used in personality estimating are the usual school report cards which include such items under the headings of "Character" or "Citizenship." The most common items are (1) cooperation, (2) initiative, (3) reliability, (4) promptness, and (5) neatness or orderliness. Sometimes the items are grouped under certain headings as "Social Attitudes" and "Work Attitudes," or "Traits Affecting Behavior," "Traits Affecting Learning," and "Traits Affecting Social Efficiency." In school reports the forms are likely to be characterized by descriptions of the traits listed, three or five degrees for each rating, cumulative records in order to show growth or change, and the requirement that teachers record only those traits that are very evident to them.

PROBLEM CHECKLISTS ARE USED FOR ESTIMATING PERSONALITY

An important approach to the study of personality is the inventorying of the felt problems of students. Many teachers and counselors have made such lists and have found them very helpful in providing the opportunity to prepare for meeting the needs suggested therein. There are problem checklists which are available through commercial channels, and some schools have used them as aids in counseling or in surveying the concerns of the student body. For the second purpose they may be filled out anonymously. A problem checklist or inventory consists basically of a list of problems which research has suggested are common to a population of the age being studied. The student doing the inventory indicates which of these problems are bothering him. Although a student, for a variety of reasons, may not be willing to admit that a problem is concerning him, these checklists, if interpreted properly, furnish interesting and helpful data for counselors. They may reveal unsuspected problems and, in many cases, their hidden causes. Their greatest value is as a basis for a counseling interview.

The conclusion regarding the personality of the individual based on information obtained from this type of inventory will depend upon the concept of personality held. If personality were considered to be characteristic behavior, all the responses would be carefully examined, and characteristic behavior would be inferred. The process would end there because the individual's characteristic behavior is his personality. If personality were considered to consist in his motives, attitudes, ideals, etc., the attempt would be to infer from his behavior what his ideals, attitudes, and motives would be, for they are his personality.

All the preceding attempts to uncover the personality of individuals approach the problem from what is called the atomistic point of view; that is, they attempt to find the elements that together constitute personality.

PROJECTIVE TECHNIQUES ARE USED FOR ESTIMATING PERSONALITY

In contrast to the previous measurement techniques, the global approach to the appraisal of personality attempts to study personality as a whole. This method is often called the "projective" technique because the individual is stimulated to project his personality into the test exercises. The stimuli used

in projective techniques attempt to arouse responses that are a projection of
the "inner self"—of motives and personality traits that are usually hidden
and often even unsuspected by the individual himself. The subject may be
asked to respond to a series of pictures, ink blots, or similarly ambiguous
stimuli. The interpretation of the responses requires a long period of training and should be done only by those who are specially qualified. Strictly
speaking, every test may involve the projection of the self in some degree,
but projective tests rely more completely on the personality signs disclosed.

AUTOBIOGRAPHY—SELF-PERCEPTION

The use of autobiographies for personality and interest estimates was quite
common several years ago, but recently their use has fallen off considerably, although many counselors still consider them very valuable. One of
the limitations of autobiographies lies in the possibility of unauthorized
people reading them. Many students have a natural reluctance to reveal to
others, especially adults, what they think and feel and what they really would
like to be. This reluctance may be especially great if they suspect that the
adult would disapprove of their goals or laugh at them. "A boy's will is
the wind's will, and the thoughts of youth are long, long thoughts."

In spite of these and other limitations the autobiography may have
many values. It aids in the interpretation of facts obtained by objective
methods and permits the client to participate actively in the counseling
process and in the development of self-understanding. The autobiography
encourages the presentation of experiences too intimate to be revealed in
a face-to-face situation by shy students. Most important for busy teachers,
it is an easy method for recording information which might be imparted in
an interview, but which the teacher might not have time to record accurately. It is invaluable in developing the longitudinal histories that are
needed to supplement our cross-sectional techniques. Finally, autobiographies
can be obtained in groups with a minimum expenditure of the time of the
counselor or teacher. This guidance technique has much to recommend it,
but it suffers, of course, from the reticence which characterizes many adolescents in their dealings with adults.

Because of this reticence, reliable information about the thoughts and the
feelings of youth may be secured indirectly. Some teachers use a character
in literature or history as topics of themes and ask students to discuss what
sort of man he was, what his purposes and ideals were, what he liked and
disliked, and in which respects was he a success and in which a failure. The
student may reveal his own ideals and ambitions by what he finds in others.
Another device used is to have students write themes on more personal
experiences and reactions such as their goals and fears, what they really want
in life, or the person in the community whom they admire most.

Still another personal document which some schools have found useful is the diary. This method of securing information about students is difficult to use because interest must be sustained over a long period of time. As a consequence teachers sometimes ask the student to simply keep a log of his daily activities over a week or so. In either activity the student is able to present to the teacher a picture of how he spends his day.

The autobiography is thought of as a valuable means of getting an overall picture of the important events in the child's life. It offers subjective information about his personality and provides an opportunity to study his basic personality dynamics. Perhaps its major contribution is that it promotes self-understanding by encouraging the student to take a close look at himself. Another special value is that the teacher can learn more about the student in less time than a structured interview would require. A major issue in the use of autobiographies is the extent to which they should be structured or unstructured. In a structured autobiography the student is provided with an outline of the kind of things he should cover—early history and family background, health and physical record, school history, leisure time activities, vocational plans, etc. In an unstructured autobiography the only directions are something like "write a story about your life." While this latter method is most apt to reveal what the child perceives as important to him, it may be difficult to obtain some of the basic data which the teacher or counselor might want.

SOCIOMETRY—PEER PERCEPTIONS

Sociometric devices which have been used in many schools with varying results are methods of determining friendship patterns and other social and psychological interaction in a group. One fundamental requirement is that the responses of individuals be kept confidential by the teacher or counselor. Types of questions like the following are used: "Who would be your choice to take the leading part in the school play?" "Who would you like most to be your partner in the laboratory experiments?" "Who would you like to have sit next to you in school?" "Who do you think would make the best captain for next year's football team?" "Who in your class seems to agree with everything that is proposed?" "Who always disagrees with what the majority wants?" The questions used should be those that are considered to be important by the group.

Such devices are useful in determining which students would be congenial as working companions for certain jobs. They are also helpful in finding the characteristics of individual students as determined both by their own responses and by the reaction of other students to them. Sociometric techniques have been very useful in the military services in organizing groups of men in airplane crews who are congenial when in close contact for many hours at a time.

By stringing together the choices of individuals, a network of school or classroom friendships is obtained. Studying this network will show "isolates"—those who are chosen by no one; "stars"—those who attract many friends; "cliques"—small groups who interact with each other but not with the rest of the group; and other phenomena which are useful in understanding the social and psychological climate of the classroom. Some researchers have merely added up the number of choices received by each student to get a gross popularity index. This index has then been related to a variety of predictor variables such as school achievement and continuation in school.

ANECDOTAL RECORDS—ADULT PERCEPTIONS

A student who meets a teacher forty-five minutes a day, five days a week, for four or five months is almost certain to be involved in some very significant incidents during this association. In order to provide some means of capitalizing on such experiences, the anecdotal report was devised. It may be defined as an "on-the-spot" description of some incident, episode, or occurrence that is observed and recorded as being of possible significance. When these reports are gathered together, they are known as an anecdotal record.

In practice the distinction between report and record is not always observed, and the two terms tend to be used interchangeably. The report itself, however, should be a clear, precise statement of what happened and of the circumstances surrounding the incident and should avoid any projection of the observer's personality. Anecdotal records, on the other hand, may consist only of a description of the incident or may include an interpretation of the observed behavior and a recommendation for action. Such records are often properly listed under "personality records" because these observations of behavior are very important in revealing personality. The description of the behavior is the most important part of the record, and some authorities say that the interpretations and recommendations should be made only by qualified experts in psychology, not by teachers.

As indicated above, there are various types of anecdotal records which are in general use. The first type contains only an objective description of behavior with no comment or interpretation. The second has a description of behavior and some comment or interpretation. The third type has a description of behavior with comments and interpretation and a description of treatment. And, finally, a fourth type may contain a description of behavior with comment, interpretation, and recommendations for desirable future treatment.

An example of the first type is as follows: "When Henry came to class this morning, he seemed very tired and just slouched into his seat. He took no part in class discussion and seemed to have no interest in what was being discussed. This was very unusual, for he has always been eager to participate and often monopolizes the discussion time."

An example of the second type is as follows: "Mary came to me before class today to say that she had written to the state department of agriculture concerning their bulletin on mammals. She had just had a reply stating that they had none on hand but would send them as soon as they were available. Mary has shown a real interest in biology since she studied the subject of birds. She is reporting her own observations to me and looking up outside material."

The following is an example of the third type: "I have found Edward day after day in the library reading magazines, yet he never has time to correct errors in his papers or to work carefully on his English assignments. He likes to read but not to work on his schoolwork. I have taken library privileges from Edward until he brings his work up to a satisfactory level. The librarian has agreed not to admit him to the library during his free periods."

The following is an interesting example of the fourth type: "John has dropped off to sleep in class three times this week. He is so obviously conscientious about his work and so helpful and cooperative that I wonder whether he is ill or spending too much time on athletics. Someone should inquire more definitely into his case and find what is the real cause of his unusual behavior."

VALUES OF ANECDOTAL RECORDS

Anecdotal reports dealing with the same student but made by several different teachers are very valuable, for they indicate whether the behavior described by one teacher characterizes the student or is a reaction to the teacher himself. Anecdotes by one teacher about the same pupil over an extended period of time are also important for showing growth and change.

The counselor secures information which he needs for conferences with individual students. The personal relationship between pupil and counselor is improved by these records, for they show the pupil that the counselor is acquainted with his problems and also point out the need for better work and study habits as well as growth in these respects. An appropriate summary of anecdotes is valuable if it is sent with a pupil when he goes to another school. Finally, a collection of anecdotal records may provide the necessary validation of various evaluative instruments.

Many schools find it helpful to distribute to teachers and counselors cards prepared especially for such records. Headings for the name of the student and the observer, time of day, and description of the incident and the circumstances surrounding it are typed on the cards for the convenience of the teachers. Forms should be short and informal, and provide space for all pertinent information, especially the objective descriptions of behavior separated from the subjective comments and interpretations. Reports are of most value when they deal with significant episodes showing a marked deviation from the normal behavior of the individual or his group. An attempt should be made to secure anecdotes about all types of students and not just those who are disciplinary problems. Because people behave differently in different settings, anecdotes should go beyond the classroom and the school to include any significant behavior wherever it is observed. Any behavior that will help in understanding a student should be noted whether it is favorable, unfavorable, or neutral. The anecdote should be written as soon after the incident occurred as possible to prevent distortions caused by memory lapses. There should be no requirement for teachers to prepare a definite number of anecdotes for any given length of time because such a requirement often results in inferior records, since incidents worthy of recording do not happen at any given time.

The writing of anecdotal reports is a skill which needs developing, and teachers need in-service training in making and using such records. Staff members who are expected to write anecdotal records should have a period of instruction under an experienced person who would help them to understand the purpose of the records and to make proper use of them.

In summary, anecdotal records provide a variety of descriptions concerning the unconstrained behavior of pupils in diverse situations and thus contribute to an understanding of the core or basic personality pattern of each individual and of the changes in patterns. Properly used, they substitute specific descriptions of personality for vague generalizations and direct the attention of teachers away from subject matter and class groups and toward individual pupils. They stimulate teachers to use cumulative records and to contribute to them. The counselor secures information which is helpful to him as preparation for counseling and which supplements information secured in other ways.

Meaning of Interest

Closely related in both purpose and method to the personality estimates just described are the various interest-finders or inventories now so extensively used. In fact, it is difficult to find any clear distinction between personality and interests because any adequate description of personality must include the interests of the individual—intellectual, physical, cultural, social, occupational, and recreational. Likewise, interests are closely related to aptitudes. Interests are elements in the total personality and aptitude patterns.

The term "interest" is rather loosely used in guidance, but it may be defined as a feeling of liking associated with a reaction to a specific thing or situation. Since it is a feeling, it cannot be objectively measured; its presence or absence can be revealed only by the statement of the individual himself. Although there is no way by which this self-report can be completely validated, we can make estimates that are, for practical purposes, very helpful.

There is a common belief that ability and interest are closely related and that one who has high ability in some activity will have a high interest in it, while one who has low ability will have a low interest. Observation indicates, however, that this relationship is not always present. A man may perform some job in which he has little interest, but he does it to make a living. On the other hand, one who has low ability in some activity may have a deep interest in it. The most important element in success is ability, not interest. Interest acts merely as a stimulant and does not ensure effectiveness of performance.

INTEREST MAY BE EXTRINSIC OR INTRINSIC

Interests may be classified as "extrinsic" or "intrinsic." Extrinsic interests are pleasurable emotions that are connected with the outcomes of an activity; intrinsic interests are those connected with the activity itself. Extrinsic interests may involve a victory over others, or money, praise, etc. An intrinsic interest is centered on the activity itself. In many cases it is difficult to determine whether an interest is extrinsic or intrinsic. In playing golf intrinsic interests are involved in the pleasure of swinging the club, hitting the ball, walking in the fresh air, and talking with friends. Extrinsic interests are involved in hitting the ball where you want it to go, making a hole in one, making a score under 80, beating the other person, or winning money.

Each type of interest has its value. An extrinsic interest provides a constant incentive to continue an activity until the goal is reached even after pleasure in the activity itself is gone. This incentive may continue to operate throughout one's life. Competitive sports and nearly every other activity where competition is involved have extrinsic interest, but they also usually have intrinsic interest. One danger in connection with extrinsic interest is that the goal may be so artificial that, after it is reached, the interest is gone. Therefore worthwhile activities are better supported by intrinsic interests because the pleasure continues even if the goal is not reached. With the different types of instruments used in the discovery of interests it is often impossible to determine whether the interest revealed is intrinsic or extrinsic.

Estimating Interest

There are three methods used in the attempt to discover the interests of people. The first method is to ask individuals what they like to do. This has some value, but answers to questions about interest may indicate only a very temporary interest, may come from the desire to please the one who is asking the questions, or may be based on the belief that certain occupations are higher than others on the social scale. The second method is to analyze the activities that a person performs. Nearly all cumulative records have spaces for indicating the interests of students as suggested by their extracurricular and out-of-school activities. The difficulty with this method is that what one is doing may not be what he would like to do but what he has to do to make a living. All acts are not free choices. When this method is used, it should be restricted to those activities that have been freely chosen by the individual himself. The third method of measuring interest is by the use of interest tests and inventories. There are many instruments now in use, and the great majority of them deal with occupational interests.

TYPICAL INSTRUMENTS FOR ESTIMATING INTERESTS

Nearly all these instruments use some form of self-report or questionnaire and cover a wide range of interests. They vary in complexity, with the simplest merely giving a detailed list of occupations and asking the student to check those in which he is interested. The more complex instruments involve the analysis of activities common in different occupations and attempt to reveal the attitude of the student toward conditions surrounding various kinds of work. Regardless of their degree of complexity, they are all directed toward the location of occupational interests or preferences. Some attempt to determine interests in specific occupations or in the activities and conditions characteristic of occupations or of families of occupations.

Although the methods used in the various blanks are fundamentally very similar, there are certain important differences. Some restrict the questions to the liking or disliking for certain types of activity and to the interest or lack of interest in different occupations; others include subjective estimates of degree of interest or ability such as "How much do you like it? How good are you at it?" Still others attempt to find how much the individual knows about the occupation or activity.

LIMITATIONS OF INTEREST INVENTORIES

Interest inventories have proved to be valuable instruments in locating general and special interests of secondary-school students, but they should be used with a clear understanding of their limitations as well as their values. Among the limitations are the following:

1. It is not possible to determine the accuracy of the statements made by the individual reporting his interests. Apparently the truth of the statements varies with the form of the question.

2. Although researchers have found patterns of interest that distinguish men from women and those engaged in certain occupations from those in other occupations and from "Mr. Average Man," there is considerable overlapping among the interests of these groups; therefore we cannot be certain that a given pattern is necessarily characteristic of a given occupation.

3. The interest of the adult worker in his activities may have been attained after he secured the job; he may not have had this interest when he was in school.

4. Meaningful interests of high-school students are, naturally, confined to those activities in which they have had experience actually or vicariously. Since one of our tasks is to broaden and create interests, the interest of a student at a given time may not be indicative of what occupation he should choose.

5. Interests are not to be confused with abilities. A person may have an interest, superficial or deep, in some activity for which he has little ability. The converse is also true. Present interest does not necessarily predict success in the occupation.

6. Interests of high-school students may not be sufficiently permanent to warrant using them even as general indicators of occupational selection.

7. No completely satisfactory method has been developed for grouping occupations into "families" which represent similar activities. Radically different occupations may involve the same or similar activities. The important element in an occupation is often not merely the activity itself but the pattern of duties and responsibilities involved in that occupation.

VALUES OF INTEREST INVENTORIES

Such inventories have value in that they require the pupil to review and analyze his interests and to find those occupations about which he knows very little and which he should investigate more fully.

The interests, the likes, and the dislikes revealed by these blanks are, in most cases, *real present* interests and as such have a great deal of value even though they are often not safe guides for the future choice of an occupation. These interests should be utilized by teachers and counselors as a means of widening and enriching the knowledge of the pupil and developing in him an understanding and appreciation of different types of occupational life.

Counselors who use the results of these interest inventories find that they are especially helpful as an introduction to the interview itself. The interest inventory helps the counselor understand the student and permits the counseling to start with a relatively nonthreatening topic—the interests of the student.

Use of Personality and Interest in Guidance:
The Case of Peg

Personality and interest estimates prove their value only in specific guidance situations. Let us look at a girl, and as we study her case, we can consider whether personality tests or interest inventories would have been helpful to teachers attempting to work with Peg, to Peg herself, or to the counselor gathering information about Peg.

PEG'S BACKGROUND

Peg is a high-school junior who was adopted by a teacher. She is a fine example for study of "background versus heredity." Peg and her twin sister were adopted at the age of four months by a childless couple who gave them every advantage. Their mother, who died several days after their birth, had fourteen children. At five, their foster father died, and at that time their foster mother revealed to them that they were adopted. (Peg feels proud and fortunate to have been selected.)

The foster mother has acknowledged that the "balance wheel" of the family was removed with the death of her husband. She has been overambitious for her girls scholastically and feels that they have let her down. The girls know that they have fallen below their mother's expectations, and their attitude is a combination of shame and resentment. This summer the girls met members of their own family for the first time and learned that their real father, who is exceedingly poor, is rearing another family and drinks heavily. He was proud of his daughters when he met them. None of the rest of the family has turned out well. One brother is now AWOL from the Army. One of the sisters has had three illegitimate children. Peg feels fortunate to have escaped this sordid background.

Peg and her foster mother get along very well, and Peg seems very fond of her; but she does not live amicably with her sister, and they were finally given separate rooms. Peg's sister was recently dismissed from a private school and is now employed as a clerk. Peg, however, is eager to complete high school. Peg sings in the church choir, plays the piano quite well, enjoys movies and reading. She apparently has few or no dates.

PERSONALITY AND INTEREST DATA

After an interview with Peg the counselor made the following notes:

> Present subjects: Spanish—A, U.S. history—C, art—C, chemistry—C, physical education—B. Regular attendance and no tardy marks. Favorite subjects: English, history, music. Least-liked subjects: math,

chemistry. Member of the Dramatic Club. Hobbies: knitting, movies, reading. Belongs to: church choir, Job's Daughters, Tri Hi-Y. Reading: fiction. Magazines: largely movie magazines. Peg expresses an interest in music and drama. Employment experience: store clerk and beauty-shop helper. She likes the beauty-shop work best because "it is interesting. You meet an awful lot of nice people."

Additional information about Peg comes from a list of occupations which she made for a report in one of her classes:

Occupation	Reason for Interest
Nursing	It is a wonderful opportunity to help people.
Dramatics	I love to act.
Make-up artist	It is a wonderful way to meet various kinds of people.
Singer	I'd love to be able to sing well.
Write	I'd love to write.

Her present vocational choice is nursing. She made this decision about five years ago. Peg feels very certain that this is the career that she would want to follow, but adds that within a ten-year period she would like to be the mother of two children. She is especially interested in social-service work, and secondly, in occupations requiring special artistic abilities. On an adjective checklist Peg characterized herself as being friendly, patient, stubborn, self-confident, quick-tempered, and cheerful. She also listed herself as being nervous and given to headaches but with no physical disabilities.

OUTLOOK FOR PEG

Peg has read many books about nursing and is very interested in it. Her interest was first aroused when she was a patient herself several years ago. Her mother want Peg to be a teacher or a hairdresser. She does not believe that Peg has the stamina to see a nursing course through to the end.

Peg has found out that she can be admitted on her present grades into a hospital that interests her, and she appears to be well acquainted with the rigorous life of a nurse.

The school adviser feels that Peg has a good chance of making a success of nursing. Peg has raised some questions, however, which suggest that her mind may not be completely made up. She wonders if her personality is one that would help or hinder her as a nurse. She has heard that some nursing supervisors and doctors are hard to work for and that a nurse has many bosses. Furthermore, she wonders if her interest in nursing would sustain her during the long and rigorous training.

As a school counselor, what are some things you could do to help Peg assess her personality and interests in a way that would help her decide if nursing would be a satisfactory goal for her?

Summary

To most people personality means individuality—what make an individual. Beyond this, there is little agreement on what constitutes personality, but there are three different meanings in common use.

1. Personality is the combination of all the physical, mental, and social traits, qualities, ambitions, aptitudes, and interests that characterize the individual.
2. Personality is the structure and pattern of the total behavior of the individual.
3. Personality can be inferred from the individual's effect on others.

The most common method used in assessing personality is observation by teachers, counselors, and fellow students. Similar methods and instruments are used in assessing the interests of students.

Most cumulative school records will have a section dealing with observed characteristics, and teachers may here record their observations and judgments about students. Similar observations are also used in business and industry in connection with the selection of workers and with promotion. This method may be called "atomistic" since it focuses on specific traits and, on the basis of the combination of these traits, some conclusion is reached regarding the personality of the student. Contrary to this is the global method that attempts to study the personality as a whole. Although neither method is completely satisfactory in describing the personality of individuals, they may be the basis for the development of instruments which would be useful in the hands of well trained and sympathetic counselors.

Interests are very important both for vocational choice and for useful and satisfying participation in the activities of the home and the community. With wise guidance, school life and community activities can be very effective tools in the development of interests that will lead to realistic occupational choices and satisfying life adjustments.

Exercises

1. One commonly used interest inventory classifies interest into six fields—personal-social, natural, business, mechanical, the arts, the sciences. From what you know about Peg, what two fields do you think would be her strongest interests? Why?

2. One commonly used personality measurement purports to describe the level of adjustments in four areas—home, health, social, emotional. How would you characterize Peg's adjustment in each of these areas? Why?

3. Read a research article making use of a personality test or an interest inventory, and be prepared to report to the class on the study. (Such articles are most apt to be found in *The Personnel and Guidance Journal, Educational and Psychological Measurement, Vocational Guidance Quarterly,* or *Journal of Educational Research.*)

References

Downie, N. M.: *Fundamentals of Measurements: Techniques and Practices,* Oxford University Press, Fair Lawn, N.J., 1967.

Gordon, Ira J.: *Studying the Child in the School,* John Wiley & Sons, Inc., New York, 1966.

Murphy, Gardner: *Personality: A Biosocial Approach to Origins and Structure,* rev. ed., McGraw-Hill Book Company, New York, 1966.

Stone, Allan A., and Sue Smart Stone: *The Abnormal Personality through Literature,* Prentice-Hall, Inc., Englewood Cliffs, N.J., 1966.

Super, Donald E., and John O. Crites: *Appraising Vocational Fitness by Means of Psychological Tests,* rev. ed., Harper & Row, Publishers, Incorporated, New York, 1962.

PART THREE

School Guidance Organizations

6

Program Management and Development

A guidance program, to accomplish the purposes for which it was designed, must be properly organized and administered. The major emphasis in the future will be on the management and development, as opposed to the initiation, of programs simply because most school systems now have guidance programs. In the late 1960s careful surveys indicated that two-thirds of the secondary schools provided full-time guidance personnel, and this figure went up above 90 percent for the larger districts. Even then, however, only one in six systems provided full-time elementary-school counselors although this proportion rose to about one in two in the large districts.

The School as a Social System

The basic principles which should guide program management and development must be congruent with the nature of the school. The school can be considered as a system of forces which not only are technical, rational, impersonal, and task oriented, but are conditioned by responsive interaction of persons and groups. These persons and groups (teachers, parents, students, etc.) interact in a social establishment which consists of a place surrounded by fixed barriers to perception in which a particular kind of activity—in this case schooling—regularly takes place. Furthermore, the interaction itself becomes a social structure which is historical in that it solidifies as a result of the experience of the particular organization; at the same time, this social structure is functional in that it reflects the adaptation of the organization to the internal and external social environments; finally, it is dynamic in that it generates new forces from the actions and reactions of its constituency.

Because the system of forces is technical there is concern for the mechanics and techniques of pedagogy. Innovations such as nongraded grouping, team teaching, and the use of audiovisual techniques are illustrative of the technical forces which shape the school. The system is rational for there is a deliberate effort to accomplish its purposes. Activity in the school is not random but rather is designed with educational goals in mind. Impersonal in this context means that students, teachers, and administrators are somewhat interchangeable from school to school. Only rarely does the individuality of a worker make marked differences in the functioning of the school. Finally, the system is task-oriented because whatever is done is directed toward the function of the institution which has been allotted to it by society. However, the technical, rational, impersonal, and task-oriented behaviors of school personnel are always colored by the fact that people interact in the work of the school. These interactions may make the work of the school easier or may in some cases interfere with that work. Counselors do not do their job in a social vacuum. Students and others have expectations of them which must be at least minimally fulfilled, for, if a school is not sufficiently congruent with the expectations of the community, it is likely that the community will demand certain changes. Counselors whose behavior is incongruent with the expectations of students will find that students will have very little contact with them. The history of the school and the individuals in it will always influence what happens under the name of education. A strong administrator, counselor, teacher, or citizen in the community may, on some occasions, have a marked impact on the activity of the school. There are schools whose guidance programs have been seriously damaged by the fact that a particular counselor did a particularly bad job some time in the past. There are also schools where counselors and the guidance program are held in high esteem because of the excellent work of a counselor who may himself no longer be in the school. When a school district changes in socioeconomic status, there are almost inevitably changes in the school program. When a rural area changes to a suburb, typically the school changes also to put increased emphasis on college preparation and selection. On the other hand, a middle-class district that becomes a slum may find that the level of teaching and counseling deteriorates. The fixed barriers to perception of the social establishment of the school are made up not only of the fences and walls blocking a view of the school but also of the "professional" behavior which shields the school from public perception. "Dirty linen is not washed in public; outsiders rarely get backstage to see it as it is; lay people don't understand and have to be shielded from reality!"

As a consequence of the forces and folklore operating in a school, sometimes rationality is tinged with the irrational, scientific techniques with superstition, behavior originally task oriented becomes justified only because it is status maintaining, and neutral decisions are biased. The school is as easy to misperceive as is an iceberg. The visible portion can only hint at the hidden reality which itself can be discovered only at risk.

This view of the school as a social system implies that the director of the guidance program must always keep in mind the many forces impinging upon his activity. He needs to be aware of the needs and wishes of the students, the counselors, the community, and other groups which he must try to satisfy. The adjustments made in a guidance program typically are in the form of administrative responses to pressures from one or many of these groups.

Program management or administration is itself one of the forces in a school system. Administration, found in all human organizations, is concerned with the directing and controlling of behavior in social enterprises. Administration may include, but is not synonymous with, leadership. Leadership is defined as the process of changing the perceptions of the work role, behavior, and goals. Such changes in perception may stem from the designated administrator or may come from peers, reading, or other sources. Actually, there is sometimes conflict between the leadership and the administrative roles. The leadership role is often concerned with initiating change; the administrative role with maintaining structure.

Confusion between administrative and leadership activities has made the conceptualization of both processes difficult. While an administrator is often the key individual in making changes in a school system, there are times when leadership not vested in the administrator results in growth or deterioration. The counselor, for example, is expected to be the major leader in guidance program management and development. Sometimes this leadership will be given directly by the counselor and sometimes he will influence the administrator to make what seem to be needed changes. Much study has been done regarding characteristics of leaders, but at the present time it seems reasonable to believe that the qualities of leadership are markedly situational. That is, in some instances a strong, aggressive, determined person may succeed in making desired changes in a program; but in other instances a more reserved, quiet, and flexible individual may fulfill this same purpose. Leaders cannot be separated from nonleaders on the basis of any clear-cut characteristics. Leadership is not discrete in the sense that blood types are. Also, leadership may manifest itself at a distance from the initiator. For example, a counselor may first need to persuade a particular teacher to consult cumulative records before other teachers will do so. The first teacher is a leader in that his behavior serves as a model for others. Such "gate-keepers" must be identified and their leadership channeled so that desirable changes follow. Most frequently, however, the counselor will need to persuade or convince the administrator to behave in a way that influences others to participate in and utilize the guidance program. This desirable administrative behavior may involve much more than leadership and is likely to consist of many facilitating activities which make available the requisite time, materials, and space and result in the appropriate motivation.

One of the basic dimensions used in thinking about administration is the extent to which the administrator initiates structure as opposed to the extent to which he gives consideration to individuals. The administrator certainly has the responsibility of seeing to it that the school does what it is supposed to do (initiate structure). At the same time, if he does not balance the institutional goals with the needs and goals of the individual (give consideration), he probably will not get the best work from the staff nor have good staff morale. This strategy of balancing individual and social goals is the highest art of the administrator.

This section has been concerned with giving the reader a way to think about schools and administration. The basic principles suggested are that the school is a social system with a multitude of forces acting on it, that administration is present in any such organization, that the administrator has a charge from society to perform certain tasks related to the purposes of the institution, that leadership and administration may support each other or may conflict and, finally, that the administrator will always need to balance the task of giving structure to work activities with the task of giving consideration to individuals' needs and desires.

UNDERSTANDING THE COUNSELOR'S BEHAVIOR

One theory of administrative systems says that we can best understand the behavior of a counselor by looking at three dimensions of the social system in which he works, the school. These three dimensions are the sociological, the psychological, and the anthropological. The sociological dimension consists of institutions (schools), the role (the occupational position of counselor), and role expectations (e.g., that he should help students get into college and talk with them about their occupational goals). The psychological dimension is made up of individuals (John Doe, Counselor), personality (the uniqueness of *this* John Doe), and the particular elements of the individual personality (needs, aptitudes, etc.). The anthropological dimension is made up of the culture (that pattern of all those arrangements by which a society achieves greater satisfaction for individuals in the United States of America in the last half of the twentieth century), ethos (the spirit which motivates the ideals and practices of a people), and the values prominent in the society (democracy, individual responsibility, the importance of work, etc.). The behavior of any individual, such as a counselor, is a function of the interrelationship between the culture in which he lives, the role in which he finds himself, and his own personality. If we are to understand why he does what he does, we must look at the various forces impinging on him. The value system of the society, the expectation of the school, and the uniqueness of the individual combine to produce behavior.

Job *satisfaction* occurs when the counselor works in an institution where the role expectation matches his needs and abilities and renders his behavior *efficient*. Job *satisfactoriness* occurs when the needs and abilities of the counselor match the role expectations of the institution and renders his behavior *effective*. This paradigm permits us to understand many conflicts which bother the counselor. There may be conflict, for example, between the counselor role and the counselor's personality, in which case we say he is the wrong man for the job. The school district may expect the counselor to emphasize getting students admitted to college. Such a counselor will need to be very well organized, a good writer of references, and a mine of information about colleges. A counselor who sees himself more as an expert in interpersonal relations and less as an expert in organization may experience some conflict between his personality and the role expectations. Additional conflict may stem from the fact that the administration expects him to handle discipline, whereas counselor educators tell him that this is not a proper activity for a counselor, and he may not wish to see himself as a disciplinarian.

There also may be conflict among the various roles which a counselor must play. To be a successful counselor he may need to stay late at school, but to succeed as a father he may need to get home early. Inter-reference group conflict stems from the varying expectations held by those individuals who have the right to have expectations of the counselor. The community may see him primarily as someone skillful at getting their children into college; the administrator may see him as someone who helps with the smooth running of the school in a variety of quasi-administrative ways; the teachers may see him as someone who can take care of their discipline problems; the students may see him as someone who can, if he will, get them out of and into certain classes; the counselor educator may see him as a clarifier of values and attitudes. Role conflict is a necessary part of every job but it may be particularly bothersome for school counselors because there is not as yet complete agreement as to what they should be doing. What they are taught in college classes in guidance, for example, may have little relationship to what they are asked to do on the job.

ADMINISTRATOR-COUNSELOR CONFLICT

The above scheme may be particularly helpful in understanding the conflict which sometimes occurs between administrators and counselors and between teachers and counselors. Considerable research has been done on the problem of differences among these three role occupants. There is some evidence of differences in personality and values between administrators and counselors. Counselors have been seen as more valuing of altruism while administrators value control more. We have no clear evidence whether the values

of administrators and counselors differed before they went into their specialization or whether the difference arose as a consequence of their jobs. Here
we have the chicken-and-egg problem. The fact that many counselors go
on to become administrators suggests that their behavior is highly influenced
by the position in which they find themselves. Behavior which may be quite
appropriate for a teacher may be inappropriate for a counselor; behavior
which is appropriate for a counselor may be inappropriate for an administrator. Anyone considering becoming a counselor will need to ask himself
whether he can assume with honesty and congruence the point of view,
attitudes, and values thought to be characteristic of good counselors. At
present it appears unlikely that there is any one personality type or config-
uration characteristic of all successful counselors—some are quiet, some
talkative; some introverted, some extroverted; some reserved, some spontaneous. Skill at using his personality to help others, rather than success at
changing his personality to fit a preconceived model, is probably the important outcome for counselors to seek.

Because the public schools generally must admit students whether they
want to or not, and because students generally must attend school whether
they want to or not, the problem of student control is a major one in many
schools. The attitudes toward such control can vary from humanistic to
controlling.

A humanistic orientation characterizes a school which is an educational
community where members learn through interaction and experience. Students' learning and behavior are viewed in psychological and sociological
rather than in moralistic terms. Learning is looked upon as an engagement in
worthwhile activity rather than the passive absorption of facts. The
humanistic teacher believes that close personal relationships with pupils
coupled with friendship and respect will lead to self-disciplined students.
Such teachers are apt to have a democratic classroom climate with flexible
rules and open communication. Both teachers and pupils in such circumstances will act upon their own initiative and accept responsibility for their
actions.

On the other hand, custodial teachers work in highly controlled settings,
concerned primarily with the maintenance of order. Students are stereo-
typed in terms of their appearance, behavior, and parents' social status and
are perceived as irresponsible and undisciplined persons who must be controlled through punitive sanctions. When a pupil does something wrong,
the teacher is less apt to try to understand him and more apt to moralize
about his behavior.

By a process of occupational socialization the counselor, teacher, and
administrator are taught to behave in the appropriate way toward students.
Preliminary research indicates that administrators and counselors are more

apt to be humanistic and teachers more apt to be concerned with controls. Furthermore, elementary-school personnel are more apt to be humanistic than are secondary personnel. Again, these differences may not stem from basic personality differences but from the demands of the job. A counselor dealing with individual students, or with small groups of students, can afford to be humanistic sometimes when a teacher faced with a large classroom cannot.

Counselors may differ from administrators in being more concerned about giving service to individual students, while administrators may demand more attention to staff and community relationships and the promoting of the general school program.

The basic administrator-counselor conflict would seem to be understood better if we focused on the job that society expects them to do. An administrator who is given the responsibility for the smooth functioning of a large institution may not be permitted the luxury of deviations from custom and the focus on individuals that the scheme provides for the counselor. The counselor, therefore, should not congratulate himself on his greater love for children but should remember and be grateful for the fact that only through the work of the school administrator is he permitted to exercise the values of individualization and concern, which are so important to him.

The basic principles in program management and development advanced here are that in understanding occupational behavior we must look not only within the individual to his unique psychological makeup but outside of the individual to the institution which employs him (which has its own peculiarities, experience, and needs), and finally to the larger society with its standards of patriotism, its historical development, and its avowed ideals. In making changes in his job, the counselor will need to know not only what he would like to do and what he is capable of doing, but what the school and society want and will permit. It is easy for counselors to blame administrators for shortcomings in the work situation but difficult for them to appreciate the burden of administration.

Organizing the Guidance Program

In developing a guidance organization there are several concepts which need to be considered. The concept of span of control is concerned with the number of individuals who can be supervised by one person. Although the span of control will vary with the institution and the function of the workers, in general it is believed that no one should directly supervise more than six people. A short span of control provides for tight administration but may produce too many authority levels. This variation in levels of authority distinguishes the tall from the flat organizational plan. In flat organizations there are few levels and few central office administrators; therefore individual school units have much autonomy and administrative responsibility is diffuse. In tall organizations the opposite occurs. Guidance specialists are *staff* personnel, while *line* personnel are administrators in both types of organization. (Line officers are those who have direct control over subordinates. For example, a principal has a line relationship with the teacher. A staff officer is one who can advise and consult but not control. It is generally conceded that it is wiser for the counselor to be a staff officer. This arrangement means that he does not have direct control over teachers but may have influence over their behavior, depending upon the merit of his ideas and the strength of his personality.)

Still another concept in organization has to do with centralization of the authority. Should the guidance program be entirely centralized from the head office of the school system or should it be decentralized so that each school unit is able to make decisions about its program? Certainly balance is needed here, and in general it is thought that the closer to the action the decision making occurs, the more apt it is to result in wise decisions.

Finally, the best organization may need to be worked out on a theoretical basis and then altered in view of the personalities involved. Textbook charts rarely fit the reality of entrenched administrators reluctant to give up hard-won power, historical accretions difficult to reverse, and situational idiosyncratic circumstances.

The accompanying chart illustrates typical organizational patterns involving guidance and other pupil personnel services. It will be seen that the counselor has only a staff relationship to teachers and therefore is in no sense their "boss." The counselor is under the direct supervision of both the principal and assistant principals. Even the directors of the pupil personnel areas do not have a line relationship with the counselor or with teachers. In short, the counselor works under the direction of the principal, and he himself has a line relationship with no one below him. This chart is in no sense a model but merely an illustration. Some districts, for example, might have a director of guidance reporting to the assistant superintendent of pupil personnel services. Some districts place their director of research under this assistant superintendent. Some will not have all the directors shown. In smaller districts the top administrator of pupil personnel may be known as the director of pupil personnel services or the coordinator of pupil personnel services. The assignment of duties to assistant principals takes a variety of forms and there is not always one in charge of service, in which case the coordinator of guidance or head counselor may report to any of several assistant principals or even to the principal himself.

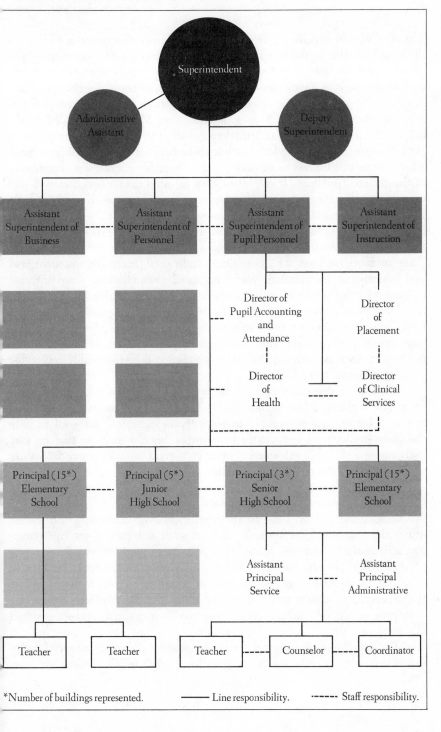

Superintendent

Administrative Assistant

Deputy Superintendent

Assistant Superintendent of Business

Assistant Superintendent of Personnel

Assistant Superintendent of Pupil Personnel

Assistant Superintendent of Instruction

Director of Pupil Accounting and Attendance

Director of Placement

Director of Health

Director of Clinical Services

Principal (15*) Elementary School

Principal (5*) Junior High School

Principal (3*) Senior High School

Principal (15*) Elementary School

Assistant Principal Service

Assistant Principal Administrative

Teacher

Teacher

Teacher

Counselor

Coordinator

*Number of buildings represented. ——— Line responsibility. ------ Staff responsibility.

The first step in organizing or developing a guidance program is to analyze the needs of the students and decide which of them can be met by the school. This analysis is followed by a survey of the present program and staff to see what is being done and what is the potential for change. Planning then begins with the maximum participation of the present staff but keeps in mind both the staff as it is and those who may be added in the future. After identifying the functions which the school will carry out, a plan of organization is needed to relate those functions to job positions. Such job positions call for job descriptions and a timetable for the instrumentation of the desired functions. It is well to keep in mind that no organization will be permanently effective and that therefore every framework needs to have built into it a method for permitting changes.

A general guide to such a preliminary analysis as a first step in organization may be obtained by the use of a standard list of guidance services. The guidance services of counseling, individual inventory, occupational and educational information, placement, and research have long provided a framework by which guidance programs could be considered. While not based completely on a theoretical consideration of what guidance should be, these services do reflect the experience of many schools, for most schools have found it wise to provide these services for their students. Definitions of the services may vary but the following ones will be reasonably acceptable to most guidance specialists.

Counseling denotes a professional relationship between a trained counselor and a client. This relationship is usually person to person, although it may sometimes involve more than two people, and is designed to help the client understand and clarify his view of his life space so that he may make meaningful and informed choices consonant with his essential nature in those areas where choices are available to him.

The *individual inventory service* consists of those activities performed to gather and to disseminate, to appropriate professional staff information about the students, which may aid in their instruction or counseling. Subsumed under the individual inventory service are such activities as testing, gathering information about the home, self, peers, and adult appraisals and perceptions. The purpose of the individual inventory must always be kept in mind for in no case is gathering such information an end in itself. While the counselor is almost totally responsible for the first service—counseling—he may be aided by others, particularly teachers, in the second—individual inventory service.

The provision of occupational, educational, and personal-social information is also a schoolwide responsibility. While the counselor may coordinate the gathering and dissemination of such information he will need much help from teachers, librarians, and administrators. Perhaps the most central and satisfactory method of providing information is through the classroom teacher who relates the content of his course to the requirements of various occupations, additional educational opportunities, and current social mores. Too many schools leave the *information service* to the counselor at the expense of an adequate service.

The *placement service* consists of those activities designed to put students into the courses which will be most beneficial to them, help them on to the next rung of the educational ladder, and help them secure suitable employment, either part-time, summer, or post school. There is much controversy over the school's responsibility for vocational placement, and some believe that such activity is better left to state employment services. In carrying out the placement service it is obvious that counselors will make much use of the individual inventory and counseling service. Some schools ask the counselor to perform this placement function while others hire placement specialists. In a few schools very much of the counselor's time may be spent on educational placement. This is particularly true in schools which have elaborate and complex tracking systems sometimes known as ability grouping systems. Such placement may, in some instances, be much better done by computers. That is, if the counselor can rationally describe how he goes about making decisions about tracking and transmit this information to a computer, it is likely that the computer can do it more rapidly, efficiently and with less cost.

Finally, the *research service* endeavors to continuously evaluate the guidance program. One type of evaluation particularly popular in many schools is the follow-up study of graduates and dropouts. Again, this service may be the responsibility of only the counselor or may be given to a social studies teacher, a business teacher, or someone else particularly qualified to do the job. Overall, it is generally felt that the counselor should coordinate these various services although he may not always carry them out himself.

To obtain the maximum effectiveness from individuals, as much freedom as possible, consistent with the overall purposes of the program, should be given them in carrying out their duties. The general purposes of an organization is to clarify and distribute responsibility and authority among individuals and groups in an orderly fashion. Therefore, organization provides answers to the question—Who should do what, with whom, when, and how? Also built into the organization should be a plan for consistent and systematic evaluation leading to continuing changes.

Regardless of the organizational structure which is decided on, there will inevitably be an informal organization which permits the staff to have access to power other than through the formal organization. An administrator of guidance needs to keep in mind that the paper structure is not necessarily consistent with actuality. In fact, individuals will tend to gravitate toward those duties which make them feel most comfortable.

In summary, the development of a guidance program will be influenced by answers to these questions. What should we be doing for our students which is not being accomplished in the regular instructional program? Who should be given responsibility for carrying out these desired functions? What space will be necessary and what budget? How will we know if the job is being done well?

The Administrative Process

Administration has been defined as the guidance, leadership, and control of the efforts of a group of individuals toward common goals. To function as a guidance administrator it will be necessary to be involved in the following six activities: planning—determining what is to be done; organizing—grouping activities into administrative units; assembling resources—obtaining personnel and equipment; directing—issuing instructions; supervising—helping staff do well the tasks assigned to them; and controlling—evaluating the program to determine that operating results conform to plans.

The administrator in performing his *planning* function will identify the needs and analyze the situation before reviewing the alternatives and deciding upon a course of action. Obviously this may be done alone or with the aid of the staff.

Some schools make use of advisory committees of teachers, other pupil personnel workers, community members, or students. Should such committees help with the planning, it is necessary to make clear to them the boundaries of their responsibility. They should not be given the impression that their advice will always be followed if in fact that is not to be the case.

In *organizing* the guidance program the administrator will be involved in dividing the activities by function, location, personnel available, and groups to be served. In many cases it will then be necessary for him to delegate responsibility for these various functions. It is not feasible for guidance administrators to retain direct control over all the aspects of the program. It is a recognized administrative principle that while he may give authority to others to act in his name, the responsibility cannot be given to others. If things go wrong, the administrator will be held responsible. It is in this organizing phase that the administrator will need to make decisions about structure, line and staff relationships, and span of control.

In *assembling resources* the administrator is concerned not only with staffing but with budget and physical facilities. The wisdom of having an earmarked budget for the guidance program has been long debated, but whether money is specifically allocated or only generally available, no planning for resources can be done without some budgetary framework. In determining the amount of resources to be obtained, the administrator will want to take account of the thinking of the staff as well as research and opinion in the field of organization and administration of guidance which suggests the percentage of the total school budget which should be used for the guidance program.

In setting out to staff the organization, the administrator will again begin by determining the need on the basis of functions to be performed and the likelihood of financial support. In selecting new staff, he obviously will want to look not only at the specific needs of the school but at those criteria which have been used to determine who is qualified to do various guidance jobs. In most states these criteria will be determined by reference to state certification requirements. Besides hiring new staff, however, the administrator may become involved in the development of the staff that is already on the job. Such development will call for in-service education activities designed to promote greater skill and understanding, better morale, and increased coordination.

In carrying out the *directing* of services the guidance administrator will need to know not only the institutional but the legal basis of his authority. Beyond formal authority, however, he may need to exercise much leadership to permit people to realize the kind of growth and change which they desire. Such direction is clearly dependent upon good staff communication which necessitates cognizance of organizational procedures as well as human factors.

In *supervising* the process of guidance the administrator may need to practice two forms of this activity. Supervision may consist of quality control which is designed to maintain, codify, enforce, and resist change. Such "hold the line" supervision is often referred to as *tractive supervision.* *Dynamic supervision* is aimed at changing, upgrading, restructuring, and innovating newer behaviors.

A school district which has well-qualified counselors (who are doing a good job of helping students think about their assets, liabilities, and opportunities and assume responsibility for their decisions) may need tractive supervision if the community suddenly decides that a much higher percentage of students should go on to college whether or not they seem capable of profiting from such an experience. Or there may be an upsurge of interest in vocational education with the concurrent demand by the community that many more students forgo general education in order to learn vocational skills even though these skills may be soon outdated by automation and other technological developments. Dynamic supervision may be necessary in a situation where counselors have traditionally been bogged down in paper work and now are being asked to do person-to-person counseling. To make changes in such a program is most difficult, and supervisors will be needed who can lead and not drive. This kind of change is perhaps the single most important problem facing guidance programs at this time. The accounting-clerk mentality has too long characterized the counselor's office! Scheduling activities are certainly necessary if the school is to function smoothly, but they do not constitute a total counseling program. If, by the use of computers, counselor aides (subprofessional workers who perform some guidance activities under the supervision of the counselor), and better trained secretaries such activities can be turned over to others, then the counselor will indeed be free to do that for which he is trained. The fact that many communities have traditionally supported counseling programs with enthusiasm does not mean that they will now support this new approach. In some districts there may be an agonizing reappraisal as the district decides whether in fact it wants "counseling" now that counselors are free to supply it.

In *controlling* the program the guidance administrator will need to know both what is happening and how well it is happening. The counselors' use of daily or weekly logs permits the administrator to learn how the counselors' time is spent. What percentage of time is used for the testing program? For personal counseling? For college placement? Answers to these and other questions are the first step in evaluating programs. Judgments about appropriate distribution of time are easier to make than those about the quality of the work done. Quality judgments, typically based on surveys of opinion though sometimes on experimental research, are extremely difficult in all phases of education but perhaps particularly so in guidance because of the absence of instrumentation. No achievement tests of the type permitting measurement in English or history are available in this field.

ADMINISTRATIVE SKILLS

Administrative skills are human-relations skills, conceptual skills, and technical skills. The human-relations skills enable the administrator to understand the needs, drives, and abilities of the staff and relate them to the fears and wishes of the larger public—community, students, teachers, and administrators. Conceptual skills permit the administrator to see the "large picture." They enable him to realize that if he makes a change in any part of the social system which is the school, he affects all other parts. By hiring a new counselor does he threaten the English department? By hiring another woman counselor does he threaten the men? By hiring only those with advanced training does he threaten those with less training? Such considerations must be taken into account in guidance administration simply because the units of such administration are people, not things. Finally, and perhaps least important, the administrator must possess technical skills. Such skills enable him to know good practice when he sees it. Technical skills will typically have been furthered by formal training in guidance so that he knows what constitutes good counseling, is aware of the uses and limitations of tests, and understands the mechanics of record keeping. While an administrator with high skills in all these three areas is not easy to find, such a person should be the ideal model for school systems looking for guidance directors.

TYPICAL PROBLEMS

Now that we have looked at some of the more theoretical aspects of the management and development of guidance programs, let us turn to some more specific illustrative problems which are generally considered in this context.

Guidance is now thought of as but one of a number of pupil personnel services. The other pupil personnel services will vary with the school district or the writer discussing them but generally include such specialties as school psychology, school social work, school nursing, attendance control and research. These pupil personnel services are frequently coordinated at the district—sometimes the county or even state—level. In the future, even more than in the present, the school guidance program will need to mesh with these broader pupil personnel activities.

A problem that continues to be of concern in some districts is whether a counselor should be assigned counseling duties full time or part time. The American School Counselors Association favors the use of full-time counselors. There are still many schools, however, that prefer to have their counselors teach part time. The argument against the part-time counselor is that it may be difficult for him to change from the teaching to the counseling role. In the classroom he may need to focus on societal concerns and be involved in discipline; in a counseling office he is more concerned with the individual student and, at least in the more enlightened districts, will not have responsibility for enforcing school regulations. Another argument against the part-time counselor is that in most areas of the United States there are not now a sufficient number of well-trained counselors to permit schools to use them as teachers as well as counselors. That is, if a school district needs ten full-time counselors, it may have difficulty finding twenty well-trained people to whom it can assign counseling on a half-time basis. The counter-argument is that counselors have difficulty in being accepted by their peers if they do not teach. This may be true in some cases, but for the most part, administrators do not teach, nor librarians, nor registrars, and their acceptance does not appear to decline. Acceptance by peers would seem to be a function of personality. As a practical matter, this decision may have to be made at the local school system on the basis of the availability of personnel.

Ratio refers to the number of students assigned to each counselor. There are variations in ratios depending on how they are calculated, but in general it can be said that secondary schools now have about one full-time counselor for every 500 students although this figure varies if we count as a counselor only those who are fully qualified or certificated by their state. The American School Counselors Association has suggested a ratio of 1 to 250 students. The sensibleness of a ratio is very much dependent upon what the counselor is supposed to do and who he has to help him do it. If he is thought of by the community, teachers, and students primarily as someone who helps children get into college and he is working in a district with very few college-bound students, a high ratio might be feasible. If he is expected to do much personal-social counseling and is in a district where many students have problems which they wish to discuss with the counselor, a low counselor-student ratio may be needed. If he has a full slate of pupil personnel specialists to help with his work, a large ratio might be possible. The best way to determine a reasonable ratio for school systems is to set down what activities the school wishes to carry out for the students, the amount of time needed to perform these activities, what help there will be among other pupil personnel specialists and community resources to aid in these endeavors, and finally of course, what resources are available to hire staff.

Data processing has become an increasingly important part of the guidance activities. Many school districts are now putting their entire cumulative records onto magnetic tapes and this has, in some cases, much reduced the clerical work previously performed by the counselor. For a long time now test scoring and reporting has been left to such electronic machines. Some districts provide occupational information by computers, and there has even been some experiments in the use of computers to actually advise or counsel. The introduction of data processing into the field of guidance may do much in the near future to liberate the counselor from the quasi-secretarial tasks, which so long have taken much of his time. The actual scheduling of students into classes, for example, has been the major activity of many counselors in many school districts for years. Now it seems quite evident that this activity can be performed better by a computer than it can by a counselor. With the introduction of these timesaving activities, more counselors are being released from paper work to actually perform their function as a counselor. Some counselors eagerly emerge from behind the "paper curtain" but others are reluctant to assume their responsibility as face-to-face counselors. In such situations, it behooves the administrator to train his staff to carry on the high level of professional activity now possible for them.

Summary

This chapter has been concerned with the organization and administration of guidance services. Theoretical positions from which problems in this area can be considered have been presented. If the school is a dynamic social system, the possible consequences to the student body and the community of change in the system are important considerations in decision making. When we try to understand why counselors and others behave as they do, it might be helpful to consider the forces on them—sociological, psychological, and anthropological. This consideration of roles leads us into the principles needed to guide us in organizing, administering, and supervising a guidance program. With that conceptualization of program management and development as a background, a very few specific and typical problems have been considered to illustrate this method of thinking about program management and development.

Exercises

1. Describe and chart the guidance organization in the school in which you are working or in any other school familiar to you. Include the guidance duties of the counselor, the librarian, and teachers. Tell what provision is made for counseling, individual inventory service, gathering and disseminating occupational information, educational and vocational placement, and research.

2. What do you perceive as the disadvantages and advantages of having (*a*) full-time as opposed to part-time counselors; (*b*) a job placement service in the school; (*c*) counselor aides; (*d*) data processing machines to aid in the guidance program?

3. Outline an ideal guidance program for the school in which you work or some other school with which you are familiar. Take into the account the school personnel presently working, the financial support possible in the district, community desires as you perceive them, and the public and private agencies available to help with guidance activities.

References

Hatch, Raymond N., and Buford Stefflre: *Administration of Guidance Services* 2d ed., Prentice-Hall, Inc., Englewood Cliffs, N.J., 1965.

Hill, George: *Management and Improvement of Guidance*, Appleton-Century-Crofts, Inc., New York, 1958.

Kowitz, Gerald T., and Norma Giess Kowitz: *Operating Guidance Services for the Modern School*, Holt, Rinehart and Winston, Inc., New York, 1968.

Peters, Herman J., and Bruce Shertzer: *Guidance Program Development and Management*, Charles E. Merrill Books, Inc., Columbus, Ohio, 1963.

Zeran, Franklin R., and Anthony C. Riccio: *Organization and Administration of Guidance Services*, Rand McNally & Company, Chicago, 1962.

7

Guidance in the Elementary School

It is difficult to gather precise figures on elementary-school guidance programs because there is not complete agreement on what constitutes such a program nor who can be considered an elementary-school guidance specialist. The best indications are, however, that by the late 1960s there were something under 3,000 elementary-school guidance counselors employed in American schools. At that time the hope was that this figure would be increased nearly ten times in another ten years. Of all the school systems enrolling 300 or more students, 85 percent did *not* provide full-time guidance counselors. This figure was much lower (60 percent) for systems with 25,000 or more students. Overall, however, it seemed clear that it was the exception rather than the rule for a school to have available an elementary guidance counselor.

At the same time there was considerable interest in elementary guidance as demonstrated by the availability of federal funds for pilot programs, the increase in training programs, and the many articles about this topic in the professional literature. These new programs took a variety of forms but there seemed to develop a consensus that the elementary-school counselor should be involved in *counseling* with individuals in small groups, *consulting* with parents and school personnel, and *coordinating* the resources available to help individual children with their development. A study by the U.S. Department of Health, Education, and Welfare indicated that the following practices figured prominently among elementary-school programs:

1. Guidance services are part of a broader program of services offered by the school system which are usually called pupil personnel services.
2. The guidance program serves *all* children.
3. The guidance consultant is at the center of the guidance program, which involves the entire school staff, and the teacher plays an essential role in the program.
4. The guidance consultant:
    a. Tests and observes children who have learning difficulties,

who are underachievers, who show signs of emotional disturbances, who need curricular advice or placement in special classes, and who are being considered for referral to other specialists

b. Counsels children with minor personal troubles that interfere with school life

c. Helps needy children obtain glasses, hearing aids, clothes, food, and other essentials

d. Consults with teachers, principal, and parents to help them understand normal children as well as children with problems

e. Refers children needing intensive diagnosis and treatment to pupil personnel specialists and community agencies, and interprets their findings and recommendations to teachers and parents

f. Provides in-service education for teachers. Through scheduled meetings and informal conferences relating to normal development and behavior in children, the guidance consultant aids teachers in meeting difficult classroom situations with understanding and composure. Other subjects included in in-service training are: mental health, administration and interpretation of tests, maintenance and use of cumulative records, and techniques of interviewing

g. Develops group guidance programs in common personal problems, study habits, occupational orientation, and preparation for the secondary school

h. Interprets the guidance program to the parent and community organizations

i. Conducts research and evaluative studies relative to the effectiveness of the guidance program

5. The guidance consultant's background usually includes successful teaching experience at the elementary-school level, certification for guidance personnel by the state, and a master's degree in guidance.

While the above statement may describe the modal counselor's duties, there are at least four common diversities. In some schools the elementary-school counselor's model seems to be that of the social worker. He will do much casework or counseling with children who are somewhat disturbed emotionally or who have severe social problems which seem to stem from their homes. Another model is furnished by the school psychologist. These elementary counselors spend much of their time in giving, interpreting, and planning for tests. A third model is that of the remedial teacher. Some counselors spend much time doing what is essentially tutoring. They concern themselves with reading skills, arithmetic skills, study habits, and other learning activities. Finally there are elementary-school counselors who pattern their day much after that of the secondary-school counselor. They may be particularly concerned, for example, with educational and vocational guidance.

The most reasonable present stance with regard to the elementary-school counselor's duties would seem to be that they will be highly situational. The particular needs of the school and the particular qualities of the counselor may determine what he does to a much greater extent then is true in the secondary school. This absence of a clearly structured job definition may result in considerable anxiety on the part of some elementary-school counselors or potential counselors. To others, however, this absence of structure may be seen as an opportunity for them to shape their job to most precisely meet the needs of the school and the community in which they work.

Importance of Guidance in Elementary Schools

Significant developments in recent decades have brought a recognition that organized guidance programs are as important on the elementary as on the secondary level. Guidance is an integral part of the total educational program, serving as a positive function rather than a corrective force, and to be most effective it must be a continuous process from the child's first contact with the school until he is ready for placement on a job or in some type of post-secondary education. Emphases may change as the growing child's needs change, but the essential process of helping each child to understand himself in relation to his own needs and to those of his environment must begin long before he is ready for secondary school. Early guidance which helps the child to make adjustments to each new situation can strengthen his ability to apply his self-understanding to the solution of problems in his later years. Guidance is no longer based on a concept of services designed to meet crises but rather on a concept of continuous development. This view emphasizes prevention and good mental hygiene and demands organized guidance services in the earliest years of the educational experience.

PREVENTIVE MEASURES CAN BE TAKEN

The present emphasis upon the development and utilization of human resources is bringing increased demands for earlier and more effective identification of individual differences. This demand for earlier identification is gaining impetus with the growing recognition that guidance services in the elementary schools are especially effective because (1) the child is flexible and has had less time for problems to become deep-rooted; (2) the parents are more actively associated with the school; and (3) many years of more successful development lie ahead for the child who can be helped to understand himself and to find acceptable approaches toward the solution of his problems. When the major guidance concern was only for the serious behavior problems, the school could look to outside agencies for assistance in providing therapeutic measures; but with the present emphasis upon prevention of serious maladjustment and upon the establishment of learning climates which encourage maximum total personal development, there is an imperative need for organized guidance services which are an integral part of the total educational program of every elementary school.

READINESS CAN BE DEVELOPED

Research findings and developments in the curriculum field point up the necessity for increased guidance services in these early years of the school experience. The concept of readiness for learning includes the recognition that educational stumbling blocks may appear if curriculum experiences are offered too soon or too late. This concept demands the earliest and best possible identification of individual differences and calls for greatly improved systems of pupil records. The emphasis upon continuous educational development, as opposed to isolated strata of educational programs which demand arbitrary common levels of development at each transition, calls for better articulation of elementary- and secondary-school experiences. Interest in greater motivation for learning and in the development of learning situations which produce creativity and leadership must result in systematic counseling for parents and pupils. This concern also calls attention to the school's responsibility to provide consultation services for the teacher in this most complex educational program. In short, time, energy, and money spent in the earliest years of the child's school life pay larger dividends in the conservation of human resources than can be expected from remedial and corrective processes offered in later years of the pupil's school experience.

The Nature of the Child in the Elementary School

All growth follows a pattern, and each child has his own built-in growth pattern and "timetable." Some mature very rapidly in all areas, and others lag behind their age group in one or more of the four areas of development—physical, mental, social, or emotional. Research shows that children exhibit every conceivable combination and variation in their growth patterns. Some grow at the same rate in all four areas, while others grow unevenly. Children may show rapid physical development with slow mental development. In addition, the same child may show both spurts and lags in his growth and development. These differences are mainly the result of the built-in growth pattern but may be influenced to a limited extent by disease, nutritional deficiencies, or other extreme environmental deprivations.

Children in the kindergarten and in grades 1 to 6 span three periods of growth and development. The kindergarten child is usually completing early childhood development, and the child in grades 5 and 6 is probably in the period of later childhood. Between these two periods is the stage of middle childhood. Each of these periods represents a specific stage in the systematic process of child development.

Because of the great variety of developmental patterns we would expect to find many different levels of development in any year of the elementary school, although in general children of any given age period will exhibit certain characteristics of growth and similar levels of development. For purposes of orientation then we need to look at the characteristics of middle and later childhood.

THE CHILD FROM SIX TO TEN

Middle childhood usually covers the years between six and ten. In this period the child is growing in all parts of his body but less rapidly than in early childhood. Muscular growth and coordination are uneven and incomplete, but manual dexterity and eye-hand coordination have developed sufficiently to allow the child to use his hands and fingers for writing, drawing, sewing, and playing musical instruments. He still has better control over the large muscles than he does over the small. The child needs opportunities for active play to release pent-up energy and a balance of rest and relaxation to meet the increasing demands which school places upon him.

The mental development in middle childhood is characterized by learning to read and by the acquisition of many other knowledges and skills. There is evidence that these children learn best when they can be active while learning.

This is the period when children begin to recognize differences in how boys and girls are expected to behave. Socially and emotionally, they are developing sexual feelings, but a divergence in interests between boys and girls results in less play together. These children are becoming more independent, are learning to take more responsibility and to show increasing control of emotions. This is a period of emerging values with some concern about right and wrong.

THE CHILD FROM TEN TO THIRTEEN

Children in grades 4 to 6 have received only limited attention in research and in the study of human growth and development.

These children are active and want to be on the move. Physical growth is slow, and health is good. Some, particularly the girls, may be maturing more quickly and may advance into the more rapid growth phase of prepubescence. The child of twelve or thirteen may show evidence of physical ungainliness and awkwardness of movement. Enlarging hips, breast development, and menstruation may present problems of adjustment for those girls who are earlier maturers. Voice changing and characteristic sex changes and developments in boys may appear in grade 5 or 6. These pupils want to be making things, want to be doing and performing in response to their need to try out their own powers.

This is the period when children are showing a tendency to draw away from adults and to turn toward their peers for companionship and for modes of living. Independence in ideas and activity is normal behavior at this age. These children need support from both adults and peers, for both help in defining acceptable limits of behavior. In many cases children show fears and worries which center in developing independence, parental and school expectations, and home problems. Competition may also be a threat to emotional well-being.

Later childhood is characterized by a desire to learn and by a wide variety of interests. The child is developing an understanding of cause and effect, forming concepts, and beginning to solve simple problems. Value judgments of right and wrong are not as well defined for the child in grade 6 as they were in grade 4. This seems to be the age when the child develops some tolerance and the ability to see things as gray rather than as black or white.

IMPLICATIONS FOR EDUCATION

Knowing about individual growth patterns and how a child grows as a whole can be of immense value. We can help our children grow to greater social and emotional maturity. Understanding the growth process can reduce much of the worry and tension besetting parents and teachers. Children can be happier when adults recognize certain modes of behavior as normal steps in the process of growing up.

In a summary of studies of how human beings grow and develop, we see the following:

Children are both similar and different.
Each individual grows according to his own time schedule and in his own style.
Growth takes time; it can be encouraged but not forced. Both nature and nurture play a part.
Growth of abilities in the same individual often varies.
Growth is continuous, following an orderly sequence in each individual.

We also learn that conditions in the environment which encourage the proper development of human beings are (1) those which support physical well-being and stimulate growth—food, warmth, air, light, activity and rest, and safety; (2) those which support emotional well-being—giving a sense of security and of worth or self-respect; and (3) those which lead to increased ability to cope independently with life situations.

Finally, the emotional needs of all human beings must be kept in mind when we attempt to understand the nature of elementary-school children. These are the need for belonging, achievement, economic security, love and affection; the need to be free from fear and relatively free from guilt; the need for self-respect and self-understanding.

The major goal for education is to help children meet the developmental tasks imposed upon them by their innate growth drives and by the society in which they live, that is, to help them to grow up capably and happily as individuals and as thoughtful, contributing members of society.

The Role of the Teacher in Guidance

The interrelation between guidance and instruction in the educational process emphasizes the key role of the teacher in guidance. The teacher is uniquely responsible for the climate of learning in which the class as a group, and each pupil as an individual in the group, finds opportunity for learning and for personal development. The school must be conceived of as the setting for learning experiences, and everything which helps to make that setting educational is a concern of the teacher. Teachers affect the lives and personalities of children, and their influence goes far beyond the academic area and what can be measured by achievement tests. If the teacher will accept each pupil as he is, with all his strengths and weaknesses, and will help him to improve where he needs to improve, the teacher will have many opportunities to help pupils understand and accept themselves and to aid them in defining reasonable life goals—two major aims of guidance. He may also influence the attitudes and feelings which contribute to making independent choices either easy or difficult.

The teacher functions primarily in his guidance role as a worker with groups of pupils and their parents; but he is also concerned about individuals in the group, and he cooperates with other persons vital to the guidance function. To provide an educational setting in which learning will take place, the teacher studies both the individuals in a group and the group itself, so that he can recognize how one group differs from another. By cherishing individual differences and by developing dynamic group processes, the teacher offers each pupil in his class an opportunity to learn.

THE TEACHER STUDIES CHILDREN

Child study is a basic guidance function and is accomplished through the use of both formal methods involving tests and cumulative records and informal methods based upon observations of the pupil in his classroom and in other settings. The teacher learns much about the child as he studies the pupil's production, his oral and written work, his art work, and his reading record. The teacher seeks to observe hobbies and interests as an aid to motivation through understanding. Observations of behavior systematized through the use of the anecdotal record provide a rich source of data for child study. The teacher in an elementary school is in a strategic position to conduct child study, for he sees the child in many differing situations and has frequent opportunity for contacts with parents.

Children enter school with wide differences in chronological age, mental maturity, physical coordination, health conditions, social and emotional readiness for formal school experiences. Children in the first grade range in age from five years and eight months to seven years. A first grade may have children whose mental ages range from three years to ten years or more. The range in physical maturity will be comparable with additional differences introduced through birth injuries, disease, or nutritional deficiencies. The differences in familial patterns and in cultural and economic backgrounds will account for wide levels of maturity in peer relationships and socialization and emotional readiness for learning. Early identification of individual differences is an essential aspect of any attempt to provide meaningful educational experiences for children. Failure to recognize levels of readiness in the early years of school life may be a major factor in the problems of underachievement, school dropouts, and even juvenile delinquency. When children begin school in a kindergarten, the teacher has an opportunity, before more formal education begins, to study levels of maturity through observations, parent conferences, health reports, and developmental records of progress in adjusting to school.

The first-grade teacher who must provide more formal learning experiences for children entering school for the first time faces a big task in studying the individual pupils in his class. Too frequently a reading-readiness score is the only objective evidence of individual differences. This score is too often interpreted as a measure of general mental maturity. The need to establish other levels of readiness and maturity must be met in order to provide a learning situation in which the child can find the satisfaction which will lead to more learning.

Readiness for learning depends upon physical and mental factors, situational factors, and the self-system of the child. The child must see what is to be learned as meaningful and useful as it relates to his needs, goals, and self-concept. The teacher must first look at the individuals in his class in order to determine each child's readiness for learning, the degree to which individual needs are being met, and how each child sees himself. The teacher also looks at himself and raises the question, "How do I feel about each of these pupils? What are my personal needs which may influence my relationship with the group or with individuals within the class?"

THE TEACHER COLLECTS DATA ABOUT CHILDREN

Early identification of individual needs makes educational planning more valid. Identification and planning, however, must be continuous and not a one-time experience.

Identification involves observation in many areas of behavior, a study of developmental records, and interviews with parents and children. One of the most useful techniques for informal study is the anecdotal record together with the roster of observations kept by the teacher. Such records, if they represent accurate and objective reporting of incidents, can help the teacher better to understand individual pupils and to recognize more clearly the relationships within the class group. Teachers need help in developing skill in this type of reporting.

The teacher will also participate in the collection of data by more formal methods and will utilize all the data in the cumulative record of the child. Such data usually cover personal and family background, health, attendance, scholarship, and activities both in and out of school. The standardized test, inventories, and rating scales may all be used in the elementary school to provide essential information for understanding children.

A test program in a school involves the selection, administration, and use of test results. Teachers should have a say in the selection of tests to be used. If the teacher is to help administer standardized tests, a program of in-service education should be provided to ensure valid testing procedures. The teacher's most important role, however, will be in the interpretation of test results. Test data can be utilized to suggest curriculum changes, procedure changes, and even changes in teacher-pupil relationships. Teachers may need help to ensure a professional and objective use of test data. There is a responsibility to give parents and pupils realistic interpretations of test results, but it is important that the school accept the further responsibility of helping to resolve emotional conflicts which may arise from such reporting of test results.

The cumulative record which the school develops is designed to help teachers function more effectively by grouping the data collected so that conclusions are more easily drawn. Effective use of pupil records is possible only when the information covers all the functional areas of human development and when it is so organized that developmental patterns are evident. Then the record can be analyzed with a reasonable expenditure of time and effort.

As the teacher studies the individual children who make up his group or class, he recognizes a multiplicity of differences based upon unique growth patterns and environmental pressures and motivations. Then he acts upon his knowledge to modify experiences to make learning more meaningful for pupils with widely varying needs. Skillful and valid planning in the light of individual needs helps each child to work on his developmental tasks in a climate conducive to greater success. Later academic achievement will be deterred or enhanced by what happens in the early years of school. The danger in these early years lies in a sense of inadequacy and inferiority which may cause the child to despair of his tools and skills or of his status. When this happens, his ego boundaries suffer, and he abandons a developing sense of industry and is thrown back on more primitive aspects of development. Thus the underachiever is born! The teacher in the primary grades can do much for children whose parents have not been successful in aiding the child through these critical adjustments.

THE TEACHER COUNSELS

The teacher works with individuals as well as groups, and there is a kind of counseling which is a legitimate function of the classroom teacher. The teacher's relationship with pupils in this class often leads to possibilities for establishing good counseling rapport. Only in the classroom climate which is really conducive to learning can such a rapport be established, because it is based on respect for the individual and reflects attitudes and not processes. The teacher's counseling role is not a therapeutic one, but he does aim at offering the student assistance in making more effective personal and environmental adjustments. When the pupil is unable to relate to the classroom teacher, or when the case calls for techniques beyond the ability of the teacher, the child should be referred to the school counselor.

Many teachers are including courses in guidance in their graduate programs, and these teachers often possess skills which make for effective counseling. If a teacher finds it difficult to accept the basic philosophy of counseling, he cannot be expected to do counseling, as such, in his work. Each teacher will have to decide for himself what limits for counseling are imposed by his own personal values and needs, his professional development, and his group or class responsibilities. He has the responsibility for using all available counseling resources as they are needed; for example, he may ask for help in recognizing the special needs of individual children. Counselors can serve as consultants to teachers, thus providing in-service education in the area of referral procedures. The case conference involving teacher, administrator, nurse, counselor, visiting teacher, and school psychologist offers an excellent opportunity to increase the teacher's skill in looking beneath symptoms to problems which need to be referred.

Besides studying children and counseling them, the teacher has other guidance responsibilities. He will study his group to discover the dynamics which are operating therein in order to improve communication, to utilize desirable areas of influence, and to relieve pressures. The teacher also works with parents in helping to promote cooperative relationships which will enhance both school and home efforts to contribute effectively to each child's development. Teachers study the school environment as it affects the the educational program and utilize resources and persons in the community to help them in their guidance work.

Although the teacher is the key guidance worker in the elementary school, he needs to recognize the guidance roles of other school personnel. The teacher is a member of a team whose function is to obtain the maximum development of each child in the school.

The Role of the Counselor

The counselor, a regularly assigned member of the elementary-school staff, is specifically charged with the responsibility for developing those aspects of the guidance function which demand an expenditure of time and the use of specialized competencies which the teacher ordinarily does not have. He is directly responsible to the principal and has only a staff relationship with the teachers and other members of the school staff. Principal and counselor working together plan an organized program of guidance services which include the following: (1) in-service education for teachers, (2) consultation services for teachers and parents, (3) counseling services for children, (4) referral services for children, (5) follow-up and research activities, and (6) evaluation studies.

THE COUNSELOR GIVES IN-SERVICE EDUCATION

An effective program of guidance services provides in-service education for teachers in the development and interpretation of pupil records. Since the average teacher will have neither the time nor the training to develop records which are complete and so organized that an analysis can be made with reasonable expenditure of time and energy, the counselor must provide assistance in the collection of data, in the methods of recording, and in the interpretation of the developmental record.

The development of a sound test program is another aspect of the elementary guidance services. Counselors can provide in-service education for teachers and can act as consultants in the development of the program and in the interpretation of results. Counselors can do some testing of pupils in the spring before the child enters the first grade. An inventory can provide data which will enable the teacher to group pupils according to levels of maturity by considering physical coordination, reading readiness, social and emotional development. Administering such an inventory requires much more time than the teacher can possibly find. The counselor also does supplementary testing for purposes of verification when results on any test seem to be illogical.

THE COUNSELOR COUNSELS

The counselor's chief responsibility is to provide counseling for all children with unusual interests or needs. Teachers can be helped to recognize these needs so that the children may be referred to the counselor. The percent of time devoted to counseling for personal adjustment will be greater in the elementary school than in the secondary school, and this is probably the greatest difference in guidance at the two levels. Children, whether self-referred or referred by parents or teachers, may need help in many areas of personal development. The excessively shy child, the socially inept child, the child whose self-concept interferes with learning, the child whose behavior interferes with work in the classroom, the child with educational deficiencies, and any child whose progress in school seems unsatisfactory— all find their way to the counselor's office.

The counselor's office should be an attractive, even if small, room, with toys, books, and manipulative materials readily available to the child. Here a youngster who is overwhelmed by the experiences he is handling or who has reached "an explosion point" may work off tensions with clay, finger paints, darts, punching bags and return to class ready to try again. Toys play an important role in helping children verbalize and communicate. Teacher and child, sitting back to back, may hold "conversations" over toy telephones even if the child is too shy to communicate in a face-to-face interview. Furnished classrooms and doll houses, erector sets, dump trucks, fire engines, and a host of other toys provide opportunities for a child to play and talk as he works with the counselor. Dominoes, checkers, and chess offer an opportunity to help the child learn more about limits, rules, and regulations. Whether the counselor works with the individual child or with small groups, his office represents a neutral setting with many aids to help the child evaluate himself, set goals, and make choices. Here the counselor uses every competence he can muster. Training which includes a knowledge of how personality develops, an understanding of counseling theories and techniques, and some supervised practice in counseling is essential if the counselor is to meet the needs of the children who find their way to his office.

Research indicates that many underachieving pupils have emotional problems and that counseling provided on a systematic long-term basis is essential before the pupil can begin to use his potentialities. Pupils respond more readily if counseling is available in the early years of school at the onset of underachieving. With the onset of underachieving occurring in the earlier years of school, there is a need to identify and provide counseling at the earliest possible time. Counseling in the secondary school may be of little help in modifying patterns of underachievement.

THE COUNSELOR MAKES REFERRALS

The counselor makes referrals of pupils to other school services and utilizes the resources available in the community. He helps to provide continuity of the educational experience through articulation services at the time a child leaves the elementary school to enter junior high school. Adequate counselor services should contribute to the curriculum through carefully planned research and follow-up activities which reveal the needs of children in the school and which provide evidence of the success with which the school is meeting these needs.

THE COUNSELOR CONSULTS

Most elementary-school counselors will spend at least some of their time as consultants to teachers, administrators, and parents. A consultant is someone who aids a peer in the solution of a problem within the consultant's special area of competency. This aid may take the form of providing information on normative child development, helping the one asking for the consultation with determining the blocks that are interfering with his own solution to the problem, or jointly trying a variety of possible behaviors to alleviate the situation.

In the school the program is aimed at assisting teachers to deal with child development problems at their own level of competency. Furthermore, it strives continuously to raise the competency level of the teacher. It does not seek to build a large case load for the counselor but rather to enable the teacher to solve the problems right in her own classroom. Such a program is built on the assumption that many problems are directly concerned with the relationship between the teacher and the child, and until this relationship is improved, outside contact will rarely be helpful.

This activity of the elementary-school counselor may be particularly difficult for him to perform because in the past our training for such activity has not been very thorough nor soundly based on theory. In short, we are not very clear about how a consultant should perform. An additional handicap is the fact that turning to a consultant for help has not long been included in the mores of the school system. Teachers tend to be autonomous in their professional functioning, and too often we see turning to a consultant for aid as an expression of weakness instead of strength. Other professions, of course, do not have this strong history of autonomy. It is considered most professional for a physician or a social worker to consult with peers or supervisors to get a different view of professional problems. Many hope this tradition of seeking consultation will grow in the school system. When it does, the specialist—elementary-school counselor, school psychologist, school social worker, etc.—will be much more valuable to the institution simply because his skills will be more widely spread. By using his skills to improve the competency of the teacher, many children are reached, whereas when he uses them to deal with an individual child only that child is helped.

Education for Elementary-school Counseling

The Association for Counselor Education and Supervision after considerable study drafted a statement indicating the kind of preparation which they believed necessary for elementary-school counselors. While the length of the training program might vary with the students' undergraduate preparation, they believe that in all cases it should be a minimum of one year. Standards were set for the staff and facilities in colleges offering such a program, and the association then outlined more specifically the kind of course work which should precede employment as an elementary-school counselor.

The didactic course work recommended would take the following form:

1. Information on the educational setting including the purposes and organization of the elementary school, school curriculum, and philosophy and sociology of schools
2. Work from the behavioral sciences including child growth and development, personality dynamics and theories, dynamics of family living, group dynamics, and theories of learning
3. Professional studies in elementary-school counseling including the following topics:
    a. Counseling theories
    b. Group procedures in guidance and counseling
    c. Professional identification, the profession, and its ethics
    d. Role definition, program development, and coordination of elementary-school guidance services
    e. The consultation process
    f. Individual appraisal
    g. Vocational development theory, including the use of appropriate materials for elementary-school children
    h. Research skills to enable the elementary-school counselor to understand the relevant research and to appraise the outcomes of his service

The association strongly believes, however, that didactic courses are not enough for such preparation. They believe that practical supervised experience enabling the candidate to deal directly with elementary-school children, their parents and their teachers, is necessary for adequate training. Such supervised experience should occur in the actual school setting. Some of these many experiences might be characterized as laboratory experiences, e.g., using pupil personnel records, conducting case conferences, and testing; some of them practicum experiences, e.g., consultation with teachers and parents, counseling with small groups, and individual counseling with pupils; and finally, some would be in the nature of an internship in which the candidate would get on-the-job supervised experience for which he would normally be paid in an elementary school.

It is doubtful that many training programs will meet these standards for some time, but they do provide an ideal toward which programs can grow. The recommendation, for example, that all students have a minimum of thirty hours actually doing counseling is probably not yet met in many training programs.

The Team Approach

A definite trend in guidance is toward a coordinated team approach under the leadership of the principal. Principals, teachers, counselors, and other staff personnel working as a team should evaluate the guidance needs within the school and assess the effectiveness of the services designed to meet these needs. Many staff people, including school social workers, school psychologists, nurses, doctors, speech correctionists, reading specialists, supervisors, and consultants, are available to the modern school. Their services can be most effectively used if the principal arranges systematic case conference procedures. In such case conferences the teacher and the counselor share with other team members the problems of children which they have identified by their close contact. Teachers get some support and consultative help in planning for these children. Referrals for other services which are the result of these case conferences are usually more valid than referrals made without such conferences. The referral report is more detailed and often more accurate, and therefore the referral services will be more effective.

Guidance in the elementary school is the responsibility of every member of the school team. Under the leadership of the principal the team constantly evaluates its objectives and plans for more effective guidance services. Follow-up, research, and evaluation activities are essential aspects of the attempt to provide an educational climate in which each child works toward a healthy personality capable of achievement commensurate with ability.

Summary

Guidance is an integral part of the total educational program and to be most effective must be a continuous process from the child's first contact with the school until he is ready for placement in a job or in a post-secondary school. Guidance in the elementary school is based on a concept of continuous development, emphasizing prevention and good mental hygiene. Traditionally the teacher has borne the responsibilities for guidance in the elementary school, but recent concern for conservation of human resources has given impetus to a demand for organized guidance services which utilize both teacher and specialist.

The major goal of education is to help children meet the developmental tasks imposed upon them by their innate drives and by the society in which they live. The chief goal of guidance is to help provide an educational setting in which learning is enhanced. Valid planning based upon identified needs, interests, and aptitudes is possible when all staff members accept their guidance roles.

The teacher is the key guidance worker in the elementary school. The teacher functions as a worker with groups of children and their parents, but he is also concerned about individuals in the group. He studies the individuals in his group using both formal and informal methods. The teacher provides counseling for individuals within the limitations imposed by time and professional and personal readiness. He works with parents, helping to plan for the development of each child. When necessary the teacher utilizes other school and community services for counseling or therapy. He works cooperatively with other members of the school team.

The counselor, as a regularly assigned member of the elementary-school staff, is responsible for developing those aspects of guidance functions for which the teacher does not have time and specialized competencies. His chief function is to provide systematic counseling for children with special needs or interests. An elementary-school counselor usually devotes a greater percentage of his time to counseling children and parents than does the secondary-school counselor. The counselor also provides in-service education for teachers in the collecting of data, in the development and use of cumulative records, and in the test program. Finally, an important aspect of the counselor's work is to contribute to curriculum development through follow-up and research activities.

Guidance in the elementary school can only be effective if it is carried on through a coordinated team approach in which all school staff members work together to provide resources for helping children with special needs. Principal, teacher, counselor, school nurse, school psychologist, and visiting teacher plan together in case conferences devoted to children with problems or unmet needs.

Guidance in the elementary school differs from that in the secondary only in points of emphasis which are dictated by the levels of development which we find in the elementary school. The goals are the same; the procedures must be adapted to the needs of childhood.

Exercises

1. The principal of an elementary school has asked his faculty to evaluate the guidance needs of the school and to make recommendations for improving the school guidance program. The school, located in a small industrial town, has an enrollment of 540 pupils. The staff has the services of a school social worker when the principal asks her to give assistance. The public-health nurse is available for limited consultant and referral services. The test program for the school consists in a reading-readiness test in grade 1, a scholastic aptitude test in grade 4, and an achievement battery in the spring of grade 6. The town has no mental-hygiene clinic. Illegal absences, underachievement, and discipline problems plague the school. Discuss the recommendations which you think the staff might offer. Keep in mind goals, program, personnel, services and procedures.

2. James was nine years old when he returned to the fourth grade in September. According to his test record he has an IQ of 126 and on a standardized achievement test in October received grade placements of 5.0 in reading, 4.8 in arithmetic, and 5.2 in language. Now, in May, the teacher is recommending retention for James because he has been doing no classwork. Discuss the guidance procedures which should be followed in working with James and his teacher.

3. You are a teacher in the fifth grade of an elementary school. The pupils listed below seem to need special help. Tell how you would handle each case. Be specific, mentioning procedures and resources to be used and giving some possible explanations for the observed behavior.

   a. Timmy's achievement is showing a downward trend. Lately he seems to be always alone on the playground and in other periods of free time.

   b. Helen is absent from school so frequently that she finds it difficult to keep up with her group.

   c. Sammy had another fight on the playground this morning. He tore up Betty's arithmetic paper. The "chip" on Sammy's shoulder always seems to be in evidence.

References

Dinkmeyer, Don C.: *Guidance and Counseling in the Elementary School: Readings in Theory and Practice*, Holt, Rinehart, and Winston, Inc., New York, 1968.

Grams, Armin: *Facilitating Learning and Individual Development: Toward a Theory for Elementary Guidance*, Minnesota Department of Education, St. Paul, Minn., 1966.

Hatch, Raymond N., and James W. Costar: *Guidance Services in the Elementary School*, Wm. C. Brown Company Publishers, Dubuque, Iowa, 1961.

Peters, Herman J., Bruce Shertzer, and William H. Van Hoose: *Guidance in Elementary Schools*, Rand McNally & Company, Chicago, Ill., 1965.

Willey, R. D., *Guidance in Elementary Education*, Harper & Row, Publishers, Incorporated, New York, 1960.

8

Guidance in the Secondary School

The guidance program in the secondary school may be thought of as consisting of the standard guidance services: counseling service, information service, individual inventory service, placement service, and research service. These services have been previously defined, but their application to secondary-school programs may best be understood by examining the status of the coordinator of these services, the school counselor. The functions of the counselor will be seen to include these five basic guidance services—sometimes under different names—as well as other functions deemed appropriate.

Status of Counseling in Secondary Schools

By the end of the 1960s more than two-thirds of the secondary schools in the United States had the services of a full-time counselor. In large school districts the provision of such services was almost universal, but there were still many small districts lacking such specialists. Throughout the United States it was estimated that there were more than 30,000 full-time secondary-school counselors or approximately 1 for every 500 students.

With the help of the federal government and the increased enthusiasm of the public for this service, it was apparent that American secondary education had made a commitment to providing specialized help of this kind for all its secondary-school students. The quality of such counseling service is certainly harder to determine but probably bears some relationship to their function and training.

The American School Counselors Association in an official statement suggested that the secondary-school counselor assume ten professional responsibilities.

1. *Planning and development of the guidance program.* The secondary-school counselor will need to be active in defining the objectives

of the program, identifying the guidance needs of pupils, assisting in developing plans of action, and in many cases coordinating and evaluating the program.

2. *Counseling.* The school counselor at the secondary level is expected to devote a considerable portion of his time to individual or small-group counseling to aid the pupil in self-understanding and in planning for the future.

3. *Pupil appraisal.* Through the "individual inventory service" the counselor will take a major role in coordinating the gathering, evaluating, disseminating, and educational use of data about pupils. Such a function may involve testing, records of experiences, contacts with parents, etc.

4. *Educational and occupational planning.* The "information service" will also call for coordination by the counselor. This service will aim at collecting and disseminating information about education and about occupations which may be useful to the student in making plans. There is no suggestion here that the counselor will himself do all this work but rather that he will aid and encourage teachers to relate their classroom instruction to the broader world of occupations and of higher education.

5. *Referral work.* Because there are limits to the time and skill available to the counselor and because there is a limited role expectation for the counselor, referral to other individuals and agencies is a necessary part of his work. These referrals may be made to other teachers who have specialized knowledge, to other pupil personnel specialists such as school psychologists or school social workers, or to community agencies offering services which are needed by the student.

6. *Placement.* Through the use of both the individual inventory and the information services, the counselor will assume some responsibilities for planning and arranging the "placement" of students in institutions of further study and in occupations. Aid in college entrance may constitute a considerable portion of a counselor's activity in some schools.

7. *Parent help.* The counselor will hold conferences with parents and act as a resource person to help them understand the growth and developmental stages of their children. In doing so, he serves as a liaison between the school and the wider community and makes use not only of the school staff but of the records available to him.

8. *Staff consulting.* It is expected that the secondary-school counselor will work closely with administrative and teaching staff to the end that all school resources will be wisely used. In doing so, he may share and interpret data to them as well as set up more systematic staff development programs.

9. *Local research.* A professional counselor will have a continuing interest in evaluating the program in which he serves and therefore may design "research" permitting a judgment regarding his program. Other research may consist of follow-up on graduates and dropouts, correlational studies designed to permit local predictions, occupational

trends in the community, and accumulation and analysis of student body demographic data.

10. *Public relations.* Like all educational workers the school counselor will need to be continuously involved in interpreting the program of the school to the community. This activity may call for publications, speaking engagements, and selected use of mass media.

Preparation of the School Counselor

Practically all the fifty states require that a secondary-school counselor have a special certificate issued by the state department of education. The requirements to qualify for this certificate vary from state to state but in general constitute a master's degree in guidance and teaching experience. Those planning to serve as school counselors will need to check with the state department of education in the state in which they hope to serve to find out the precise requirements they will need to meet.

The Association for Counselor Education and Supervision has set up a model program which they think should be followed in preparing a secondary counselor. The program of studies provides for learning regarding the foundation and dynamics of human behavior and of the individual in his culture, the education enterprise and the processes of education, and ten areas of professional studies in school counseling and related guidance activities: (1) philosophy and principles underlying guidance and other pupil personnel services, (2) the nature and range of human characteristics and methods of measuring them by individual appraisal, (3) vocational development theory, (4) educational and occupational information, (5) counseling theory and practice, (6) statistical and research methods, (7) group procedures in counseling and guidance, (8) professional relationships and ethics, (9) administration and coordination of guidance, and (10) supervised experience.

This last mentioned activity—supervised experience—is thought by many to be the central part of counselor education. Simply studying books and taking examinations will never prepare an individual for the task of sitting across from a student and helping him understand his own nature and the situation in which he finds himself. The Association of Counselor Education and Supervision believes that every counselor in training should have from thirty to sixty hours of actual counseling experience under careful supervision. In most cases the counseling student will be observed through a one-way glass while he does his work so that a supervisor may discuss his techniques and approaches with him. Practically all schools also use tape recorders to record the interview and make it available for analysis during the supervisory session, and many now use closed-circuit television for the same purpose. The important part of the supervised experience requirement is that learning to be a counselor involves affective and skill learning as well as knowledge.

Importance of Guidance in the Secondary School

REMEDIAL GUIDANCE

Much guidance at the present time might be characterized as remedial. A student who is failing in his classes may talk with a counselor to try to understand whether his failure is a function of his own characteristics, the class in which he finds himself, or some other cause. Students who have great difficulty in their contact with their peers or family may also talk with the counselor in an attempt to make a better adjustment to their situation. Theorists in counseling, however, suggest that guidance programs which are designed either to prevent malfunctioning or to aid the individual in the course of his normal development are to be preferred to remedial programs.

THE NEED FOR PREVENTIVE GUIDANCE

The need for guidance is universal; it is not confined to the period of childhood and youth. It is present whenever, at any age, help is needed in making choices or adjustments or in solving problems. The recognition of this truth is shown by the increasing efforts to provide guidance for older people who have retired or who are about to retire. It is also seen in the phenomenal development of all kinds of assistance to the handicapped of all ages. Guidance should be a continuous process throughout life for those in need of help. However, it is very apparent that the most important and effective period for such help is at the time when habits, attitudes, and ideals are being formed and when techniques for self-help are being developed. Guidance given at this time will greatly reduce the need for help later and will increase the ability to choose occupational, civic, and social activities wisely in adult life. Preventive guidance in the secondary school lessens the need for remedial guidance later.

DEVELOPMENTAL TASKS AND GUIDANCE

Among the special tasks which our society imposes on the adolescent are those of selecting and preparing for an occupation and preparing for marriage and family life. These tasks necessitate making important decisions which will do much to shape the entire course of the student's life. If guidance is to play a part in increasing the individual's happiness and effectiveness, it must do so at this time. Adolescence is the period of choice making, and guidance is the systematic effort to improve the quality of choices; therefore it is important that the secondary school have a program of guidance for the adolescents it serves.

Guidance Needs Related to Education

The guidance needs of students in the secondary school are basically not very different from those in any other part of the educational system. What differences there are stem from the degree to which the student is able to participate in the solution of his problems, their urgency, and the facilities available for help.

The organization of secondary schools is undergoing much experimentation. We cannot say with certainty in what kind of school the adolescent will be. Some districts now provide an elementary school of kindergarten through grade 5, a middle school of 6 through 8, a high school of 9 through 12. Older organizational patterns included, of course, the six-three-three pattern, the eight-four pattern, and the six-six pattern. Some schools in communities that provide junior colleges also have such patterns as six-three-three-two or six-four-four. The main point here is that the organization of the school may, to some extent, influence the guidance needs of the student.

ADJUSTMENT TO SECONDARY SCHOOL

Although the change from the six-year elementary school to the junior high school is not so abrupt as that from the eighth grade of the old elementary school to the first year of high school, there are several very important differences between the two schools. Because of the departmental organization usually found in the junior high school, the pupil must adjust himself to a variety of teachers instead of to only one teacher. Instead of remaining in the same room for all classes, he moves from room to room. The character of the junior-high-school building itself is often quite different from that of the elementary school. The student is plunged into a different type of school life and school discipline. There are various types of clubs and group activities; there is usually some form of student government; the school library and the school gymnasium provide new experiences. The student is expected to take more responsibility both for his own activities and for some elements in the life of the school.

The junior high school is so organized that in the first year there is likely to be little or no choice of subjects because nearly all students are required to take the same work. Starting with the eighth or ninth grade, however, the student must make decisions about courses which may have lasting results for his occupational adjustment. Out of this situation many important problems arise which require that the student have guidance.

Many of these same problems arise in the transition from the junior high school to the senior high school. Where the entire six years of the secondary school are housed in one building and considered to be a six-year school, there is no problem of adjustment to a new building, but other more important problems remain. For example, a student may need help in deciding whether to leave school at the end of the compulsory attendance age or to remain for graduation.

DECISIONS ABOUT LEAVING SCHOOL

Soon after starting secondary school some children will begin to reach the place where further schooling of the kind available may not be desirable because each year brings them diminishing returns. How long to remain in school becomes an important problem for these students. Research indicates that students who do not graduate from high school are at a disadvantage for the rest of their lives, particularly with regard to employment. It is essential, then, that every possibility of adapting the school program to serve the individuals be explored before the reluctant conclusion is reached that leaving school is the best available method of "continuing education."

LEARNING PROBLEMS

Although the learning problems encountered in the secondary school are not always new, many now become of increasing importance. Reading difficulties; rate of reading and comprehension; likes and dislikes of studies, teachers and types of literature; differences in aptitude for different school subjects—all are very important factors in the student's adjustment to the secondary school. A guidance program will help diagnose the learning difficulty and plan steps to overcome it. The student may need remedial reading, help in arithmetic, a different course of study, a change of teachers, or perhaps prolonged counseling to overcome emotional barriers to learning.

DECISIONS ABOUT COLLEGE

At graduation from the secondary school a decision must be made regarding enrollment in some type of post-high-school institution, such as business school, technical school, or college. Such a complex and crucial decision should be made with adequate guidance from teachers and counselors. At present it seems likely that, with the limited facilities of colleges and with the great increase in the number applying for admission, the problem of being accepted for college work will be a very serious one. This means that the marks earned in the last two or three years of the secondary school and the quality of work done there will be of extreme importance. The unprecedented demand for trained men and women in science and mathematics and the millions of dollars provided by the federal government, the states, and private enterprises for increased educational facilities and scholarships place an added responsibility upon the schools for the guidance of students who have the abilities to succeed in such specialized training and who have the desire and the ambition to enter this specialization.

The choice of a college is one of the very important problems facing parents and high-school students, and it merits far more consideration than is usually given to it. Colleges are not all alike in entrance requirements, cost, atmosphere, or opportunities offered. Proximity to the home of the student is often a controlling factor. Some students do need a continuance of home influence, but others need to get away from home and learn to be independent. Some need a small college; others, a large one.

Some colleges have developed an aura of respectability, a halo of superiority that is often mistaken for unusual merit. This halo may be the result of long tradition, difficulty of entrance, long waiting lists of candidates for admission, or propaganda. The recent attempts to rate colleges according to certain predetermined elements are, in many ways, helpful, but the ratings typically do not take into account the elements that are of greater importance—the quality of instruction, the personal influence of the faculty on the students, and the atmosphere of the college.

Institutions do differ in real effectiveness of instruction, and some that have high prestige really merit it, but others do not. Leaders in all walks of life are by no means confined to graduates of so-called "high-ranking" institutions. There are hundreds of good small colleges scattered about the country where a student may secure a really fine education. Indeed, some of the men and women who have received their graduate training in large universities of high reputation and are, therefore, claimed as their product have taken their undergraduate work in a small college. It is often a blessing, rather than a tragedy, that a student finds himself unable to gain admission to a college that has a high reputation. Much depends upon what the student brings with him, and admission by itself guarantees nothing in the way of learning and success.

Two of the most frequent reasons for the choice of a college are that the father or the mother graduated from that particular college or that some friend, possibly the teacher or the counselor, did. These reasons are emphasized by the propaganda organized by nearly every college and broadcast by the alumni. "Harveton University wants the best. Alumni, be on the lookout for good strong men: scholars, athletes. Get hold of them, send them to Harveton." This activity may be entirely legitimate, but the result is that Mr. Brown, an alumnus of Harveton, principal of the Jonesboro High school, picks out the best students and the finest athletes and tries to influence them to go to Harveton. Now Harveton may be a good university, but it may not be the best place for these particular boys. Alumni are very likely to want to send the best candidates to their own university, saying, "Let the others go to Podunk College."

Colleges and universities differ in spirit, offerings, and suitability for certain types of young men and women. No choice of a college should be made without a very careful study of the institution and of the student to determine the suitability of one for the other. The decision should be made on the basis of the needs of the student and the degree to which the institution meets these needs. When two institutions are equally suitable and equally good, other reasons may then properly enter into the decision. The question is altogether too vital, and means too much in the life of the young man or woman, to be decided upon any other basis than the needs of the individual.

Information about college entrance requirements should be known by students and parents long enough in advance of graduation from high school so that subjects necessary for entrance may be taken. The parents of a young man may plan for years to send him to a certain university, only to find when he is a senior in high school that he cannot qualify because he has only two years of Latin and four years are required. Such a situation is entirely inexcusable.

At present the unprecedented demand for college education and the limited facilities throughout the country have sometimes changed the question for many from "What college shall I choose" to "What college will take me?" This condition has made it necessary to plan well in advance and to make applications intelligently. This situation places an added responsibility on the secondary school for considering more carefully the type of college which is best suited to a student's ability and needs and for preparing him to adjust himself to the scholastic and social life of the college. The difficulty, importance, and complexity of decisions about college argue strongly for the need for guidance services in secondary schools.

DECISIONS ABOUT WORK

Nearly half of the students who graduate from high school will enter the work force. Frequently, this first entry job is selected on a purely fortuitous basis. It has been estimated that more than half of these first jobs are taken when the student knows of no other possible opening at that time. This means that some friend or neighbor has told him about the job or that perhaps an employment agency has sent him to it with no real consideration as to whether it is a suitable position for him to take. The secondary-school guidance program assumes some of the responsibility for helping students make decisions about the kind of work they should get into. Many programs make use of the state employment service to test their students and help them understand their characteristics and also to make them aware of the kinds of occupations which they may enter in the community.

Guidance programs have long been accused of being only concerned about the college-bound student. Much ingenuity is needed to make the secondary-school guidance program more valuable to the workbound student.

Guidance Needs of Secondary-School Students Related to Personal Development

EMOTIONAL DEVELOPMENT AND GUIDANCE

Emotional disturbances may occur in any stage of a person's development and in any part of the school system. Some have their origin or at least become more pressing in the secondary school. Physiological development, bringing with it increased size and strength, sex impulses, responsibilities resulting from approaching maturity—all are very important causes of emotional changes and emotional instability. Such emotional conditions are often the causes of much maladjustment and unhappiness. The student needs help in his growth toward "emotional maturity," that is, in the ability to direct his strong basic emotions into channels that lead to the attainment of ends that are socially desirable and individually satisfying.

PHYSICAL DEVELOPMENT AND GUIDANCE

The physical needs peculiar to secondary-school pupils center around the period of rapid growth and physiological maturation. Along with these changes we may find lowered vitality, fatigue, lethargy (often mistaken for laziness), impaired coordination and awkwardness due to unequal growth of different parts of the body, and physiological changes caused by maturing. Serious maladjustments often result from these conditions. Students undergoing such development need information, understanding, and guidance to help them adjust to their changing bodies.

SOCIAL DEVELOPMENT AND GUIDANCE

The special social needs of the young adolescent arise partly from expanding vision resulting from more extensive experience, wider contacts, and approaching maturity. Timidity, self-consciousness, overaggressiveness, dislikes, "crushes," and "wanderlust" are among the difficulties often apparent in the adolescent. He needs help in the establishment of wholesome relations with the opposite sex. He needs to be understood and accepted even when his conduct cannot be approved. What he does and what he thinks should be viewed with an understanding of the physical and mental changes that are taking place in him. He needs to have a sense of belonging to some group, a sense of being needed and wanted. He needs help in freeing himself from the fears and the sense of guilt that beset him. The narrow personal loyalty that he feels toward his gang should be respected, but he should be helped to widen this loyalty to a larger group—to his school, to society, to an accepted ideal. He needs to understand more clearly his responsibilities toward others and toward constituted authority. He needs help in the development of responsibility and independence of judgment.

Guidance has a major responsibility in assisting youth to organize or choose groups that have useful objectives and that are suited to the desires, needs, and abilities of the individuals of the group. Assistance to youth in social adjustments is a function of the entire school. The administrator, librarian, teacher, and counselor all have a definite responsibility for giving such help. Every pupil should feel that he is accepted by his teacher and by every other member of the school staff who has contact with him. The entire atmosphere of the school should be permeated with this spirit even though corrections, restrictions, and punishments may be necessary. Pupils should always feel free to come to any member of the school staff for help. The desire to be accepted by someone is universal. We all want to have a feeling of belonging, to be needed and wanted. Nonacceptance or open rejection often results in reprisals and in destructive activities.

Guidance can also help in assisting in the organization of such activities as student clubs in the secondary school. Very often the organization of clubs that are constructive and useful prevents the formation of clandestine groups that have undesirable objectives. In many schools certain clubs are purely traditional and, although once useful, do not now meet real needs. Such clubs should be eliminated or their purposes changed. A pupil who wishes to be chosen for a certain club should be helped to realize the necessity for developing the qualifications required by the club he hopes to join and of being the kind of person who will be accepted by the members of the group.

The members of clubs should also be helped to realize their responsibility for the selection of new members. A member should not be chosen or rejected merely for personal reasons or because he lives on a certain side of the railroad track, nor even entirely for the contribution he can make to the club. The help that the prospective member can get by membership in the group should also be a factor in a decision about his selection.

The problems occasioned by organizations and other elements in the school program designed to increase social adjustment call for guidance services. The finest program of clubs, classes, and activities will not help the student who has not been guided in making best use of his available opportunities.

Summary

However effective the guidance given in the elementary school, it will not eliminate all the problems that appear in the secondary school. The period of the junior–senior high school presents a challenge for guidance workers. The differences among secondary-school students in height, weight, physiological maturity, and social and emotional characteristics are very great. All are approaching maturity, but there are often mixtures of immaturity and maturity not only among the pupils in a class but also in the same pupil.

Just ahead are important choices regarding education, occupation, and marriage. Study, discipline, social life, and available school activities are quite different from those found in the elementary school and must be varied for different students in the same class. This is the last opportunity for the school to give the majority of students any material help in learning to make wise choices.

When we consider the nature of the secondary-school student, we see that our culture makes great demands on him. Basic decisions must be made at this time which will have lasting repercussions. Guidance must be available to increase the quality of the vocational, educational, personal-social experiences which the school offers the adolescent.

Exercises

1. List some decisions you made in high school that have had lasting effects on the course of your vocational or personal development. How might guidance have helped you with these decisions?

2. There is much controversy regarding the extent of the school's responsibility for the personal-social development of its students. What is your position with regard to this problem?

3. Interview three secondary-school students regarding guidance. Ask to whom they go to discuss (a) personal-social concerns, (b) educational decisions, (c) vocational plans. Be prepared to discuss the implications of your findings.

References

Downing, Lester N.: *Guidance and Counseling Services: An Introduction*, McGraw-Hill Book Company, New York, 1968.

Fullmer, Daniel W., and Harold W. Bernard: *Counseling: Content and Process*, Science Research Associates, Inc., Chicago, 1964.

Hatch, Raymond N., Paul L. Dressel, and James W. Costar: *Guidance Services in the Secondary School*, Wm. C. Brown Company Publishers, Dubuque, Iowa, 1963.

Ohlsen, Merle M.: *Guidance Services in the Modern School*, Harcourt, Brace & World, Inc., New York, 1964.

Roeber, Edward C.: *The School Counselor*, The Center for Applied Research in Education, Inc., Washington, D.C., 1963.

PART FOUR

Counseling—Techniques and Philosophy

PART
FOUR

9

Counseling with Individuals

The point of view presented in Chapter 1 indicates that the authors do not consider guidance to be the concern of the counselor only. Collective efforts of the administrator, librarian, English teacher, and school nurse, among others, are needed if students are to be provided with a comprehensive, effective guidance program.

Counseling is the component of guidance for which the school counselor takes primary responsibility. Others assist him in gathering the data that comprise the individual inventory and maintaining community contacts so that a placement service may be effective. The task of assisting students to examine conflicting values that are the root of a personal problem or to weigh information as they make plans about schooling and work is one which requires specific education, supervised practice, and experience. Students may find genuine benefit in talking with friends and teachers. If the conversation is to be beneficial for the student, it should have a number of characteristics, such as the establishment of objectives or goals toward which the conversation might point, the quality of *opening up* the area of concern rather than glossing it over, effective use of the decision process by formulating alternatives and projecting consequences of each, and terminal structure that allows the student to review critically what has taken place and makes provision for future meetings if they are needed. Social conversation may or may not be marked by any of these characteristics, depending upon the people involved and the nature of their relationship. Counselors, because of their specialized training, can develop relationships with students that contain all of these characteristics. Further, they can use accumulated information, test results, and knowledge of community resources as they help the student to understand himself, his environment, and the process of change.

Traditional Differences

Two traditions that have their roots in the early years of this century are represented within the field of counseling. The first grew initially out of a need to assist immigrants and those living in slums to become employed. This humanitarian purpose was increasingly supported by tools of assessment that were developed within the growing field of measurement and evaluation.

Frank Parson's founding of the Vocational Bureau in Boston in 1908 is frequently cited as the birth of this tradition. Vocational guidance, with its broad interest in social reform and specific skills to help workers obtain employment, gradually blossomed into counseling psychology, with attention given to the normal individual's development in personal and social, as well as vocational and educational, areas.

The second tradition also had its beginnings in 1908 with the publication of Clifford Beers' book, *A Mind That Found Itself*. This led to the establishment of the National Committee for Mental Health in 1909. The National Committee first championed adequate living conditions and humane regard for those who had succumbed to serious mental disorders. Later it turned public attention to those with less severe disorders and persuaded educators to become more cognizant of developmental problems such as self-doubt and alienation tendencies among their students.

Each tradition has influenced the other during the sixty years since their beginnings in 1908. Vocational guidance early demonstrated tendencies toward orderliness and quantification through development of a scientific approach to extensive occupational classification systems, vocational surveys, research methods, and assessment instruments. Mental health programs placed stress upon assisting the individual to develop, change, and cope.

Gradually, as vocational guidance developed into counseling psychology, it was shaken from its authoritarian approach to individuals and became aware of the person as well as his problem. Stress, as never before, was placed upon counseling processes and techniques. At the same time, greater emphasis upon research and publications caused those within the mental health tradition to become more involved in research of the counseling process and assessment of outcomes.

Each tradition is being now advanced by new proponents. Many of the original distinguishing features have been blurred as each has taken on some characteristics of the other. But differences exist. Current interest in environmental manipulation, computerized counseling, and systems approaches to the process may be traced to vocational guidance origins, while those who focus upon the counseling relationship and the personal qualities of the counselor more nearly follow the mental-health tradition.

Orientation of Students to Counseling

School counselors could spend a considerable portion of their available time in orienting students to the counseling process unless they organized some formal system or plan. To introduce each student to counseling through the experience of the interview alone not only is an inefficient use of the counselor's time, but also may prevent students who need to see the counselor from knowing of his availability and cause anxieties on the part of students who do see him and are unfamiliar with the process. The counselor's attempts to be seen as one who treats students as his equal and is willing to meet with them whenever they have a concern, a doubt, or a decision to consider may be seriously harmed by the paternalistic act of calling in a student at the counselor's convenience, according to a checklist, and without regard to the need of the student.

The problem, therefore, is one of allowing students to visit the counselor's office as they desire and yet having them familiar with the counseling service in order that they might avail themselves of it. A number of practices have been developed to make the nature of counseling services known to students, parents, teachers, and administrators. First, the counselor may present programs at school assemblies, before parent groups, or in faculty meetings. In addition to verbal explanation, slides that indicate the various aspects of the counseling service, role-playing interviews, and the playing of model tapes may be used.

Students, however, need to become acquainted with the person, not a figure standing before them in an auditorium or a sequence of slides that show a smiling face and no action. An interim step is to have teachers send small groups of students to see the counselor for a "get acquainted" visit of a few minutes' duration. If the counselor is new to the school, this may be done with all students. The experienced counselor may use this as an ongoing practice of orientation for the class of students just entering the school each fall and students who transfer from other schools during the academic year.

The counselor introduces himself to the students, lets each student introduce himself to the group, and makes certain that they understand the purpose of the visit. Conversation is focused upon the purposes of counseling, why students might wish to visit the counselor, how the counselor might assist them, and what resources he has at his disposal. Although the interaction is not counseling, the counselor attempts to enter fully and openly into the discussion. To give them the "feel" of the counseling relationship, he may ask one of them to role-play a student who is concerned about English or wondering about his future. The informal nature of the meeting and the security of having peers at his side helps the student to remain calm until he becomes familiar with the counselor's manner and the physical surroundings. As a terminal exercise, the counselor shows students how they may sign up for interviews and asks them to visit him when they feel he may be of assistance.

Most students will be receptive to this introduction and visit the counselor at a later date. Some, however, may express interest in knowing more about the process. The counselor may then wish to meet at greater length with the student or provide an audio-tape of an interview that can be played publicly, in order that the student may gain further insight.

The Counseling Process

Counseling, as a process, has been defined variously by authors and professors for nearly fifty years. While no single definition has stood the test of time, most contain some reference to difference in role of the student (who is to be assisted or helped) and the counselor (who is more experienced, frequently older, and has as his function to help). Also, mention is generally made of the objective or goal in terms of improved adjustment, higher functioning, and greater happiness. Finally, focus is usually placed upon the process involved, the learning that occurs, and the assistance that is given.

Four basic assumptions must be accepted if counseling is to be successful. First, it is assumed that the student is willing to participate in the process. He may have a concern, a wonderment about the world around him, or curiosity about what he is experiencing. While the process may be unfamiliar to him and he may display resistance at moments, counseling will not be successful unless he participates fully.

Second, the counselor must possess appropriate training, experience, and personal attitudes to function effectively. He must be able to relate easily with the student, assist him in establishing objectives and goals, and employ any ethical means that will assist the student to change or learn behaviors necessary to cope with his environment and work toward the objectives they mutually have established.

Third, an appropriate environment is necessary. Depending upon the nature of the interview, this environment must provide assurance of confidentiality, a mood of contemplation, and/or adequate information resources.

Finally, as the term is used in school settings, counseling must provide a relationship that allows for meeting both immediate and long-term needs. The counselor must be available at moments when the student needs him for specific assistance. Also, he must work cooperatively with the student in identifying and altering behavior to meet long-term goals and maintain contact throughout a year or several years, depending upon the organizational structure of counseling services within the school.

Like the student, the counselor also has objectives which are the outgrowth of his professional value system and his assumptions about human behavior. They do not conflict with student objectives because the counselor's objectives are concerned with the process of counseling rather than with establishing specific goals toward which the student might work.[1]

One of these objectives is *clarifying the helping process.* The counselor, because of his training and experience, is able to do this by providing the student with an overall structure that explains who the counselor is, what he is able to do, and what he expects of the student. He can assist the student in perceiving what the student believes to be his concern or what he might explore with the counselor. In order that he may understand the student and his world, the counselor may focus less upon the cognitive or content aspects and attempt to understand how the student really feels, what he is attempting to say, and what he is unable to verbalize. The counselor may assist the student in talking at times. Should the student wander in talking and lose focus, the counselor can intervene and bring focus back into the conversation. One client described the process as follows: "It was kind of like going down the highway on a foggy night. I drove my own car, but the counselor provided the illuminated white line in the middle of the road for me."[2]

Another objective toward which the counselor works is *assisting the student to examine the psychological dimensions of what he is thinking and saying.* The counselor's approach in this regard is quite the opposite of that of a person engaged in social conversation. In social situations we react to remarks of self-doubt or anxiety by attempting to "close down" the display of emotion. We may interject mirth, change topics, give words of comfort, or suggest that things really couldn't be as they seemed. Counselors do quite the opposite. Rather than "close down" the student, the counselor will focus upon the central concern of the student and help him to *open up.* When a test-anxious student suggests that he will fail, the conversationalist reassures, "I can't imagine you failing. You've always done so well." The counselor, however, probes, "You're certain you'll fail. Why?" The counselor must be mindful of limits in time and his ability to assist the student. Assisting the student to *open up* carries with it the obligation, on the part of the counselor, to have the time and skill to follow through and terminate the interview successfully.

[1] Adapted from Leona E. Tyler, *The Work of the Counselor,* Appleton-Century-Crofts, Inc., New York, 1961, pp. 54–55.

[2] Lawrence M. Brammer and Everett L. Shostram, *Therapeutic Psychology,* Prentice-Hall, Inc., Englewood Cliffs, N.J., 1960, p. 183.

Finally, and most importantly, the counselor must work to *develop a sound relationship with the student*. When the student arrives in the guidance suite, the counselor may greet him cordially and introduce a topic of common interest and experience during the time that they are walking to the counselor's office. A relationship cannot be based upon small talk, however. The student has come to the counselor because he understands he will receive professional assistance, and the relationship must be based upon mutual understanding and respect. The eager apprentice counselor may work hard to be ingratiating and feel needed. He vows, "This student will like me before we're through." The experienced counselor, through his skill in putting strangers at ease and getting the relationship going, will ponder, "I'll like this student if I get to know him and draw upon what the student wants, what he prides himself in, what he considers important and is really concerned about."

The three goals must be used in concert. A counseling relationship cannot be developed without structure and the process of helping the student to *open up*. Similarly, counseling will not be successful if the counselor concentrates upon developing the relationship and assisting the student to open up, but provides no structure.

During the course of practice, counselors find themselves operating at various points along four dimensions. The nature of the relationship of the student's awareness may determine, in part, the counselor's behavior. However, the counselor's basic philosophy concerning human development and the translation of this philosophy into a theoretical approach to counseling also influences his behavior. Examination of these dimensions is not made to determine which is appropriate and which is inappropriate; rather, they are stated here to help the counselor order his thinking and understand the meanings and purposes of the four continua.

1. *Diagnostic–developmental.* Our problem-solving nature sometimes causes us to attempt to "diagnose" and "prescribe" in the best tradition of the family doctor. The counselor's insight may prove immediately helpful to the student. He may be able to make a specific observation that causes the student to view himself more clearly. More than one-shot problem solving is involved in counseling, however. Concerns frequently are of a developmental nature. The student may wish to explore subtleties of his environment and culture or learn how to relate effectively with peers. In these instances, he will learn more effectively through experiencing than being told.

2. *Cognitive–affective.* Both intellectual content and personal feeling are the substance of counseling, and a relationship seldom develops in the absence of either. Again, it is the responsibility of the counselor to assist the student in focusing upon facts and descriptive content at one moment

and their affective meaning to the student at another. The counselor can sometimes combine both in his response. He may say, "You see that you're not accepted, can understand why, but feel pretty angry about it."

3. *Observer–participant.* The counselor must, at all times, view himself as operating in two distinctly different ways. A part of him must remain the detached, scientific observer who takes account of student behaviors, formulates thoughts as to their implications, and subjects these thoughts to tests by questioning the student or observing whether or not behavior is consistent. However, the counselor is fully involved in the relationship, must act and react, and cannot remain a stoic observer if the relationship is to be marked by involvement and movement.

4. *Ambiguity–structure.* Stress has previously been placed upon the need for structure within the interview. That the student may need some assistance in understanding the purpose of counseling and what is expected of him in general terms is not argued. At the same time, he needs freedom to decide what he feels is important and how he wishes to proceed. The counselor, therefore, may vacillate from stimulating student responses through general, ambiguous leads (such as, "And what did this mean to you?") to providing structure when the student's thoughts have wandered ("I'm not sure how that related to your wanting to work").

The Counselor's Attitudes and Skills

One may ask, "What sort of personal characteristics would I need in order to become a counselor?" Extensive research has sought to determine which characteristics would be appropriate and in what combination. Most personality assessment instruments and many screening techniques have been used in this effort. The results have discouraged continuance of this search for a standard personality pattern and, instead, have caused researchers and counselor educators to view the attitudes and skills of the counselor as of importance rather than his personality type. The following represents a description of some of the counselor's basic attitudes and skills.

Ethical Behavior. The most basic of attitudes that a counselor possesses is his ethical behavior. Because he is concerned with helping people and often is given information of a highly confidential nature, the counselor must demonstrate a *professional* attitude toward his work and be ethical in his every act. Unless the student is convinced that he can completely trust the counselor, he will be inhibited in talking and not participate fully in the relationship.

Flexibility. Because of the fluid nature of the counseling relationship, the counselor must not be rigid. He must be alert to changes in student attitude and student expectation of him. The student at one time may look to him as a peer; at another, an authority figure. The flexible counselor will find himself moving back and forth along the four dimensions previously discussed as he adapts himself to these changes.

Intellectual Competence. The counselor's skills are built upon a thorough knowledge of human behavior, perceptive mind, and ability to integrate present events with training and experience. An ability to think in an orderly, logical manner is essential if he is to assist the student in setting objectives, placing events in perspective, considering alternatives, and assessing outcomes.

Acceptance. Researchers have rather commonly reported that little is accomplished in counseling through advice, persuasion, or threat. Students come to the counselor for understanding and help. They bring with them the hopes, fears, doubts, and anxieties with which they are concerned. Brammar and Shostram suggest that the counselor, if he is to convey acceptance, must have made some basic assumptions about the student with whom he is working. He must (1) regard the student as a person of infinite worth and dignity, (2) accept his right to make his own decisions, (3) believe that he has the potential to choose wisely, and (4) understand that he is responsible for his own life.[3]

Understanding. The counselor must understand the student on two levels. Observation, conference notes, and test results provide a preliminary understanding. The student, however, will feel that he is understood only when the communication of the counselor moves to a level of feeling, and he indicates that he understands the world of the student and perceives his doubts or hopes as the student does. He will then be thinking *with* rather than *for* or *about* the student. Communication may be nonverbal as well as verbal. The counselor who understands will be able to integrate the student's words with his use of nods and gestures. The counselor's communication skills assist the student in (1) establishing objectives, (2) freeing up his thinking and exploring aspects of the concern that were previously closed to him, (3) formulating alternatives, (4) changing or learning behaviors, and (5) assessing possible consequences.

Sensitivity. The counselor must, above all, be honest and sincere in his attitudes. The student is accustomed to the mild deceit that is so much a part of the social conversation "game." If the counselor hopes to have the student be "open" and candid, the relationship must be marked by com-

[3] *Ibid.* p. 157.

plete honesty on the part of the counselor. Some discretion is needed, of course. The counselor who remarks, "I can't stand pink shirts on men," merely because this is one of his biases may find that he has alienated a pink-shirted student rather effectively. The counselor's attitude can therefore be described as one of *appropriate openness*. That is, he is open in all matters that pertain to the relationship and, as with other attitudes, doesn't project his biases about extra-counseling matters into the interview.

Evaluating the Effectiveness of Counseling

The effectiveness of counseling is determined by the evaluation of counselors, supervisors, and students of the behavior of the counselor. Students participating in research projects are sometimes asked, "What did the counselor do to put you at ease?" or "What characteristics did he have that you liked or didn't like?" If we wished to enlist the aid of students in changing the behavior of counselors, as is frequently true during the early phases of *training*, these would be the type of questions we might ask. However, the questions are not directly related to counselor effectiveness because our primary purpose in counseling practice is not to produce changes in *counselor* behavior.

Student change or development is the purpose of counseling. This implies that an assessment be made, independent of the interview, as to whether the student has altered his behavior with regard to the objectives he set for himself in counseling. The effectiveness of counseling with the student who seeks help because he needs to improve his grades could best be determined by looking at the grades he has received since termination of the counseling relationship. He may report that he feels happier, has more friends, or no longer worries about skipping church. These changes cannot be considered as indicative of counselor effectiveness unless one or more of these were objectives he set for himself in addition to obtaining improved grades.

Helping the student to clarify his objectives and state them in terms which are observable is the first essential for determining effectiveness. Developing a system that produces data concerning the student's development since counseling is a second step. This may entail meeting briefly with the student, monitoring his progress through grades assigned and teacher reports, or observing the student in learning and social situations. Measuring outcomes by determining whether or not the student has changed or learned the behaviors necessary to meet the specific objectives that he set for himself at the outset of counseling provides the counselor with evidence of his effectiveness. Students and school staff, if told candidly why the monitoring is conducted, will be more receptive to the counselor's method of evaluation.

Initial Interview Procedures

Most counseling within a school setting is, in a sense, initial interviewing. School counseling is not marked by a long series of weekly or biweekly interviews. The student visits the counselor, for example, in November for one or two interviews, and they may not have another conference until spring of the following year. Although the counselor follows the student's progress and may have several brief chats in the corridor or at an athletic event, their next meeting starts the process all over again. Quite likely, the objectives established for the first interview or interviews will bear no relationship to those established at a later date. The school counselor, therefore, must be particularly skilled at initial interviewing. Basic procedures are presented and commented upon.

1. *Preparing for the interview and getting started.* Counseling can hardly be expected to be effective unless both counselor and student are prepared for what is to take place. The counselor may need to review background data concerning the student or read notes made after the last meetings. He may know of some materials or information sources that he could have readily available. The student, if he is aware of the purposes of counseling, should consider how he can best use the time available. As described earlier in the chapter, the counselor uses his skill in communication to draw upon what the student wants, what he is attempting to say, and what he considers of current primary importance.

2. *Developing opening structure.* The student needs to know who the counselor is, what he is able to do, and what he expects of the student. This should be done briefly and simply. Experienced counselors know how to communicate quickly and effectively, but the novice might well write out and commit to memory what he wishes to say during the opening moments. Although it may never be used quite as it was prepared, it provides a guide that will be helpful in getting started. For example:

COUNSELOR: Scott, I'm Mr. Jansen. I've been counselor here three years. Before that I taught science at South High. Because you've recently moved here, I'd like to get us started by asking about your contact with counselors at your previous school. Could you tell me what counseling means to you as the result of these experiences?

STUDENT: Well, I met once or twice to talk about schedule changes. That's what the counselors seemed to do most of the time.

COUNSELOR: It's good that I asked. Scheduling here is handled by our assistant principal and I spend most of my time in meeting with students about whatever concerns seem most relevant to them. It may be wondering about their development, broken friendships, getting into college, or a host of other areas. What we say will be held in strictest confidence. We'll have about thirty minutes to talk today and I'm wondering if there is a particular place you'd like to start.

Such a statement might be used in most interviews with strangers. However, the counselor should be sensitive to the needs of the student and not allow the structure to get in the way of the student's expression of concern. If he seems anxious to talk, a more appropriate opening would be, "Hi, Scott. Let me close the door and we'll get started."

3.   *Establishing the objectives.*   As a product of his training and experience, the counselor will be aware of objectives he can set for himself in counseling. These stem from his professional value system and the way he conceptualizes human development. They are manifested in the ways that he can effectively behave and communicate with students.

During the opening minutes of the interview, the counselor and student need to establish objectives or goals toward which they can work in the time available. The objectives are not of a fixed nature and may be revised as the interview develops. An objective must be attainable and realistic in order to be a goal worth pursuing. The student who suggests, "I'd just like to be liked by everyone," will need assistance from the counselor in making the objective realistic. "I wish I had two friends who cared" would be a goal toward which they might work. Counseling without process objectives on the part of the counselor and student objectives in terms that are meaningful to him is a futile endeavor.

4.   *Building the relationship.*   As the interview progresses, the counselor must continue to build upon the relationship that has been established. His honesty, expression of interest, humanness, and perceptiveness will allow the student to realize that the counselor is fully committed to assisting him. At times, however, the novice counselor needs to remember to let a little of himself out. A warm smile, a touch on the hand, a nod of understanding, any act of caring that is shown will help the student to invest a little more of himself and be more honest in his communication.

5.   *Helping the student to talk.*   The counselor may perceive that the student is reluctant to discuss some concerns or some aspects of concerns even though a sound, trusting relationship has been developed. When this occurs, the counselor may need to give particular assistance to get communication going. The threatening nature of the concern probably prohibits approaching it frontally. The counselor must therefore rely upon spontaneity and sensitivity in (*a*) assisting the student to express his feelings, (*b*) understanding why the student is experiencing difficulty, and (*c*) help-

ing the student to recognize feelings of which he is unaware or has difficulty accepting. The counselor's own relaxed and reassuring manner will convey more than the words he uses.

6. *Terminating the interview.* The counselor must use his skill in developing closing, as well as opening, structure. He initiates this phase of the interview by pausing longer between responses, focusing more upon cognitive than affective aspects of the student's concern, and not encouraging further exploration of subtleties or tension-producing areas. His sensitivity assists him in determining when the focus might be changed to the summary and plans for subsequent meetings. This may be initiated by his suggestion that "our time is all but up." The counselor asks the student to summarize those aspects of the interview that were most meaningful and assists him, as necessary, in reviewing the objective and whether or not it was achieved. Plans for the future must then be made. Will there be another interview? When? Where? Or should there be a referral? Should tests be taken? Information sources tapped? When counselor and student have reached an understanding concerning how they might handle matters such as these, the counselor stands up (an excellent way to prevent a reopening of concerns) and sees the client to the outer office.

7. *Planning the follow-up.* After each interview the counselor should make some brief notes as a check upon his own faulty memory and in order to keep a running record of what has transpired through the series of interviews. These can be reviewed briefly before the next formal contact with the student. Even though no immediate contact is planned with the student, a note can be made to see the student briefly after a week or a month to learn whether the established objectives have been reached and whether the counselor can be of future assistance. This informal, individual follow-up can be structured to give the counselor some evidence of whether or not he was effective. A more comprehensive, mass follow-up is conducted separately as a guidance service to study groups such as all seniors, all recent graduates, or all students now in technical schools.

Summary

Counseling is a process through which a student works with a professionally trained person in establishing specific objectives and changing or learning the behaviors which he must possess in order to attain these objectives. The counselor is able to assist the student because he is intellectually competent, flexible, accepting, understanding, and sensitive to student needs. He will have little success in developing a relationship, however, unless the student is willing to participate fully in the process.

Students, like adults, are bound up in their fears, dreams, disappointments, and hopes. A student comes to the counselor bearing the thoughts and feelings with which he is struggling. The counselor assists him to get started in talking, but stresses that the student must set the objectives toward which they might work. He will help the student to clarify the objective and state it in attainable terms. At the close of the interview, the counselor helps the student to summarize those parts which the student considers most significant, and mutually they consider whether they should terminate the relationship, continue to meet, or seek a referral source.

The counselor evaluates the effectiveness of counseling by monitoring the extra-interview behavior of the student. Counseling is effective when the student attains the objectives he established at the outset of the relationship.

Exercises

1. Interview a practicing counselor to learn his perceptions of the counselor's work. What does he find particularly rewarding? What are the causes of his greatest frustrations? How does he spend his time? What aspects of counseling does he find most demanding?

2. Discriminate between counseling and conversation. What are the purposes of each? What specific characteristics does counseling have that conversation does not? What skills does a person use in counseling that are not usually used in conversation?

3. Develop an opening statement that would be useful with most students in your school. Without referring to your developed statement, make a list of specific information items concerning the process of counseling which you should communicate to the student during the opening minutes of the interview. Next, check your statement. Revise it until it will adequately communicate your intentions to the student.

References

Blocher, Donald H.: *Developmental Counseling*, the Ronald Press Company, New York, 1966.

Miller, Carroll H.: *Foundations of Guidance*, Harper & Row, Publishers, Incorporated, New York, 1961.

Patterson, C. H. (ed.): *The School Counselor; Selected Readings*, McGraw-Hill Book Company, New York, 1967.

Tyler, Leona E.: *The Work of the Counselor*, Appleton-Century-Crofts, Inc., New York, 1961.

Wrenn, C. Gilbert: *The Counselor in a Changing World*, American Personnel and Guidance Association, Washington, D.C., 1962.

10

Counseling in Groups

Traditionally, counseling has involved a counselor working with one student, as discussed in the previous chapter. The work of counselors with groups in a *counseling* relationship is a relatively recent development and is not yet acknowledged by all. The belief continues to exist that the goals of counseling can be met only through a one-to-one relationship. Little evidence exists to suggest that the learning processes involved in counseling can be better stimulated through this mode than through interaction involving peers as well. Rather, the increasing body of knowledge concerning human behavior strongly suggests that group membership has great psychological significance. Those who insist counseling is restricted to a one-to-one relationship have eliminated the motivational potential which the group possesses for assisting one of its members in the process of changing or learning behaviors.

Students come to counselors with hopes, doubts, dreams, and fears. From these are established objectives which are meaningful to the student. A problem that exists in counseling is that while students are able to formulate attainable goals, identify changes, and specify desired skills, these necessary steps are not helpful to the student unless the dialogue, verbal promises, and actions within the interview result in a transfer of learning that affects the student in his daily environment and relationship. Saying it is not enough. Interview behavior must lead to changes outside the counselor's office if counseling is to be effective.

The group presents a student with a microcosm of social reality in which he might attempt to bridge the gap between his insight at a counseling group session and his daily pattern of experience. Transfer of learning can be immediate in that the student can *test out* plans for changed behavior within the safe and confidential confines of the group prior to an attempt at exhibiting the same behavioral and attitudinal change in the student's environment.

As an example, Jim, a junior, may realize that he is afraid to express tender emotion. He reports that he frequently torments his younger brother, while he is unable to relate at all to his affectionate older sister and attempts to freeze her out by ignoring her completely. The objectives and desired changes may be identified rather easily. How, though, would he take next steps? In individual counseling, the counselor might attempt to assist Jim in formulating plans and then testing them out, either through considering possible consequences or engaging in some role-playing activity. His repertoire of thought, experiences, and models is limited to himself and Jim.

The group adds versatility at this crucial point in attempting to effect change. Males within the group may help Jim to understand how they relate to their younger brothers. They might engage in role-playing with each other as well as with Jim in order that he might sense how best to attempt new behaviors which might be initially awkward, but appropriate, for a fraternal relationship. The group quite likely would also contain female members. They could add another dimension to his learning through helping him to understand his sister's way of relating. Through interacting with them, Jim could acquire behaviors that would be necessary to effect adequate brother-sister communication and understanding. Interacting with male and female group members and learning of their experiences may provide him with a far more realistic vehicle for transfer of learning than could the individual counselor.

Definitions and Distinctions

Varying forms of group activity have been associated with the guidance and counseling movement since its inception. Tracing the emergence of group innovations in some ways provides one with a history of the movement itself. Early attention was given to working with students through clubs, homerooms, and guidance classes in order to disseminate information largely of an educational and vocational nature. Concurrently, focus was placed upon discussion of social etiquette and normal patterns of growth and development.

Pioneering efforts in group discussions of personal concerns are threaded throughout the movement's history, but only in the past decade has its use become popular among counselors. Even today many experienced counselors have never attempted group counseling.

At the present time there are a number of different models with somewhat varying purposes that hold promise for the school counselor. Of the many that are available, three forms of group interaction have been selected and will be discussed. It is acknowledged that any attempts to define and distinguish between the many models presently being used is an arbitrary task in view of the fact that a given term or procedure may be used quite differently from one setting to another.

Group Guidance Model. Varying forms of group guidance have been used by educators since the early years of this century. Today, its usefulness continues. Counseling, as stated in the previous chapter, is only one task of the counselor and one mode of assisting students. It may be just as effective and much more efficient for the counselor to meet with a class, homeroom, or similarly constituted group upon some occasions. Group guidance refers to the interaction of the counselor with a relatively large group of students through the media of the lecture, discussion, and question-and-answer communication. Some basic purposes are to:

1. Disseminate information that will assist students to make effective use of the school environment, develop a strategy for the attainment of long-term educational and vocational goals, and understand the purposes, format, and reporting procedures for mass testing.
2. Provide factual sources for the discussion of growth and development concerns peculiar to the group.
3. Stimulate student thought about his biological, psychological, and sociological worlds.
4. Orient the student to the availability of guidance services, purposes of counseling, and operational procedures of the counseling office.

A number of leadership models may be used to conduct group guidance. The leader may serve only as an agent to sponsor meetings such as group discussions, clubs, student forums, or parent discussion groups. In these instances the counselor may function primarily as one who "keeps things going" and provides a supportive atmosphere. Through the establishment of guidance or occupation courses and homeroom guidance meetings, the counselor usually takes a more active role, represents "expert opinion," and functions more as an instructor than as a peer.

The obvious value of group guidance to the counselor is that it allows him to reach many people at once. He must realize, however, that he is sacrificing depth for breadth, working with a group that may have no choice but to participate, and probably meeting with them only occasionally. Participants may have difficulty in involving themselves at more than a superficial level, and the counselor will be challenged to develop a climate of acceptance and permissiveness with a group of this size. His contact with students in this setting, however, may be instrumental in motivating those who have specific concerns to meet with him individually or in counseling groups.

Group-process Model. A more sophisticated, intimate form of interaction may be provided through process groups. As used here, the term refers specifically to those group experiences which have as their objective the development of the group as a functional unit. Through the process of becoming a group, each member has learned his role within the group, learned something of behaviors of which the group approves and disapproves, and learned how he might affect change in the group.

Process groups have their origins in the group-dynamics movement. Business and industry have frequently used this model, and rather recently its use has been proliferated among groups of many types, including those comprised of teachers as well as of students.

Primary focus is placed upon group development rather than individual change in the group-process model. Indicators of progress are member cooperation, attainment of group goals, and group unity. Assisting members in meeting personal needs is a secondary purpose. Process groups differ from counseling groups, then, in the priority placed upon individual as opposed to group needs. Group counseling, as described in the next section, exists primarily to meet individual needs. Group cohesiveness is developed only to the extent that it is necessary to provide effective assistance for individual members.

Process groups differ from group guidance in purpose and size. Most use verbal interaction as the vehicle for achieving a sense of unity and cooperation, although nonverbal exercises are used increasingly. Focus is basically upon affective dimensions, and relatively little attention is given to developing life plans or discussion of topics not central to the group's purpose. Communication frequently centers upon current concerns of members, their interaction with their environment, and their interaction with each other.

The intense nature of the interaction means that the group must be relatively small. Some favor group size as small as four or six in order that member verbal participation can be maximized. The argument for larger groups is based on the assumption that some people are natural leaders, enjoy verbal expression, and learn best when pressed to express themselves, while others have become adept at learning through observation. Further, these advocates suggest that observational learners may not benefit from participation in a group where somewhat equal verbal participation is expected of all. Within a group of twelve to fifteen, the argument continues, roles become more nearly like those in environmental experiences. Each is then afforded the opportunity to learn in the manner in which he has become adept at learning.

It is not necessary that participants either have had previous experience in counseling or have expressed any particular problems or concerns that have motivated them to join the group. Generally, heterogeneity is seen as an asset to the group because it increases the variety of contacts and potential, helping relationships that might be available. Male and female, young and old, aggressive and passive may all be represented. Membership is restricted only in that an attempt is made to screen out those who might be affected negatively by the experience.

Leadership roles for process groups vary widely. Occasionally, leaders attempt to facilitate group interaction through rather structured approaches that emphasize a clear statement of purpose and specification of precise leader and member roles. Much more frequently a highly unstructured format is followed in which the leader, although more experienced in group interaction, may choose to participate exclusively as a group member and share the task of leadership with other members who wish to exercise it.

Process groups represent an excellent vehicle for learning about oneself and one's interaction with others. When mild curiosity about oneself and a general desire for personal development is the motivator, the relatively short-term and nontherapeutic nature of process groups may be ideal. For those who are aware of specific and immediate needs, group counseling with its focus on individual growth as opposed to group development and its more structured approach may be preferable.

Group-counseling Model. The most complex form of group interaction and the most demanding counselor tasks are those involved in group counseling. In the restricted sense in which the term is here used, the purposes of group counseling are closely parallel to those of individual counseling as described in the previous chapter. The term "group" suggests that the counselor is working with more than one person concurrently and that others may offer helping relationships to the individual.

If the purposes of individual and group counseling are common, why do both exist? First, efficiency and economy of counselor's time is involved. Most counselors are very conscious of demands upon their time. If the counselor found that he could work as effectively with a group of students as he could with an individual student during a given time period, then he would be making more efficient use of his time and assisting more students by engaging in group counseling. Second, a group environment is sometimes more conducive to learning new behaviors than is individual counseling. Group interaction is a more effective learning mode for some students or for students struggling with some problems.

One way of distinguishing group counseling from group guidance would be to view how each group would handle a common problem. Career planning might be considered by a guidance group with appropriate emphasis placed upon information sources and typical entry requirements. The counseling group would focus directly upon the psychological implications of varying alternatives for the individual, and he would be encouraged to examine the psychological realities of the choice for him. They might assist a girl to clarify whether she is interested in the helping professions because she wishes to help or be helped. Has she learned to enjoy dependency relationships? What do they mean to her? Specific and detailed probing may be needed to uncover and examine the implications involved.

Group process and group counseling have much in common. Both have group cooperation and individual development as components. The crucial difference rests in the priority assigned to each component. Process groups are organized to develop group unity and cooperation and have as a secondary purpose the meeting of individual needs. In contrast, group counseling has no group purpose. Each member participates only in order that his individual purposes might be met. Group cohesiveness is developed by the counselor only in order that the group might maximally assist each individual member. Only when a sense of cohesiveness is achieved can the full force and effectiveness of the group be brought to bear upon each individual's concerns. In this sense, the objective of each individual member is shared as a common objective of all the group members.

Groups Structured to Meet Specific Objectives

Debate has been raging for years whether groups should comprise members with the same or highly similar problems as opposed to members with quite different problems. Ample support can be found for either argument, and a more important consideration is the manner in which the group is originally structured. Encouraging results have been reported by a number of investigators working with homogeneous groups whose objectives were determined and clearly outlined to the potential members before the group began to function. These studies illustrate some of the varying needs of students which are met through group counseling.

Underachievement and motivation of able students has frequently been studied. Outcomes have been somewhat discouraging in that the grade-point average of those participating in group counseling has seldom differed from those who did not. Too few group meetings is frequently given as the cause. Some studies indicate that those who participate received lower grades, but showed increased acceptance of self. The group offers support, not motivation, it would seem.

Increased attention is being given to the original structuring of the group. Chestnut[1] reports encouraging results from a study in which groups were structured in two quite different ways by the counselor. Those whose format was counselor-structured (similar to group counseling as described in this chapter) reported improved grades as compared with

[1] W. J. Chestnut, "The Effects of Structured and Unstructured Group Counseling on Male College Students' Underachievement," *Journal of Counseling Psychology,* vol. 24, pp. 388–394, 1965.

those whose format was group-structured (comparable to group process as the authors use the term) and a group which participated in neither activity. No differences in study habits and attitudes or achievement needs were found between the three groups.

Problems of college attendance have often caused high-school students to be anxious and uncertain. School counselors frequently have structured groups to provide information that would reduce the anxiety and uncertainty experienced by high-school seniors. In a more comprehensive study than most, McKendry[2] compared students who participated in groups for this purpose with those who did not. Participants met for six weekly meetings of sixty minutes each during the spring term of their senior year to discuss problems of college attendance. They showed greater knowledge of general college requirements than nonparticipants and made a more appropriate curricular choice. Participants who entered college had six meetings of sixty minutes each during the following fall term. During this term participants as a group received higher grades than did nonparticipants.

Students classified as disturbing in the classroom frequently are referred to the counselor by the teacher. Groups have been formed to meet this need. Benson and Blocher's[3] study shows the combination of techniques that a group counselor may use. Working with a group who had been identified by teachers as low achievers and negative in school attitudes and classroom influence, Benson led discussions about specific study skills, presented three "how to study" films, arranged for a reading specialist to meet with the group, and capped discussion of authority figures by arranging a confrontation of the group with the school principal. Participants increased their grades, had fewer referrals for disciplinary action, and reported fewer problems on the SRA Youth Inventory. All participants continued in school the following year, while one-fourth of the nonparticipants dropped out.

Information-seeking behavior also has been a frequent focus of concern. Large group lectures fail to motivate most students to become active. Individual counseling is too time-consuming. Krumboltz and Thoresen[4] used groups of two males and two females in an attempt to increase the vocational and educational information seeking of eleventh graders. Two meetings were held with each, and the frequency and variety of information

[2] A. W. McKendry, "The Effects of Group Counseling on the Educational Planning of College-bound High School Seniors," *Dissertation Abstracts*, vol. 25, no. 7, pp. 3978–3979, 1965.

[3] R. L. Benson and D. H. Blocher, "Evaluation of Developmental Counseling with Groups of Low Achievers in a High School Setting," *School Counselor*, vol. 14, pp. 215–220, 1967.

[4] J. D. Krumboltz and C. E. Thoresen, "The Effect of Behavioral Counseling in Group and Individual Settings on Information-seeking Behavior," *Journal of Counseling Psychology*, vol. 11, pp. 324–333, 1964.

seeking was measured three weeks later by an independent evaluation team. Counselors, using reinforcement counseling, increased information seeking both when a social model tape was used and when it was not employed. Further, they found that the use of the model tape with reinforcement counseling was more effective for males than females and more effective for males in a group setting than in individual counseling.

Each of these studies illustrates careful structuring by the counselor to assist the group in reaching a specific objective. Techniques were tailored to maximize efficient use of group time. Far less encouraging results are obtained from studies and practice in which no counselor structure is provided and group purpose must be determined concurrently with individual development.

Attitudes and Skills of Group Counselors

The attitudes and skills which a counselor finds effective with individuals closely parallel those desirable for group counseling as well. Ethical behavior, flexibility, intellectual competence, acceptance, understanding, and sensitivity are among the basic attitudes and skills of the group counselor. Each was described in some detail in the previous chapter.

As is the case in working with individuals, the counselor is concerned with helping. His function differs from that of other group members in that he neither seeks nor expects the group's assistance in facing his primary concerns. He gives his full attention to whoever is talking, attempts to assist him in working toward his objective, and generally serves as a model for group members to follow in terms of attentiveness, understanding, and assistance.

Individual counseling, although the best single background experience, may cause problems for the counselor who attempts to apply this experience directly in the group situation. Communication within a group is far more complex. Experience in counseling individuals may well have taught him to be aware of the student's every verbal and nonverbal act. Attempting to pick up and respond to the every nuance of several group members concurrently would prove impossible. Those who choose to continue the intensive one-to-one interaction learned from the previous counseling experience are forced to treat the group as a succession of individuals. His intensive personal interaction with a single member deprives the counselor of the opportunity to be sensitive to the needs of others, and their participation cannot be properly encouraged. Other than its observational value for group members, the counselor is essentially conducting a series of individual interviews. Group counseling is built upon the assumption that members are assisted by helping others as well as being helped by them. The counselor, therefore, must facilitate student-student communication as well as counselor-student interaction.

This is done through what is termed the *linking* function of the counselor. As members talk, the comments of the second speaker may have relevance to those of the first that are not readily apparent. Unless the counselor is able to link these comments by emphasizing their common purpose, the contributions of the various members will lack cohesiveness. Linking, further, helps the individual to feel a common bond with other group members. As each member, in turn, attempts to link his comment to what has previously been said, he feels more inclined to assist his fellow member. The experienced counselor, then, is able to enlist the efforts of group members so that the individual receives help from many members as well as the counselor.

Responsibilities of Group Members

Counseling, individual and group, will be more successful when its purposes and the responsibilities of all participants are understood before its inception. The act of joining a group can only be accepted as an indication of commitment to counseling when the student is aware of why the group is being organized and how he might benefit from participation. Four responsibilities are basic to all counseling groups and group members.

First, each member must determine a purpose for group participation that is meaningful in terms of his current concerns and circumstances. He may receive assistance from the counselor and group members in making this more specific, but the responsibility for determining the objective and attempting to reach it must be his. He must also recognize that objectives of other group members are also being individually determined and may be compatible or contrary to his own.

Second, each member must involve the group directly in working toward his objective. His participation in the group will not be optimal until he is able to express himself to others and actively seek their support. However unpalatable they may seem, he has no choice but to interpret the perceptions and suggestions of others as attempts at assistance. Some may seem deprecating, some offensive, and some inconsequential. The temptation to discount them or to raise one's defenses against them will be great at times. The advantage of group assistance can easily be tossed away during moments of anxiety.

Third, by the act of electing to take part in the group, each member has accepted a responsibility to attentively listen to the concerns of others and attempt to assist them. His contribution will be more meaningful if he follows the counselor's example in linking his comments to those of others whenever possible. He must remain aware of the right of others to have equal time to seek the assistance of counselor and group. Concurrently, he must respect the right of each member to remain silent at any time even though he may question the reason.

Fourth, each member must follow the consensus of the group with respect to rules and procedures. Basic rules may be developed at the group's inception. Special circumstances may cause procedures to be altered at a later time. Confidentiality and the rights of members must be respected.

Commitment to group counseling is somewhat different in the psychological press it places upon the student than is the case in individual counseling. An individual, impatient of results or dissatisfied with his experience in counseling, can terminate the relationship with relative ease. The responsibility a group member has accepted to assist peers and the "hole" his departure may cause are factors which make termination from group counseling somewhat more difficult.

Procedures in Group Counseling

Counseling, individual or group, can be effective only when an objective or terminal behavior has been identified and is understood by both counselor and student. Group counseling further implies the involvement of other group members in assisting the individual. Procedures that follow are those which the counselor must understand thoroughly and be able to implement before he involves students in group counseling.

1. Identifying each member's objective. Group counselors frequently organize a group and then expect members to find group and individual purpose while participating. The wide range of interests and purposes that an individual may express diminishes the likelihood that sufficient time can be concentrated upon a given objective to ensure its attainment.

No doubt should exist about the purpose of group counseling. The counselor may need to meet with potential members individually and determine the purpose of each in joining the group. This often requires specific probing as to whether the objective is fully understood by the student, whether it is attainable, and which conditions or activities are deemed necessary if the objective is to be attained.

The counselor can then assign the individual to a group when objective attainment seems possible. He might decide, however, that more individual counseling is in order or no appropriate group is presently available.

2. Organizational decisions. The counselor needs to consider the optimal size, physical site, and length and frequency of meeting for each group with which he works. Too often the counselor applies the same alternative to all groups.

Ample conjecture and some research indicates that a group of five or six is optimal for counseling purposes. As group size increases, the leader tends to become more dominant and addresses himself to group rather than individual needs, members become more dependent and talk less, and feelings of frustration, threat, and inhibition concerning participation increase. There may well be cases, however, where a larger number would actually be advantageous to the group. For example, a number of individuals might be meeting with a counselor because each has expressed a desire to participate more effectively in classroom discussions. A group size of ten or fifteen might prove more effective in this instance than a group of five because the larger group more nearly approximates the classroom situation. If a student could participate effectively in a counseling group of fifteen, he should have less difficulty in transferring this newly learned participation skill to the classroom.

Similarly, many settings other than the counselor's office may prove better for particular groups. Students who have difficulty in addressing strangers might better hold some sessions in a school cafeteria, activity room, or even the main lobby or corridor. Confidentiality may not be possible, but increased opportunities for trying out behaviors and receiving immediate reinforcement counterbalance this factor.

The counselor may vary the length and frequency of sessions, also, in order to enhance goal-directed behavior. During the early stages of a group, he frequently finds that two or three meetings each week are beneficial. As more intensive attempts are made by the individual to reach his objective outside the group setting, formal group meetings may be reduced to once weekly. Length of sessions may also be reduced as the group continues. Some groups have sessions as long as four, eight, or twenty-four hours soon after they are established. As communication channels are cleared and interaction becomes more open, sessions may be shortened to ninety minutes or less. The counselor should attempt to have flexible time limits available to him in light of these considerations.

3. *Forming the group.* Two potential sources of group members exist for the counselor. First, he might make the opportunity for joining a group available to students with whom he or his fellow counselors are working individually. Second, he could make announcement of the opportunity to students more generally. As an example, he may be working with two students who are unable to communicate effectively with members of the opposite sex and might benefit from working on this objective with a group. He could obtain the names of other students who had this concern from fellow counselors or through public announcement. Students

would meet individually with the counselor and be encouraged to enter the group only if this seemed to be a primary concern and if they seemed motivated to work toward effective communication with the opposite sex.

The counselor may, on the other hand, consider it advantageous to have a group composed of people with *different* primary concerns. A girl who has trouble conversing with boys might well gain more insight from an effective communicator than from another like herself.

The critical issue for the counselor is in determining the group composition that will maximally benefit each member. The complexity and unpredictability of human behavior may force him to rely more on hunch than scientific observation. His knowledge of people from previous counseling contacts may guide him.

4. *Getting started.* The counselor can get the group started by giving a brief but clear description of his role and clarifying the role of members. Some counselors place primary emphasis upon counselor-student communication and discourage extensive contributions from members. Others stress student-student communication, use themselves primarily to structure and facilitate communication, and verbally are relatively inactive at times. Students should be aware of the counselor's preference and reasons for his choice of primary communication pattern.

Each member has already discussed with the counselor his objective in joining the group. He needs to share this purpose with other members of the group and also inform them of what he expects of them or how he feels they might be most helpful. The counselor may supplement these individual statements by suggesting how those with similar or dissimilar problems may be of maximum assistance to each other.

Care must be exercised that the time and place of subsequent meetings is agreeable to members' schedules. Cautionary words must also be given concerning the importance of confidentiality and the opportunity provided for setting any other rules or procedures that seem appropriate.

As is the case in individual counseling, the counselor must be able to assist the group in starting to talk. Attention to natural difficulty in getting started may release tension a bit. To state, bluntly, "Where shall we get started?" may be threatening and cause members to be needlessly uneasy. From prior contact he may be able to identify a member who has little difficulty in communicating and encourage this student to begin. The use of open-ended leads rather than specific questions will assist the individual as he begins to speak. Concurrently, the counselor must be sensitive to other members and encourage them to participate.

5. *Building the relationship.* As the group develops, the temptation is great for a member to wander from his original purpose and confuse his

own objective with that of another. This is somewhat akin to "intern's disease." As we hear of another's specific symptoms and concentrate upon the manifestations, we begin to believe that the problems are ours, not theirs. The counselor may have to be rather direct in reminding a member of his objective.

Concentrating upon one concern at a time may seem needlessly restrictive. Not so, says Krumboltz.[5]

> People can talk about only one thing at a time. By concentrating on the problem that each individual considers most serious at the moment, a group can often devise solutions. Success at resolving one problem often enables the person to take similar constructive steps in dealing with his other problems. It is true that every person's problems are interrelated. However, merely talking about all the complex interrelationships does not enable the client to get a handle on his problems so he can resolve them. One of the problems must be selected, isolated, and attacked systematically so that the subject can experience success in handling the one problem that is currently troubling him the most. Subsequent efforts can focus on other problems as the client desires.

The counselor's transparent honesty and sincere interest will allow the student to realize that the counselor is fully committed to assisting him. The counselor, through the linking function, must assist other members to participate effectively also. The pooling of insights and mutual encouragement will help members to attempt new behaviors outside the group as they gain more confidence. In some instances a member may be accompanied by another in order that he might have immediate reinforcement for attempts at changed behavior. Other circumstances may suggest that this is unwise or that the member is able to act more independently.

6. *Terminating group membership.* The rate of development varies greatly among group members. Some will attain one objective, then identify and attain another before others have made much progress. Inevitably, some will have exhausted the group's potential, and the counselor must concern himself with terminal alternatives for the group and probably will wish to involve the members in discussion of the alternatives prior to reaching a decision.

A primary decision concerns whether members will leave the group singly or whether all will stay until the entire group is terminated. To ask members to remain after their purposes have been served may seem to be an imposition. These members, however, have a commitment to assist their

[5] John D. Krumboltz, "A Behavioral Approach to Group Counseling and Therapy," *Journal of Research and Development in Education*, vol. 1, p. 10, 1964.

peers and frequently will be among the more active contributors. If they are allowed to leave, some of the most beneficial helping relationships may be eliminated and the effectiveness of group counseling may be reduced.

When members are allowed to leave a continuing group, a second decision must be made. Would it be to each member's advantage to allow newcomers to enter the group? The addition of new members may cause problems of communication, mutual trust, and reduced group effectiveness. On the other hand, the new recruits should benefit from working with those who have experienced group counseling previously, and they may provide forms of assistance to veteran members that were unavailable from those who left the group.

The counselor's experience and assessment of needs of remaining group members will guide him as he faces these decisions. The group should be reconstituted only if it can continue for sufficient time to assist members, new and old, to attain the objectives they have identified.

7. *Evaluating outcomes.* The effectiveness of counseling, individual or group, can only be measured by observing how successful the student is in attaining the objective outside of counseling that he established at its outset. Observations of a counseling group at work or members' ratings of their peers are not indicative of effectiveness.

Assessment is not a particularly difficult task if the objective has been stated in terms that are measurable. This explains the need for counselor assistance in developing a specific objective prior to entering the group. "I hope to generally get along better with people" represents an objective that could only be measured by inference. No direct way exists of measuring attainment.

An objective that states the conditions for attainment might be: "I am shy and awkward with strangers. My objective is to be able to carry on a five-minute talk with a stranger in the student union in which I introduce myself, reveal my thought on at least two current issues, and recall the stranger's name after he leaves." A simpler, yet equally measurable objective might be identified by a person whose nervousness in tense situations causes him to stutter. If, as the result of group counseling, he could deliver a two-minute speech to a class without stuttering, counseling would have been effective.

Evaluation conducted in this manner allows the group member to know immediately and specifically whether group participation has been effective. He may identify new objectives or continue present efforts based upon the outcome. His efforts and those of the group are not consumed in repeating ineffective procedures. Those that are helpful are continued. Those that are ineffective or inefficient are replaced.

Summary

Group counseling affords the student a greater potential number of helping relationships than is the case in individual counseling. Because the group is a microcosm of social reality, the student is able to use this confidential and trusting atmosphere to try out changed or newly learned behaviors.

Group counseling differs from leader-centered group guidance and group-structured process groups in that each member identifies a primary concern that he feels might be alleviated through group participation. This concern is specifically worded as an objective, frequently through the assistance of the counselor, prior to group involvement. When the stated objective is attained outside of counseling, the student may wish to identify and work on succeeding objectives in similar fashion.

The counselor's sole criterion in organizing a group is to develop an environment that will provide optimal conditions for each member's attaining his stated objective. Skills and attitudes necessary for successful individual counseling are also applicable in working with groups. The group counselor faces the task of maintaining many relationships concurrently. He must be perceptive to the behaviors of silent members as well as the person speaking. Through his own example he is able to involve others in the discussion, encourage them to share their insights, link the comments of one speaker with that of another, and develop group cohesiveness.

A counseling group has no purpose other than to assist each member to attain his individual objective. As members assess whether or not they have fulfilled the purpose for which they joined the group, those methods which are inefficient and ineffective are replaced by new procedures. The counselor, as well as the members, learn effective group techniques through this process.

Exercises

1. List ten concerns that are common to students with whom you work. Suggest whether group guidance, group process, or group counseling would be most appropriate and specify reasons for your choice.

2. Develop a precedural outline that might be used to interview prospective group members. Include an assessment of their knowledge of why counseling is conducted in groups and of their objective in joining a group.

3. Interview a student who is interested in group counseling, Assist him in developing an objective that specifies the conditions for attainment in measurable terms.

References

Bennett, Margaret E.: *Guidance and Counseling in Groups*, McGraw-Hill Book Company, New York, 1963.

Bradford, L. P., J. R. Gibb, and K. D. Benne: *T-group Theory and Laboratory Method*, John Wiley & Sons, Inc., New York, 1964.

Goldstein, A. P., K. Heller, and L. B. Sechrest: *Psychotherapy and the Psychology of Behavior Change*, John Wiley & Sons, Inc., New York, 1966.

Kemp, C. Gratton (ed.): *Perspectives on the Group Process*, Houghton Mifflin Company, Boston, 1964.

Mahler, C. A.: *Group Counseling in the Schools*, Houghton Mifflin Company, Boston, 1969.

11

Counseling in Community Agencies

Although most counselors work in schools, many are employed by other private and public agencies. Both the number and proportion of counselors employed in these related agencies will probably increase in the next few years for it is apparent that the counseling needs of our society cannot be met if we confine counseling only to the formal educational institutions. Therefore, many counselors now in training will use their skills in these nonschool settings. Furthermore, school counselors will need to collaborate with counselors in agencies and therefore may be helped by understanding these newer developments in the field of counseling.

United States Employment Service

The United States Employment Service (USES) employs over 3,000 counselors in its 2,000 offices. This organization is clearly the largest purveyor of vocational guidance services in the United States.

The USES has two major functions in the area of vocational guidance. The primary function is the placement of job seekers. But a major secondary function is that of selecting persons for other training programs, such as the Manpower Development and Training Act.

The counselors working in USES are of divergent backgrounds and skill levels. However, there is now considerable press to upgrade the Employment Service counselor by encouraging him to secure at least a master's degree.

The Employment Service counselor works with a variety of clients. Some clients are young people entering the labor market for the first time who have no work experience. Others are adults who are changing occupations either because of desires on their own part or because of technological unemployment occasioned by advances in science and industry. A third category of clients are those who have special job handicaps which require particular attention. In this category would be those handicapped by age or physical and mental disabilities.

The approach to vocational counseling and placement in the employment service has five identifiable phases. The first phase has to do with the identification and delineation of the problem. At this point a decision may be made that the Employment Service cannot be helpful until other agencies have done their part. Such a decision might be made, for example, in the case of very severe emotional or family problems which interfere with employment behavior. If, however, the clarification of the problem results in a decision that the Employment Service can be helpful at the present time, the counseling moves to phase two, which deals with vocational analysis and appraisal. In this phase an analysis may be made of such matters as the worker's background, experience, and education. Frequently, the General Aptitude Test Battery (GATB), developed by the USES, is used to help the counselor learn more about the applicant's aptitudes and enable the counselor to compare him with employed normative groups. The GATB yields ten scores: intelligence, verbal, numerical, spatial, form perception, clerical perception, aiming, motor speed, finger dexterity, and manual dexterity. The test norms purport to predict job performance by expressing minimum levels of essential aptitudes for each of a large number of occupations. The third phase of the counseling involves such assistance to the counselee as giving him information about job situations and trends, referring him to other agencies, or making available to him the placement services of the office. The fourth phase involves decision making on the part of the client who obviously is ultimately responsible for his own future. The decision itself tends to be a joint process involving the counselor and the client with the counselor helping the client to make sense out of the personal and economic data which has been discussed. The final phase of the process involves the implementation of the plan which the two have worked out. This implementation may require placement in an occupation or a training program.

A special concern in USES counseling is the problem of testing job applicants from disadvantaged groups. Charges have been made that tests are unfair to some types of applicants, particularly those lacking the usual cultural and educational advantages given to middle-class Americans. These charges have been analyzed as referring to four types of disadvantages: anxiety in the testing situation resulting in lower scores; unfairness of the test content for other than middle-class children; improper interpretation of scores by failure to realize that the same score has different meanings depending upon the background of the person taking the test; and lack of relevance to the requirements of the job.

The examiner must try to allay test anxiety should it seem to interfere with test performance. Giving practice in taking different tests may reduce the anxiety of the applicant, but these practice exercises must not resemble the test closely enough to bias test results. Tape recordings of directions for taking tests have been used to reduce test anxiety in the belief that the applicant may feel more comfortable when the examiner is not present, particularly if the examiner is a member of a different racial group.

The argument about cultural bias in testing has been with us for some time, but the generally reached conclusion is that so-called "cultural free" tests reveal the same differences between social classes that other tests do. Certainly the preponderant weight of research evidence indicates that non-verbal tests do not result in measurable benefit to disadvantaged groups, for the disadvantaged score no better on them than they do on conventional tests. Perhaps the most plausible solution to this dilemma is to strive rather for tests which are "culture-laden" with those items important in the work culture and therefore highly related to the criterion of work success.

Some have suggested that disadvantaged applicants be given a bonus of raw score points to make up for the deprivation in their environment. There would be difficulty of course in deciding who would get such a bonus and what it should be. Certainly an improvement in accuracy of prediction may well result from determining optimum weightings for each group in the population, but to date such weightings have not been determined.

Finally, the major problem with regard to testing and the disadvantaged is whether testing and test scores are really relevant to the work to be done. Tests, like other predictive instruments, must be evaluated in terms of how well predictions made from them conform with reality, as represented by such criteria as measures of success on the job. Without adequate criteria, meaningful and free of bias, it will be difficult for anyone to know what predictors are effective. It is obvious to professional users of tests that criteria must be studied and refined; others may occasionally need a reminder not to forget the criteria while they are busy attacking the predictors.

This problem of testing and the disadvantaged has entered the courts and the total civil-rights struggle. It is becoming increasingly difficult to separate the professional from the political aspects of the problem. The acceptable answers would seem to vary with the job market. If, in fact, there are not selections to be made because of a very tight market, the question becomes irrelevant. When a job market permits fine discriminations, the question arises whether the employer is to be given complete or limited freedom in making determinations about who would best fit his needs.

One position advocated by students of testing is that it is clearly the obligation of an employer not to discriminate among persons on the grounds of race, religion, or national origin, but it is not the obligation of an employer to hire or to promote the less qualified in an attempt to compensate for some injustice of society in general.

Vocational Rehabilitation

Approximately 3,500 counselors are employed doing vocational rehabilitation largely through federally supported but state-managed agencies. These counselors tend to form a bimodal distribution with regard to training. Some of them have had very little training and cling to their jobs by virtue of seniority. More recently hired counselors are apt to have a full training program of two graduate years in carefully selected institutions. The outlook is for expansion and upgrading of these services, and such an outlook seems justified by the fact that the government is now spending considerable money to train rehabilitation counselors at both the master's and the doctoral level. Such trainees receive stipends and participate in well-funded programs.

Although the counseling will vary with the skill level of the counselor, in general it will include the following steps: (1) determination of the client's eligibility for this service based on the extent and nature of his handicap, (2) an appraisal of his current status as it relates to working, including an evaluation of his experience, education, and potentiality, and (3) a systematically evolved plan for upgrading his work skills to the point where he can be of optimum value to society.

In performing these functions, the rehabilitation counselor may make considerable use of referrals to physicians, to psychometrists and other psychological examiners, and to any agencies or individuals which may be useful to him in doing his job. A distinct advantage of the vocational-rehabilitation approach is that it centers on one person—the rehabilitation counselor—the possibility of obtaining for the client a variety of services—therapy, counseling, education, job placement, etc.

Strengths of this approach are integration of personal and vocational adjustment counseling, concern with psychological aspects of vocational behavior, the use of other vocational guidance techniques to supplement and extend vocational counseling, delineation of appropriate occupational behavior as a major criterion, and utilization of school facilities as counseling adjuncts to provide guidance. Limitations of the approach appear to be a tendency to constrict the perspective of the client to the counseling setting, lack of attention to significant persons in the counselee's family and environmental factors influencing vocational development and adjustment, limited use of community nonschool resources for guidance, limited use of vocational experience as a technique for fostering vocational growth, and the tendency of the client to choose goals and make decisions which he feels are in accord with the counselor's expectations and which will, therefore, ensure continued support.

Counselors in training with special interest in working with the handicapped—physically, emotionally, mentally—would do well to search out the possibility of federal support for their training. Not only do such federally supported programs provide the student with money which will permit him to concentrate on his studies, but they also tend to be located in institutions with particularly strong programs of training in vocational rehabilitation.

Federal Programs for the Disadvantaged

By the late 1960s the federal government was supporting various programs designed to aid in the development of children and adults who were being characterized as disadvantaged. Typical of such programs were the Job Corps, residential vocational training centers for young men with special vocational needs; women's residence centers, parallel institutions for young women; youth opportunity centers designed to provide part-time employment and training for urban youth; and VISTA, which was the domestic equivalent of the Peace Corps. Counselors and those using counseling skills were employed in all these programs, and the outlook was for their continuation and expansion.

The activities of these counselors vary from situation to situation, but in general it can be said that they are probably more active and reach out more than counselors in schools or in private practice.

COUNSELING THE DISADVANTAGED

Personnel in one Job Corps center developed a statement regarding the work of the counselor in their organization, which is included here because it gives a clear delineation of the adaptations which need to be made in the usual counseling practice for the counselor to be of maximum value to these clients.

> The aim was to motivate the counselee toward a continuous learning situation by teaching problem-solving techniques that would enable the individual to meet the exigencies of future living situations. The counseling staff was problem-centered rather than technique-centered; i.e., the problem dictated the technique that would be used to correlate and direct the desired solution through persuasion and suggestion. The counselor's goal was to make the counselee independent, responsible, employable, and most of all, to give the counselee the courage to develop to his full potential. The counselor's job was to motivate the counselee to pick meaningful goals and encourage simple goals that were easily attainable. Because the trainees had had very few

successes, it was important to give them some minor successes to whet their appetites for larger ones. We attempted to motivate the counselee for continued learning; i.e., we helped the counselee to visualize the changing world we live in and how one must keep growing or stagnate.

The term "counselor" as used in our job-training program had a much broader meaning than it does in most professional organizations. In addition to the typical activities of having sessions with individuals and groups for their betterment, and sometimes testing, our counselors also helped trainees find clothing and homes, take care of their health problems, and even provided transportation to doctors', lawyers', and dentists' offices. Counselors also developed job prospects in the community, helped trainees find jobs, and followed them up later in the program. In other situations some of these needs would be handled by a social caseworker, home visitor, or rehabilitation agency. Although we received some assistance from welfare workers and vocational rehabilitation, it was felt that the immediacy of the trainees' problems did not permit the time required to work through the regulations of these agencies. In short, it was quicker and more efficient for our counselors to assume some of these roles, while working with existing agencies when time permitted it.

From the initiation of our project, the staff looked upon counseling as a very essential part of the program, at least as important as any basic education or vocational training that the trainee would receive. The counselor's position was defined so that he would be the one person immediately responsible for a given trainee and the closest person to that trainee. If the trainee was missing, the counselor should know why; if the trainee was troubled, the counselor should find out the source of the trouble; if the trainee was progressing, the counselor was there to point this out and encourage him. The counselor became as familiar as possible with the trainee's home, family, abilities, interests, and background.

The quality that best describes our counseling staff's activities would be mobile, relentless pursuit. Although a counselor working with middle- and upper-class clients may be very successful working solely in his office and primarily by scheduled interviews, this manner of operation does not adapt well to the hard-core poor. Our counselor was not seen as a deskbound or office-centered person, but a person who went to the problem and was primarily concerned with handling problems rather than keeping hourly counseling appointments. Some schedules were kept, especially for group counseling, but the primary emphasis was on a flexibility that permitted the counselor to see any trainee at any time, either in or outside the training center, so that the pressing problems could always be met at the right moment. Instead of having a counselor and a home visitor who would have to coordinate their work, the counselors assumed home visiting as part of their job. A low counseling ratio of one counselor to from thirty-five to sixty trainees made this possible.

The term "pursuit" as used in football, describes well the staff's working relationship. Counselors and teachers were always backing each other up. Communication was constant and easy.

The relentless nature of the counseling needs comment. A counselor with a college or high-school orientation might object to this, but it must be kept in mind that the hard-core unemployed person is a particular breed with background and problems different from those of the average college or high-school student. Our counselors were aggressive in some aspects of their dealings with trainees. Initially, when recruiting, the counselor did everything possible to interest a needy person in training. If necessary, as many as six home visits were made to get a person into training. During the program, counselors would make home visits as soon as possible to an absent trainee, particularly if it was believed that sickness was not the reason for the absence. The idea was to stay on top of the trainee's situation as much as possible, and not to be caught by surprise by events.

One of the strong assets of our counseling program was the close working relationship among the members of the counseling staff and between the members of the counseling and teaching staffs. There was a minimum of friction present although there were very strong personalities on both the teaching and counseling staffs, and their work often overlapped. The basic reason for this was that all the members of the staff had a fairly clear idea of their roles, and they had a strong common goal—the employment and full development of all our trainees. This was stronger than personal goals of self advancement. In addition to having a real feeling for other people and their needs, the counselor should be a mature, secure person who will be flexible enough to adapt to ever-changing situations. A less than secure person will often react with an inflexible attitude toward trainees because he feels that otherwise their failure will threaten his adequacy. This kind of counselor must be prepared for frequent failures because he will lose many battles before he wins the war.

The insecure counselor will hesitate to become too personally involved, and this will hurt him, since trainees have had too much contact with impersonal agencies and respond very well to a warm, down-to-earth approach. It is easy for trainees to detect a lack of sincere interest on the part of a counselor.

No attempt was made to assign trainees to counselors according to sex, since it was obvious that many trainees related better to someone of the opposite sex in a counseling relationship. After a random assignment of trainees to counselors, the counselors attempted to have an interview with each trainee once a week. This formal interview soon stretched out to once every two or three weeks, but the breaks between classes permitted a relaxed chat with trainees daily. During these ten-minute breaks, coffee was available and everyone milled around in our large foyer. The atmosphere was friendly and casual, and the counselors often found this period more profitable than the counseling interview, since many of the trainees seemed threatened in a small office situation but were more relaxed when talking to the same counselor in a less structured situation.

A technique which our counseling staff credited with effecting much of the change in trainees was group counseling. Group counseling was a process involving approximately eight trainees with a counselor for two hourly sessions a week. In these sessions the counselor's role was simply to see that the discussions were profitable. The group did most of the talking and would often decide the initial topic, although the counselor would usually come prepared with some stimulating material in case the trainees did not have a topic of their own.

The initial sessions were spent getting acquainted and deciding the rules the group would use in regard to confidentiality. Initially, topics would center around life at the training center: classes, absenteeism, setting goals, choosing an occupation, making new friends, adjusting to schedule changes. As the groups got better acquainted with each other and with the counselor, the range of topics became very broad: why do people lose jobs, what does it feel like to be a welfare recipient, drinking and alcoholism, understanding oneself, communication with others, understanding your children.

Later in the program some experimental groups were tried, e.g., a group of mothers who had no husband in the home, a group composed only of Indians (because many of the Indians had been extremely quiet in integrated groups), a group of teenagers, and vocational groups, such as welder trainees and auto mechanics. The mothers without husbands in the home had several very successful sessions on topics like the difficulty of raising children alone, sex education, and the social difficulties of the unmarried mother.

Group counseling permitted the staging of role playing acting out interviews for employment, questioning social behavior patterns, etc. We do not feel that there is any *one way* to do group counseling. Utilization and experimentation with many techniques produced, for us, a synthesizing and new approach to the group counseling effort.

The success of group counseling came from the fact that although a counselee looked upon an individual counselor as someone who for some reason "had it made" (no matter what the counselor's real background may have been), the counselee could not dismiss his classmates in the same way. They were his neighbors and many of them were worse off than he was. Their remarks, comments, and opinions had an effect on him that individual counseling sessions may not have had. If several of his mates felt that it was a disgrace for an able-bodied man to live off welfare, this struck him harder than if he knew his counselor felt this. This is only one example of how group counseling aided in effecting change in the trainees.

Training for such work might be very similar to that given the usual school counselor providing it is supplemented with considerable opportunities to increase in self knowledge and considerable sociology and anthropology, which enable the counselor to look beyond his subculture to an appreciation and understanding of others.

WHO ARE THE DISADVANTAGED?

Of course, the nature of the counseling will need to rest on a conception of what constitutes a disadvantaged person, but here again, there is not complete agreement on definitions. Material advantages—good clothes, good furniture, homes, etc.—are generally absent from the lives of the disadvantaged. Their self-concepts are not apt to be at a high level because their entire lives may have taught them that they are not valued. Stable families are less frequent, and the absence of a father in the home is not as rare as in other families. The child's self-confidence and motivation is characteristically less high than that of his more advantaged fellows. The modal family is that of the poor white or an ethnic minority, particularly Negro. Many of these families live in urban slums. They are economically in the lower class, and the father, when present, is most likely to work as an unskilled or semiskilled laborer.

As a consequence of these and other disadvantages, the child may frequently have a distorted perception of reality both in terms of his handicaps and his opportunities; a deep sense of inferiority built up in the community and in the school as well as in the larger society; an unrealistic self-depreciation, particularly if he accepts the valuations of the larger society; and much confusion and frustration, resulting from conflict between the democratic ideals he hears about and the discriminating practices which "keep him in his place."

A child subject to these pressures will typically have lacked succorance, will have early independence from his core family, will look to peers for many of his values, and will have chronic problems at school. There are a variety of ways to adjust to his situation. Some will do so by apathetic compliance, some by aggression and acting out, some will simply withdraw from the situation as best they can, while a few will assimilate the charges which have been made against them and consequently develop some self-hate.

Workers in one institution spelled out their own perception of the disadvantaged which grew from long and intimate experience with them.

1. Many of the older trainees just plain look and act beaten. The younger trainee often wears a thin veneer of insolence and sneers at the idea of rules and regulations, but usually conforms after a time, after a fashion.
2. The lower the mentality of a group, the harder to make any change in routine. Any change in time and place for holding classes and, worst of all, a change of teachers, creates a major crisis.

3. Certain characteristics ran through the group. Little interest in other parts of the city or other areas was displayed, and a definite reluctance to move outside the confines of the existing living area seemed general. This presented a stumbling block to effective placement.

4. Interests of many of the trainees are narrow, communications poor. Their culture includes many old wives' tales, passed verbally from person to person. Their fantastic ideas on cause of change of season, length of day and night, health problems are proof of this.

5. Newspapers and magazines are not in many homes. A newspaper article regarding a trainee and his people caused concern among the staff lest it arouse antagonism. It was totally ignored by the trainees. No one had read it.

6. Money management is a problem to this group. In many cases, these poverty-ridden trainees were not in need of money nearly as much as they were in need of guidance in planned spending. They exhibited no foresight in long-term or on-time buying. Interest paid on debts was never taken into consideration. They may buy a car for $50 that runs 75 miles and then quits running. "Can't come to school. I have six cars here but they are all apart." Welfare agencies and job training centers would do the taxpayer and the trainee a tremendous service if the welfare family was helped with a budget and was expected to make an effort to follow this. The Better Business Bureau might also lend a hand by looking into unwholesome deals and questionable sales habits carried on by some local business men in the area.

7. Group giving is frequent. Trainees were always generous and anxious to "pass the hat" for any event, a new baby, a teacher leaving, or a funeral.

8. Arguments or disagreements, whether within the family or within or outside of school, were often settled in physical combat. Males and females used fists, teeth, fingernails and feet. Both sexes showed up at different times, if able, with black eyes, bad hands, lame legs, and scratched faces.

9. Little value was placed on jobs or on training even though trainees in general expressed themselves as eager to find work. The least excuse was sufficient cause to stay home. Dislike of fellow workers, need for sleep, unseasonable cold, a minor ache or pain would, in their thinking, justify an absence.

10. There was little self-discipline on the part of some in such matters as promptness, consideration for others, toilet habits, smoking habits.

11. Many lived simply from day to day with no future goals.

12. Most of the trainees were not civic minded; they never voted. Hunting out of season, fishing with no license, driving with an expired license or no license were facts carelessly and openly discussed.

While these generalizations will not fit every disadvantaged person, for stereotyping of any group is dangerous, they are the considered conclusions of a staff with much firsthand experience.

The goals of counseling with these disadvantaged children and adults have not been clearly defined, and there are differences of opinion about them. The counselor will need to keep in mind the anxiety and shock attendent upon movement away from the comforting support of like-minded peers and family. Some believe that counseling should raise the level of aspiration of the disadvantaged, but the extent to which this goal should be tempered by the reality of his ability and opportunity is not clear. Particular controversy swirls around the extent to which counseling should try to substitute one set of values for another. Is the lower class without worthwhile values? Is it not possible that their more immediate and spontaneous way of life may have worth that the middle class does not see? Finally, anxiety and guilt are often part of the internalized personality of the disadvantaged, and the counselor will need to ask himself the extent to which he wants to make use of these characteristics as motivators and the extent to which he wants to remove them.

Typical techniques include much parent involvement, a systematic attempt to raise the level of the self-concept, placement in a realistic curriculum, and an attempt to relate with the client at a warm human level. In doing so, the counselor will need to be aware of the perception the client has of the usually middle-class counselor. Such perceptions may not always be flattering, and the counselor will need to face his own attitudes toward people who are different, such as the following representative.

E. C., who is eighteen years of age, illustrates the extra mile that counselors must sometimes be willing to walk. The mother, C. C., was in the program. She faithfully attended classes even though she worked nine hours per day, went home in the evening, prepared dinner for three children, then attended our night program for 1½ hours. She was underemployed, having no skills, but is now employed by one of the better clothing stores in alteration work. She worked part time during the last phase of the program, and upon her graduation went to work full time.

The assigned counselor of the tailoring and alterations class made daily calls to the vocational site. During these visits, the counselor was made aware of C. C.'s extreme nervousness. She broke into tears for no apparent reason on several occasions. Upon questioning her, it was learned that her son had been arrested for being drunk and disorderly and had received a ten-day jail sentence.

The counselor went to the County Jail to visit E. C. and from there to the auto-wash where he was employed. Discussion with his employer led to his agreeing to take E. C. back and give him a 25-cent raise. E. C. was released, went back to work, and about three weeks later was arrested again on the same charge. This time the counselor was not called until after E. C. had been sentenced to fifteen days in jail. Again, the counselor went to the jail, talked with E. C., and then decided it would be better to pick him up on his release.

Following his release, he went to the home of the counselor. They talked for over three hours. After some probing, it was found E. C. was bitter, and justifiably so, at certain racial injustices against him. (He was a Mexican-American.) His drunkenness was open defiance of authority. The counselor decided at this time that he needed a better job, i.e., one with status and certainly more money. A job was secured at an automobile factory. He worked for about a month and then "fell off the wagon." This time, he called the counselor immediately from jail. When he went to court, the counselor accompanied him, talked with the judge, explained the program we had outlined for E. C., the length of time he had worked in the factory, and impressed upon him the fact that any time spent in jail would lose the job for him. The judge was very cooperative and gave him only a fine as a fourth offense—drunk, $60. E. C. had about $80, which left him $20 to meet his needs until the next payday.

This time, E. C. was quite frightened about losing the job. For the first time, he realized he had something worthwhile to lose. Fortunately, he did not miss a day of work because he was working afternoons, and the case was terminated in the morning. At least three hours were consumed in court on that one day, which indicates how much of the counselor's time is required for such activities. At this time, it was felt that E. C. needed more motivation, so it was suggested that he buy a new car. This was exactly what he wanted. His mother's pay rate required a co-signer, so the counselor co-signed, and E. C. is presently purchasing his car. He is working two jobs, and his mother (the trainee) is doing excellent work because her greatest anxiety has been removed. E. C. is now a contributing member of the family and has a great deal of status. The younger siblings look up to him, whereas before he was in constant disgrace. It has been suggested that he enroll in night courses to earn his high-school diploma. After this, we shall encourage him to attend adult evening school or community college.

This young man could not have been redirected without the full support of all social institutions, the judge, prosecutor, probation officer, and employment personnel. The longer time period between E. C.'s third and fourth offense can definitely be attributed to his job, according to his counselor. This again illustrates the tremendous importance of meeting the total needs of an entire family. Had this young man not obtained assistance, not only would he have been adversely affected, but his mother and her younger children would also have been hurt by his continuing misbehavior. Because of her concern for her son, the mother might have lost her job, and the total family situation would have become even more desperate.

VETERANS ADMINISTRATION COUNSELING

Since the end of World War II the Veterans Administration has provided counseling for those who wish to take advantage of their rights to it.

Veterans eligible for special training because of disabilities were sometimes required to take such counseling in order to qualify for extra benefits, but it was also made available to others who believed they could profit from it. This program, which now employs approximately 800 counselors, is probably the most elaborate and complex attempt to provide vocational counseling that has ever been attempted. Counselors at the beginning of the program were frequently ill trained at the time they accepted their assignment, but there has been a continuing upgrading in the requirements for a position as a counselor for the Veterans Administration until, at the present time, most counselors have very high qualifications. Originally, the counseling was highly structured, frequently test centered, and designed to overcome the inexperience and lack of training which characterized the counselors. More recently, the Veterans Administration counselor with his high level of training and experience has been liberated from this tighter structure and is free to pursue his counseling in the manner which seems most suitable for him.

While it is impossible to stereotype the thousands of veterans who have taken advantage of this experience, some generalizations seem justified. Many veterans feel pressed for time because of the fact that their vocational lives have been interrupted by their service experience. They may want to know possible shortcuts which permit them to avoid the traditional lock-step of American education. The General Educational Development Test (GED), for example, has enabled many veterans to receive a high-school diploma or its equivalent without putting in the time in classrooms which is usually demanded. The GED is a test measuring five areas of achievement which has been widely used to enable veterans to secure high-school diplomas by establishing the extent of their knowledge and skill independently of school transcripts. The results are also used as the equivalent of a high-school diploma in some situations and to determine qualifications for jobs or for college entrance.

Related to this feeling of pressure is the fact that the veteran has more maturity than the usual student. Experience has indicated that for many veterans this maturity pays off in more responsible academic behavior. He may question academic practices to a greater extent than does his younger classmate, but at the same time his sense of urgency leads him to be a good student.

Although there is much variation with the individual, many veterans find adjustment to civilian life difficult and react unfavorably to it after their years of regimentation. This readjustment does not usually require therapuetic counseling, but it may call for understanding on the part of the counselor, the school, or the employer. To overcome the difficulties of readjustment, the veteran may need a period in which he is permitted to work through some of his values, beliefs, and interests.

A counselor planning to work for the Veterans Administration will be advised to plan on getting a doctor's degree in counseling psychology because this has come to be more and more the norm for this organization. Certainly, the entire field of guidance and counseling is indebted to the Veterans Administration for its many counseling innovations and its broad support of the vocational counseling movement.

COUNSELING IN PRIVATE AGENCIES

A variety of private agencies such as the Urban League and the Jewish Vocational Services also provide counseling and hire counselors. In some cases, the counseling may take a form very similar to that of social work, and in others it may be more directly vocational and patterned after the counseling provided in the United States Employment Service. The level of counseling skill found in such agencies is increasing, and for the most part, counselors are required to have a master's in guidance or a related field.

The general objectives of such agencies usually include helping the client increase his problem-solving capacity, particularly in vocational areas, and helping him assume an adequate vocational role. To reach these objectives, the agency may provide not only counseling but work training experiences to increase his vocational desirability. The services of other agencies for recreation, job placement, etc., will also be made available to the client. While agencies vary in their approach to such problems, many of them seem to be characterized by a high level of counseling and psychological sophistication.

Many clergymen have found that their religious duties require them to serve as counselors for parishioners and others who turn to them for help with a variety of problems. It is apparent to such clergymen that religion is not enough to aid them in these duties, and they need counseling skills also. As an indication of the importance of this connection between religion and counseling, the *Directory of Approved Counseling Agencies of the American Board on Counseling Services* shows that nearly 20 percent of the approved agencies have a religious affiliation. Counselors in such agencies will have been trained specifically for their counseling duties. While many seminaries may offer an orientation course in counseling, the well-trained pastoral counselor will go beyond such a course to a systematic training program which includes careful supervision in the counseling process itself.

There seems to be no end to the kinds of problems presented to clergymen. Those with difficulties in their marriage, with life goals, with vocational problems, all may turn to the pastor as the first line of defense against overwhelming anxieties and difficulties. The clergyman himself has the difficult task of deciding which problems he is capable of working with and which should be referred to a better-trained specialist. The major concern is that the pastor not overwhelm the client with guilt but rather strive to help him cope more effectively with his problems. For such a difficult psychological task the pastor will need special training.

Summary

This chapter has illustrated the fact that many counselors work in institutions that are not strictly educational. The recent increase in concern for disadvantaged adults and youths has led to the establishment of a number of agencies with special interest in these groups. In all cases a central part of the service offered is counseling, and more people in the future will probably be employed in counseling special groups of citizenry. Some of these groups well be disadvantaged culturally or physically, while others may be eligible for services because they are veterans or because they are unemployed. The individual in training as a counselor may well want to consider the possibility of employment in these newer counseling agencies.

Exercises

1. Analyze the case of E. C. and discuss how you might have tried to help him. What agencies in your community might have been useful in this task? What special knowledge of the subculture in which E. C. lives would have been useful to you?

2. Visit at least one agency providing counseling in your community, and report to the class on the clientele served, the requirements for the counselors, and the source of support for the agency. What do you see as the pros and cons of working as a counselor in such an agency?

3. Identify at least one group in your community characterized by ethnic background, religion, or special cultural characteristics which might make use of a counseling agency other than schools. What should a counselor understand about this group before attempting to be helpful to it?

References

Barry, Ruth, and Beverly Wolf: *An Epitaph for Vocational Guidance*, Columbia University Press, New York, 1962.

Borow, Henry (ed.): *Man in a World at Work*, Houghton Mifflin Company, Boston, 1964.

Lofquist, L. H.: *Vocational Counseling with the Physically Handicapped*, Appleton-Century-Crofts, New York, 1957.

Thoroman, E. C.: *The Vocational Counseling of Adults and Young Adults*, Houghton Mifflin Company, Boston, 1968.

Williamson, E. G.: *Vocational Counseling: Some Historical, Philosophical, Theoretical Perspectives*, McGraw-Hill Book Company, New York, 1965.

12

Vocational Development and the Work of the Counselor

The most important job of the school counselor, at least in the eyes of parents and students, is that of helping students to plan for and secure employment satisfying to them and requiring activity which they are able to perform in a satisfactory manner. Such is the meaning of counseling to the lay person, and such the major justification for counseling to those who supply the money and facilities which undergird its practice.

The conceptualization of how a dependent child becomes an economically independent worker has engaged the attention of many guidance theorists. The school counselor who helps a student make vocational decisions must work from some theory of how the process occurs if he is to choose those activities which will facilitate good decision making and eschew those activities which will interfere with good decision making. Too often, however, the theory is not explicit, its assumptions are unexamined, and hence its correction or validation unlikely. Only after a clear theory of vocational development has been set forth is it profitable to examine the major questions of vocational guidance. How did it happen that you are working at your present job? How is it that your brother became something else? And the man across the street still a third kind of worker? Concern with these questions is central to guidance, and answers depend on clear models of the process of vocational development.

Trait and Factor Approach

The most common formulation with regard to vocational development is based on the idea that the traits of an individual which have vocational salience are somehow matched with those requirements of the occupation in which he works. Recent statistical techniques have permitted the grouping of traits into basic, relatively independent, factors. This advance has permitted more economical measurement methods and clearer understandings of relationships among traits. Early expression of this formulation is found in the work of Frank Parsons, who in his book *Choosing a Vocation* (Agathon Press, 1967) wrote, "In the wise choice of a vocation there are three broad factors: (1) A clear understanding of yourself, your aptitudes, abilities, interests, ambitions, resources, limitations and their causes; (2) a knowledge of the requirements and conditions of success, advantages and disadvantages, compensation, opportunities and prospects in different lines of work; (3) true reasoning on the relations of these two groups of facts." Such is the approach of most vocational counselors in schools and elsewhere.

The first step is to discover the characteristics of the individual. This process usually involves a careful interview designed to reveal the interests, experiences, and wishes of the individual. In schools the cumulative record will usually contain much of the basic information desired. The school counselor will use this information, supplemented as necessary, to delineate more clearly the work-oriented characteristics of the student. In most cases standardized tests will be used to give more precise estimates of his abilities, achievements, interests, and personality dimensions. After gathering such data, inferences will be made about the nature of the student and predictions assayed about the kind of work in which he might find satisfaction and in which he might perform in a satisfactory manner.

The second step calls for analyzing the requirements of various occupations and making judgments about the long-term outlook for employment in these occupations. Sometimes such analysis is based on psychometric data which tells us the ability level and special aptitudes of current workers. More generally the analysis is based on "conventional wisdom" and is not subject to empirical testing. Counselors frequently, by the use of "common sense" or their professional intuition, make judgments about the necessary characteristics of workers in various occupations. What does an individual need in the way of abilities to be a good truck driver? Department store salesman? Bookkeeper? Certainly, the judgment of experienced professionals is better than that of the lay person, but it should be kept in mind that many of the opinions given by counselors in the counseling interview are based on nothing more than their own limited experience, or worse, their biases. The task of discovering the necessary characteristics of workers in an occupation entails a difficult research procedure. Which worker characteristics are present but not really necessary? Which "good" traits are not functional for productivity, but are useful for smooth interpersonal relationships among the workers? Which characteristics are simply examples of featherbedding and designed to lower competition rather than increase production? Were the traits observed in adult workers present when they were adolescents? Is technology changing the job so that tomorrow's worker will not need to be so strong, or so bright, or so skilled as was yesterday's? Without answers to these and other questions the counselor will need to hold very tentatively and gingerly his views regarding the characteristics needed by workers in any occupation.

The possibility of predicting the outlook for various occupations is also a very difficult task. After World War II, it was generally believed that there would be an oversupply of engineers because many veterans were attracted to engineering because of technical work they had done in service. Clients were often told that this would be an overcrowded field and were admonished to seek different forms of work. In fact, of course, there never was such an oversupply, and the predictions proved quite false. Research is not available which shows how accurately long-range occupational predictions can be made. The government, through various publications such as *Occupational Outlook Handbook*, supplies predictions, but the method of validating them has not yet been devised. We know when we give a standardized test to a student the limits of its accuracy, but when we give a student a prediction of the job market of the future, we are not able to tell him with equal certainty the parameters of our judgment.

The third step involves the matching of the characteristics of the client with the requirements of the occupation through "true reasoning." In common parlance, this step consists of "fitting the square pegs into the square holes and the round pegs into the round holes." Such a consummation is devoutly to be wished, but much more difficult to do than it seems at first blush. We do not know the likelihood of our having discovered the crucial characteristics of the individual. Is his low reading level really a fatal flaw in his desire to be a teacher, or can it be outweighed by his personal charm? Is every teacher someone who speaks clearly and correctly, or are there successful teachers who do not have this seemingly essential characteristic? This matching process based on "true reasoning" may have to take account of many irrational motives in the individual and irrational hiring practices in the occupation. How many students are in college because "true reasoning" disclosed the wisdom of higher education and how many because their family and friends expected to find them there? How often is "true reasoning" engulfed by emotion, persistence, and denial of what appears to others to be the "facts of life"? In your own vocational decisions what part was played by "true reasoning" and what part by social pressure? By economic circumstance? By whim and accident?

We no longer think of the process of vocational development as putting together a jigsaw puzzle. We recognize that the pieces change shape and that the design is organic and not fixed.

ASSUMPTIONS OF TRAIT AND FACTOR APPROACH

A number of assumptions often not clearly stated underlie the Parsonian (or trait and factor) conception of vocational development. The major assumption is that vocational development is largely a cognitive process in which the individual uses reasoning to arrive at his decision. But thinking is not the only process used by decision makers for it is apparent that many important decisions, including vocational ones, are made on the basis of emotion. An anecdote about Freud says that he handled decision making in two ways. When he had a minor decision to make, he gathered all the facts and came to a logical conclusion. When he had a major decision to make, he simply listened to his unconscious! How many choices of college, major, or occupation are based on what one's friends are doing, family wishes, and minor fortuitous circumstances?

Another assumption is that occupational choice is a single event. At some point in life the individual "decides" what he shall do for a living. It seems more likely that vocational choice is a slow process through which an individual moves by imperceptible stages from no notion of what he will do to certainty with regard to what he will do. The Parsonian view stresses development very little and choice very much. A counselor working from such a position might overvalue the series of interviews that he has with a client at any one time just as he might overvalue the "facts" that are to be discussed as opposed to the emotion surrounding the facts.

A third assumption is that there is a single right goal for everyone making decisions about work. A parallel might be drawn with sentimental novels that imply that a girl goes through her teens looking for "Mr. Right," because she believes that there is only one man that could make her happy as her husband. Or, another analogy might be that of the salmon leaping upriver to find the single right stream in which to lay its eggs. It is now more generally believed that any worker might fit well into a number of occupations. The final choice of an occupation is often made on the basis of unforseeable and unpredictable circumstances.

A fourth assumption—really a mirror image of the preceding one—is that a single type of person works in each job. While there may be some minimal truth in the idea that there is a "teacher type," "salesman type," "engineer type," etc., it is evident that many different kinds of people manage to be successful as teachers, salesmen, or engineers. While this idea of a single type for each job is not necessarily inherent in the total theory, many counselors have been misled into believing it.

The final assumption is that there is an occupational choice available to each individual. An alternative view is that social and economic forces guide a person's vocational development, and he has little control over it. Given the fact that you were born into a particular family of a particular race, a particular socioeconomic level, a particular religion, at a particular time in our history, how much choice did you really have? Were you equally free to be a fisherman or a psychiatrist, a tenant farmer or a teacher, an artist or an accountant? If we believe that many of the choices that seem to be made during a vocational history are not, in fact, choices at all, then we look at the vocational development process in a new and different way. The naïve client's request "I'd like to take a test to find out what I'm best suited for" becomes not only impossible to fulfill, but irrelevant. We recognize that while vocational development may involve the minimal presence of appropriate characteristics on the part of the individual and minimal knowledge of the requirements for a vocation, there is no high correlation between the two necessary for development into a successful worker in the field.

The trait and factor theory of vocational development has a long and honorable history and still constitutes the rationale for most vocational counseling in schools. However, counselors approaching their work from this point of view too rarely examine their assumptions to learn the base on which this approach rests. This theory has given great emphasis to test development so that traits and collections of traits—factors—could be measured. It has also given great emphasis to the analysis of worker characteristics and job requirements. The field of vocational psychology is closely allied with this point of view, as are the scientific aspects of vocational counseling.

Developmental Theories

The publication of *Occupational Choice—An Approach to a General Theory* (Columbia University Press, 1951), by Eli Ginzberg, Sol W. Ginsburg, Sidney Axelrad, and John L. Herma, gave the field of guidance a systematic way of viewing vocational development. On the basis of the research and conceptualization done by these authors, the counselor was asked to view vocational development as a long-term process, largely irreversible, and resulting in eventual compromise.

The process was seen as starting in early childhood and continuing until the twenties. This period of vocational development is divided into three general stages: the fantasy period, the tentative period and the reality period. In the fantasy period, which continues until about age ten, the child responds to the question "What will you be when you grow up?" with fantasy answers selected from the culture to which he has been exposed. These answers represent only a childhood view of the society in which he lives and not his own capabilities or desires. The little boy may say "I want to be an astronaut," or "fireman," or a "cowboy," and none of these answers tell us much about him or his plans. The little girl may say that she wants to be a movie star, a teacher, or an airline stewardess, but again, her answers tell us something about her culture rather than her as an individual.

After the fantasy period there is a tentative period from approximately ages eleven to seventeen. This period is characterized by the expanding recognition of the several dimensions of the problem of deciding on a future occupation. The solution must be sought in terms of probable future satisfactions rather than in terms of current satisfactions. This period is subdivided into four stages. When he is eleven or twelve, the boy's choices and plannings are apt to be made largely on the basis of interest. The boy has learned what he likes to do and may make his tentative choices on the basis of such a subjective factor. The next stage, thirteen and fourteen, is that in which choices are made on the basis of recognized capacity. Here the boy may have learned that he is better in school than most and so may plan on high-level occupations; or he may have learned that he is not good in mathematics and may drop from consideration occupations which he thinks call for this skill. He may have learned that he is good on the playground and may begin to think of himself as a professional athlete. The third stage is characterized as the value stage and is placed at approximately ages fifteen and sixteen. Here the boy begins to delineate what is really important to him. Does he most want money, prestige, a chance to be creative, the opportunity to work in a particular setting, or some other value which is enhanced by his vocation? Considerable research has shown that these value commitments actually occur even earlier than these authors believed, are rather stable, and show some relationship to eventual occupational choice. While it is difficult to accurately measure and define values, evidence suggests that counselors and teachers should be striving to help the student clarify his values and see the bridge between what he thinks is good and what are the requirements and consequences of various kinds of work. Finally, the last substage in this period is that of transition when reality considerations which were on the periphery of consciousness move into a more central position. This shift reflects the fact that the values which an individual hopes to realize through work are deeply embedded in the social and economic structure to which he must adjust himself and, therefore, which he must understand, test, and know through experience.

The reality period which begins in late adolescence continues until the person has finally settled into an occupation which he will hold for some time. During the first part of this period, he explores various occupations either by direct work experience or vicariously. He does so in an attempt to link his decision making to reality. After sufficient exploration, his choices become crystalized and he moves into the vocation in which he will work. This crystallization is culminated by the stage of specification in which he selects and enters into a particular job with a long-range commitment to a given type of work, perhaps even in a particular company or geographic area.

These three stages provide a framework useful in thinking about vocational development. To the extent that they are accurate, they enable us to know the kinds of learning experiences which may be useful to vocational decision making at various ages. They also give us a rough index as to whether the individual child is "on schedule" in his vocational development.

The general theory embodied in this book may be stated in this way: First, occupational choice is a *process* which takes place over a minimum of six or seven years and more typically over ten years or more. Second, since each decision during adolescence is related to one's experience up to that point, and in turn has an influence on the future, the process of decision making is basically *irreversible*. Third, since occupational choice involves the balancing of a series of subjective elements with the opportunities and limitations of reality, the crystallization of occupational choice inevitably has the quality of a compromise.

Although much criticized for what has been seen as an inadequate research design, this book has had a considerable influence on the field of vocational counseling. It has been relatively unchallenged in its basic theses (1) that we should consider vocational development, not occupational choice, in striving to be helpful to students; (2) that some kind of synthesis or compromise typically occurs because no one can do all that he would like to do, and no one is without some, though perhaps limited, freedom; and (3) that decisions are irreversible in that we cannot step into the same stream twice. The concept of irreversibility, often attacked, is best understood as a belief that every decision we make has an influence on future decisions and that there is no way of going back and expunging or erasing the past. This theory is almost entirely concerned with the vocational development of middle-class males, a limitation it shares with practically all vocational theories. Of girls, it is usually only remarked that "they are different"— a difficult proposition to refute. The vocational dynamics, patterns, and motives of girls have been less studied and are less understood than those of boys. The vocational lives of the lower class and the upper class have attracted less attention from theorists than have those of the middle class. It is moot whether these omissions stem from bias and leave the counselor without needed formulations for his daily work. Possibly vocational decision making is a more crucial developmental concern for middle-class boys than for others. All in all this developmental framework has been found useful by many counselors who are trying to understand the process by which children become working adults.

Robert Havighurst has also become identified with a conception of stages of vocational development that imply appropriate kinds of development for each age level. These stages might be thought of as an extension and particularization of his better known "developmental tasks."

The first stage is that of "identification" and runs roughly from ages five to ten. During this period the boy identifies himself with the worker in the family who is an adult male, that is, in most cases with a father. As he begins to understand that he will grow into an adult male, he realizes that this role typically requires going to work regularly and supporting a family. Havighurst points out that in many disadvantaged homes there is not a father who is a regular worker with whom the boy can identify. The absence of such an identification figure may well interfere with the healthy or "normal" vocational development of the boy.

From ages ten to fifteen the boy is in a stage where he is acquiring the basic talents of industry. The child begins to learn responsibility and to organize his life so that it includes the notion of work. Work at this stage may include part-time jobs such as carrying papers, chores around the house, or school homework. To pass through this stage successfully, the boy needs to learn to do some work without being specifically told what to do. He learns to organize his time and energy and to put "work before play." Because many of the rewards for industriousness at this stage are given in the school, the child who is not successful in school may have difficulty acquiring the basic talents of industry. He will not learn that it "pays" to work.

The next vocational stage, ages fifteen to twenty-five, is given over to acquiring identity as a worker in the occupational structure of society. At this time the boy selects an occupation and begins to prepare for it. In most cases, he will enter into work during this period. He now sees himself not as a prospective worker but as an actual worker. Again, if there are not jobs for him to pursue, because of his own lack of ability or because of economic problems in society, he may have difficulty moving through this stage.

From ages twenty-five to forty the individual is a productive person and, in most cases, reaches the peak of his skill. He will move up the vocational ladder and most men at this time find that work has become the dominant force in their life. However, those who have not successfully moved through the prior stages cannot reach this peak of productivity.

The individual maintains his productivity from roughly ages forty to seventy. He may be, at this time, not so much concerned with personal productivity since he is more certain and secure about his vocational status. His attentions are now concentrated on his contribution to society so that the major task of this period is to "maintain a productive society." He takes more active interest in professional organizations, labor unions, service organizations, and general community projects. His concern is with raising his own children, providing a better society for them, and his total role as a citizen.

Finally, the last role is that of contemplating a productive life. If he has been a productive person during the first five stages, he will likely be more contented during this stage.

Havighurst's conception of vocational development is particularly valuable in its emphasis on the importance of supplying the boy with a proper figure for identification if he is to learn to be a productive worker. He also emphasizes the importance of the school and its influence on the individual's vocational development. A secure and interested teacher or counselor may contribute a good deal to the boy's vocational development, primarily by demonstrating socially acceptable adult male behavior and by rewarding industriousness and responsibility.

Havighurst's views have special relevance for society's concern with the disadvantaged. How do we aid the child in overcoming the deprivation of the home which does not provide a stable, working father for his identification? What can schools do to teach the child that industriousness pays off in immediate rewards as well as the greater likelihood of later satisfactions? Is early interference with vocational development irreversible, or can compensatory programs help the late starter catch up with his more favored peers?

Still another vocational development framework is that advanced by *Donald E. Super,* particularly in *The Psychology of Careers* (Harper and Row, 1957). Super's theory involves both structural and developmental aspects, but only the latter will be considered at this point.

Super posits five stages of vocational development: growth (to age fourteen), exploration (fifteen to twenty-four), establishment (twenty-five to forty-four), maintenance (forty-five to sixty-four), and decline (after sixty-four). Super elaborates these stages by suggesting that at least three of them have substages. The (growth) stage is subdivided into a fantasy stage (ages four to ten), an interest stage (ages eleven and twelve), and a capacity stage (ages thirteen to fourteen). The exploration stage is subdivided into a tentative stage (ages fifteen to seventeen), a transition stage (ages eighteen to twenty-one), and a trial stage (ages twenty-two to twenty-four). The establishment stage has two substages: a trial stage from ages twenty-five to thirty and a stabilization from ages thirty-one to forty-four.

The names of these stages suggests the nature of vocational concerns. Such concerns start in late childhood with tentative probes and questions, become stronger stirrings in early adolescence as recognition of the importance of vocational decisions grows, and finally lead to educational, and sometimes preliminary vocational, decisions. These decisions in turn are evaluated, either are modified or become crystallized, and lead in the mature stages to elaboration and embellishment of vocational behaviors. Each of these stages has its characteristic behavior and attitudes, and therefore the vocational maturity of an individual may be estimated by relating his chronological age to his vocational behavior. For example, during the tentative and transition terms of the exploration stage, the individual is engaged in crystallizing his vocational choices. This crystallization is characterized by an awareness of a need to make decisions, the appropriate use of resources, an awareness of factors that need to be considered along with the contingencies which may affect his goals. During the establishment stage the individual is particularly concerned with stabilization for the first ten years (twenty-five to thirty-five) and interested in consolidation after that. The stabilization process is marked by an awareness of a need to stabilize, planning for stabilization, accepting the inevitability of some instability, and obtaining a stable, regular job. The consolidation period is characterized by an awareness of the need to consolidate and advance, securing information on how to consolidate and advance, planning for consolidation and advancement, and executing consolidation and advancement plans. These illustrative attitudes and behaviors show how Super has been able to make concrete and specific his formulation of vocational development. Such specificity has led others to develop instruments to measure an individual's vocational maturity.

These three formulations by Ginzberg, Havighurst, and Super of vocational development all focus on the developmental process by delineating the stages through which an individual passes. Although ages are associated with these various stages, none of the theorists interpret the age limitations rigidly. There is no thought that a boy is somehow abnormal if he still is fantasizing about occupations at age fifteen or that he is greatly precocious if he takes account of his capacities at age ten. The ages given are simply very rough approximations of when certain vocational behavior typically occurs. These vocational development theories give some basis to the counselor or teacher upon which to consider the vocational development process and help students understand their present and expected decision-making behavior. Super's formulations have resulted in more research than has that of the other two, and we may hope for more precise and operational statements of his stages.

Less is know about the developmental stages characterizing the vocational life of girls, but that problem too may yield to additional formulations and research. Also cross-cultural consideration of vocational development is largely unexplored. Do boys in Ghana, Japan, Russia, or Panama move through these same stages? What of Havighurst's identification stage in a kibbutz in Israel? At what age does exploration occur in nations where very few go to school? These and other questions not only are not answered, but remain largely unasked.

Structural Theories

A number of vocational development theories have been advanced which purport to explain the process of vocational development by specifying that part of the structure of the world of work toward which an individual will gravitate. In the broadest sense these theories attempt to explain why an individual ends up in a particular occupation.

Anne Roe believes that every individual has a tendency to expend his energies in a particular way which is dependent upon innate predispositions as they are altered by childhood experiences. The combination of these two factors permits predictions about the kind of work in which the individual will find himself.

She makes particular use of the "need" theory associated with Maslow. Childhood treatment by the parent is the prime determiner of eventual vocational placement, she believes. These childhood experiences largely revolve around the satisfaction of needs. Needs which are routinely satisfied do not become unconscious motivators; higher-order needs will disappear entirely if they are unsatisfied, while lower-order needs will become dominant motivators if they are only rarely satisfied. Finally, needs that are satisfied after unusual delay will become unconscious motivators under certain conditions.

The core of her theory consists of spelling out the kind of childhood treatment which will result in various occupational placements. She first divides early childhood experiences into those which take place in a psychologically warm home as opposed to a cold home. Next a home may be designated as one in which the parents are accepting of the child, are avoiding of the child, or concentrate emotionally on the child. A home in which there is much emotional concentration on the child may in turn be either overprotecting or overdemanding. A home in which the child is accepted may be one in which the relationship is casual or loving. Finally, a home in which the parents are avoiding of the child may be one in which he is neglected or rejected. The child will be motivated to seek occupations in which he works with persons if he comes from a home where the climate is loving, overprotecting, or overdemanding. Examples of such occupations are those in service, general cultural, or arts and entertainment. Conversely, a home in which the attitude toward the child is casual, neglecting, or rejecting will tend to lead him toward occupations which are in the fields of technology, outdoor work, or science.

In summary, her theory says that the development and meeting of needs in the early years of childhood determines the general vocational direction toward working with people or away from working with people. Motivation rests largely on the intensity of needs and is a function of the degree of deprivation of an individual combined with his genetic structure.

The level at which an individual will work will vary from unskilled labor to professional and managerial occupations. This level is determined largely by differences in intelligence and in the socioeconomic status of the child's home.

Theoretically, if we examine the child to learn much about his intelligence and if we examine his relation to his parents, we will be able to make accurate predictions of his eventual vocational status, both in terms of its level and in terms of the kind of work which he will do.

What research has been done as a result of this theory does not tend to support Roe's original ideas. She has now begun to revise her theory into a three-dimensional paradigm with the axes being loving versus rejecting, casual versus demanding, and overattention versus neglect. She believes that the casual-demanding axis is probably not important in determining whether an individual will go into an occupation where he works with people. She further has expanded her views; she now states that, generally, satisfactory early experiences with interpersonal relations both with parents and with others should permit individual development, which allows free play to individual aptitudes within a wide range of culturally approved activities. These satisfactory experiences are no longer limited just to those with parents but may be with teachers or peers or other significant people in the environment. A further elaboration of the theory takes account of the fact of differing behavior of the two parents or inconsistent behavior by one or both.

Her present position seems to be that differentiations among members of the groups can be shown, but the typical personality pattern is never a universal one for any occupation. Furthermore, personality is only one factor in vocational decisions, and its importance may vary from situation to situation. It now seems more important to her that we take into account sex stereotypes and the possession of appropriate abilities as well as the childhood experiences of the worker. She now is more concerned with the total career of the individual and recognizes that a number of choices throughout the years are made which result in the total lifework history of the individual. Her greatest contribution has been in pointing to the importance of the satisfactoriness of interpersonal relations in determining the general direction in which an individual will seek further satisfaction in the vocational realm. She also has contributed greatly to our under· standing of the relationship of occupational fields. She believes that these occupational fields can be arranged to show their relationship by conceiving of them as making a wheel in which service occupations are next to business contact occupations followed by organization occupations, general cultural, arts and entertainment, science, outdoor, and, to complete the wheel, technology occupations, which are also next to service occupations but on the other side from business contact occupations. Research has shown that when people change college majors, they are most apt to either stay within one of these eight occupational areas or move to one of the areas next to it in the above arrangement. These findings suggest that the relationships of occupations posited by Roe mirrors their actual relationships as seen by prospective workers.

John L. Holland in *The Psychology of Vocational Choice* (Blaisdell, 1966) and elsewhere has given us a theory of vocational development, the central concept of which is a typology related to work. Holland believes that we can characterize people by their resemblance to one or more personality types and that the closer a person's resemblance to a particular type, the more likely it is that he will exhibit the traits and behaviors associated with that type. He also believes that the environments in which people live can be characterized by their resemblance to one or more model environments. Finally, he believes that the pairing of persons and environments leads to several outcomes which are predictable from our knowledge of the personality types and the environmental models.

The six orientations or types into which Holland divides people are the realistic, intellectual, social, conventional, enterprising, and artistic. The realistic type is characterized by aggressive behavior, capabilities in motor coordination, and masculinity. The realistic person tends to act out his problems and avoid tasks involving interpersonal and verbal skills. He seeks concrete rather than abstract problem situations. Such people tend to be low on social skills and sensitivity. The intellectual person tends to think rather than to act, to understand rather than to persuade, and to avoid close social contacts. The social type gravitates towards teaching and other close personal relationships. He avoids occupations requiring intellectual problem-solving or physical skills and seeks out occupations calling for skillful interpersonal relations. The conventional person has great concern for rules and regulations, great self-control, and tends to subordinate his personal needs while identifying with power and status. He likes structure and order and seeks out occupations where structure is available. The enterprising person is verbally skillful but uses these skills to manipulate and dominate people. He is concerned with power and status, as is the conventional person, but they differ in that the former aspires to power and status while the latter honors others for having it. Finally, the artistic type has strong needs for self-expression and tends to relate with people indirectly through their artistic expression. He dislikes structure and prefers tasks which permit him to express himself. He tends to be more culturally feminine than masculine, show little self-control, and express emotions more readily than most people do.

Holland's theory is not very explicit in explaining how people develop into these various types. The presumption is that some combination of genetic and environmental influences result in a given type, but this matter is not very well explained. He is clear, however, in saying that if one of these orientations is much more highly developed than the others, the individual will tend to seek out an occupation in that orientation. Furthermore, if he goes into a school or job which is characterized by the presence of many people with a given orientation, he will tend to become more like them. That is, the student at a teacher's college will be more apt to go into teaching, the student at a school with many engineering majors to go into engineering, etc.

The environments posited by Holland tend to fall into the same six types as the individuals. These types are identified in educational and other environments largely in terms of the vocational goals or status of the people in that situation.

Although Holland has not classified all the occupations, he has sorted many of those requiring a college education into his six typologies. In the realistic class are found such occupations as engineering, farming, and forestry; in the intellectual class such scientific occupations as biology, chemistry, mathematics, and physics; in the social class counseling and guidance, education, social work, and religion; in the conventional class accounting and finance; in the enterprising class law, business management, and sales; and in the artistic class, art, drama, literature, and music.

It is Holland's thesis that if we know an individual's type, we will be able to predict not only his vocational choice but other things about him. His research has shown that his typology permits predictions about the competencies that individuals have (technical, business, social and educational, artistic, and leadership), their life goals, their self-concepts, and their attitudes.

He also is concerned with the level at which an individual will work and believes that intelligence and self-evaluation are the prime determiners of the individual's occupational level.

While typologies are generally suspect, Holland has provided for degrees of purity in his types by taking account not only of the prime orientation, but in some cases, of the second and third most important orientation. His studies of environments have enabled him to classify colleges in what seems to be reasonable fashions. Most of all, his conceptions must be taken seriously in light of the wealth of research he has done, most of which has resulted in many positive findings.

His views might best be summarized by saying that he believes that his six types somehow develop distinct and different life-styles. These differences in life style result in differences in vocational development and in many other factors which are measurable. When a given type is matched with a sympathetic environment, the result is apt to be satisfaction for the individual and satisfactoriness for his work. When this does not happen, the individual tends to change himself and his goals so that they become more congruent. Again, his research has demonstrated that he can predict the kinds of changes that an individual will make as he moves through college. These changes in major tend to result in his moving into an environment where he is more like the others. This theoretical combination which considers life-style and the influence of reference groups makes Holland's vocational development conceptions plausible to many and useful to the counselor who is engaged in helping students make vocational plans.

Donald E. Super has not only contributed to the developmental theories of vocational behavior, but is also regarded as a major figure relating personality to occupational choice.

Drawing from differential psychology, self-concept theory, and career patterns, Super has evolved a statement which in essence says that a person strives to implement his self-concept by choosing to enter the occupation he sees as most likely to permit him self-expression. Although there are obvious reality limitations to an individual's choice, as far as possible he will select that occupational role which permits him to be what he sees himself as being. Vocational development then becomes essentially a process of developing and implementing a self-concept. Super believes that people differ in their abilities, interests, and personalities and are therefore qualified for a number of occupations. Each possible occupation requires a given pattern of characteristics, but with tolerances wide enough to allow some variation for individual differences. Because a person's self-concept changes with time and experience, his preferences for vocations may change, and therefore, we should study not his occupational choice, but his career development. The stages through which a person moves in implementing his vocational self-concept have been previously discussed, but the nature of his career pattern is a function of his socioeconomic level, mental ability, personal characteristics, opportunities, and most of all, his everchanging self-concept. The school and the counselor can aid in this vocational development by facilitating the individual's process of maturation and by helping him to test his views about himself against reality. This process of implementing a self-concept by vocational choice is characterized by a synthesis between the individual's characteristics and his opportunities. To the extent that his vocational role playing meets with the approval of superiors, he will be encouraged to continue movement in a given direction. This role playing may be in fantasy, in the counseling interview, or in real-life activities such as courses, part-time work, and trial jobs. Finally, Super believes that work and life satisfactions depend upon the extent to which the individual finds adequate outlet for his characteristics in a work situation, thus, permitting him a way of life in which he can play the kind of role which his growth and exploratory experiences have led him to consider congenial and appropriate.

Super's major research is a longitudinal study of students as they move through school and into work. In this study, he has endeavored to assess the vocational maturity of his subjects at various ages. The vocationally mature individual will be doing different things at different life stages. For example, the vocationally mature fourteen-year-old will be concerned with evaluating his interests and abilities to help him decide on further educational plans, while the vocationally mature forty-five-year-old man will be attempting to maintain his occupational status.

A major contribution of Super is seen as that of viewing vocational adjustment as a developmental process. He has wedded vocational development to self-concept theory in a way that enables us to see the economy of the translation of self-concept into work behavior. Finally, by his emphasis on career patterns, he has pointed out that the process of vocational development is lifelong. This conclusion means that individuals at all ages may profit from vocational counseling because they need to continually reassess their self-concept and test it against reality.

Super thus becomes one of the few theorists with a reasonable explanation for occupational changes in adults. Why does the teacher decide to become a counselor? Why does the accountant quit his job and go back to college to qualify as a teacher? In both cases, Super would say that the individual's self-concept has changed and he is attempting to implement this new view of himself.

The counselor's function thus becomes one of aiding his client to clarify his self-concept. Only after a person knows who he is can he determine what he wants to do vocationally. Counseling is thus focused on self-concept clarification and reality testing. This reality testing might be done through the use and consideration of tests and occupational information or by exploratory courses and trial work situations.

Assumptions of Recent Approaches

The assumptions underlying the theories explicated here are quite different from those upon which the trait and factor position rests. Those more recent theories assume that vocational development is not strictly a cognitive process, but also involves affect. As a consequence, the counselor is expected not just to provide "facts" but to provide a climate and a series of skills which permit the individual client to explore his emotional world. Only after he can come to terms with what he is and what he wants from life can he make reasonable vocational decisions.

A second assumption is that vocational development is a process and not an event. These latter-day theorists concern themselves not so much with occupational choices as with careers. They believe that vocational development is a lifelong process and not something which is gotten out of the way once and for all in adolescence.

Stemming from this assumption are the further beliefs that for each individual many possible occupations are available and that in any one occupation there is room for various types of people. Any who have worked can attest to the truth of this last assumption. If you walk down the hall of any school, you will find various kinds of people successfully performing as teachers.

Finally, these more recent theorists take more direct account of the possibility that careers are not based solely on the wishes of the individual, but are to some extent determined by the kinds of things that have happened to him—that is, the experiences he has had. These experiences are not always chosen by the individual, but may be thrust upon him by the exigencies of life. The behavior of his parents or other significant people toward him, the reactions that he elicits in others, however unwittingly, all determine the kind of person he is. From such a view stems the possibility that it is the job of the counselor not only to aid an individual in decision making, but to aid him in an acceptance of what life has brought him in the way of characteristics and opportunities.

Summary

In considering vocational development theories, we look first at the work of Frank Parsons and others who believe that individuals end up in occupations as a result of learning about themselves, the world of work, and logically deducing an appropriate connection between the two. From such a position, the counselor would concern himself with testing and interviewing to help the client know himself. Added to this self-knowledge would be information about various occupations, including the characteristics presumed to be needed for success and the outlook for the future. This experience in cognition is presumed to guide the individual to that vocational location which is most suitable for him.

Some of the more recent theorists, however, have devoted themselves to explaining the stages through which an individual moves in his vocational development. These developmental theorists seem to agree that predictable, although not precise, stages are characteristic of usual vocational development. The major contribution of these developmental theorists is to provide the counselor and the client with a scheme by which he can assess vocational maturity. We do not expect the fourteen-year-old to have made an ultimate decision about his occupation. At the same time, we do not expect the thirty-year-old to be completely without knowledge of his abilities, interests, and values. Without appropriate life experiences, the process of moving through vocational-development stages becomes difficult, if not impossible. It thus becomes the obligation of the counselor, the school, and society to provide experiences to the young which permit them to turn into productive working adults.

Another group of theorists have been concerned with the relationship between personality and vocations. Some have put special emphasis on the parent-child relationships, others on the self-concept, and still others on the life-style most comfortable to the individual. Out of these personality characteristics, it is assumed, comes the direction in which the individual will move vocationally.

At the present time, vocational-development theory is still not well developed, and there are many unanswered questions. Little is known about this field, and therefore the appropriate behavior of a vocational counselor cannot be specified in any detail. He must learn to live with ambiguity and to help his client do the same. There does seem to be agreement, however, that self-knowledge must precede vocational selection. The counselor and the client work together to enhance that self-knowledge so necessary for proper vocational development. Self-knowledge is generally thought to be a necessary but not sufficient condition for satisfactory metamorphosis from dependent child to independent producer. There is less agreement regarding the other necessary conditions.

Exercises

1. Write your vocational autobiography. Include answers to such questions as these:
    What was your vocational goal when you were seven years old?
    What was your vocational goal when you were in high school?
    When did you first decide on your present occupation?
    Who influenced your choice?
    What satisfactions and dissatisfactions do you find in your present work?
2. Interview an adult who seems satisfied with and satisfactory in his work. Apply the concepts of one of the theorists discussed in this chapter to his vocational development. Does the theory fit the facts in this person's case?
3. Most of the vocational-development theorists concern themselves only with males. How do you think the vocational development of women would differ from that of men? Why? What are the implications of these differences for the work of the school counselor?

References

Borow, Henry, (ed.): *Man in a World at Work*, Houghton Mifflin Company, Boston, 1964.

Nosow, Sigmund, and William H. Form (eds.): *Man, Work, and Society*, McGraw-Hill Book Company, New York, 1962.

Osipow, Samuel H.: *Theories of Career Development*, Appleton-Century-Crofts, New York, 1968.

Peters, Herman J., and James C. Hansen (eds.): *Vocational Guidance and Career Development*, The Macmillan Company, New York, 1966.

Slocum, Walter L.: *Occupational Careers*, Aldine Publishing Company, Chicago, 1966.

PART FIVE

Emerging Guidance Areas

13

Leisure-time Guidance

One of the most important problems arising out of our complex social, economic, and industrial conditions is the effective use of leisure time. With increased life expectancy, shorter working hours, and more systematic retirement plans the place of leisure in American society has assumed increasing importance. Many feel that the schools, along with other institutions, need to take greater responsibility for preparing students for leisure and giving them guidance in its satisfactory use.

Place of Leisure in Society

Others have pointed to the paradox of considering leisure—a subject associated with reward and relaxation—as a "problem," but a problem it is in the affluent American society of today. The vast majority of mankind would, of course, welcome such a "problem," but this fact does not lessen the dilemma leisure poses for many in this country.

MEANING OF LEISURE

Although the concept of leisure has varied in some respects from time to time, it has always carried with it the idea of free time, that is, spare time at one's disposal. It is usually interpreted as time not spent on the activities of making a living, keeping alive, or maintaining one's efficiency—eating, sleeping, and the ordinary care of the body. Leisure is synonymous with idleness or with time spent on avocations, hobbies, or recreations. These are merely ways of employing leisure time. It is often difficult to distinguish between one's vocational and avocational activities, but the distinction can be made with sufficient definiteness to give a fairly clear idea of the meaning of leisure.

A common definition of leisure says that it is an activity freely pursued without pay which brings an immediate satisfaction. The three major functions of leisure are relaxation, entertainment, and personal development.

VARIATION IN LEISURE TIME

The amount of time for leisure is largely dependent on the time it takes to supply one's physical and social needs. Leisure time may be increased by decreasing needs or by increasing the speed of producing what is needed. Diogenes increased his leisure time by reducing his needs to a bare minimum. We can increase our time for leisure by taking less time for eating, sleeping, and making our toilet. We could also increase our leisure, as some do, by quitting work before the regular time, but this practice usually is not to be commended. We often combine the satisfying of physical needs with social satisfactions, by not gulping down food as fast as we can at meals, by taking time to enjoy beautiful settings and interesting conversation. Although human needs have a way of increasing with increased power to satisfy them, human ingenuity has developed ways of greatly increasing the power to satisfy them. The satisfaction of our needs has been accomplished by increasing man's ability to produce, by increasing the quality and quantity of products of the land, by the discovery of new sources of food, and by the invention of tools and machinery that enable one man to do the work of fifty in gathering and processing food materials.

EARLY ATTITUDE TOWARD LEISURE

There was a time when leisure was considered to be the prerogative of the privileged class. In ancient Athens and Rome and even in America in times of slavery this may have been true. This class, through wealth, power, or tradition, could commandeer the services of a large number of people for the production of sufficient goods of all kinds to enable them to live a life of leisure, free from the necessity of making a living.

It is singular that, in America today, although we have a large group of people who have enough wealth to buy luxuries far beyond the dreams of the richest man in ancient Athens, we have practically no leisure class— at least none that is at all comparable to that of the wealthy citizens of Athens, the powerful barons of feudal times, or the leisured English gentlemen in the time of Locke. Many of our wealthy men are the busiest men we have and have little or no time for leisure. The reason for this anomaly is that we have made a god of work and think chiefly in terms of work, power, and money. This attitude is an outgrowth of our beginnings and of our surroundings. The early New England settlers found life in the new country unexpectedly severe. The soil was poor, the Indians hostile, and the climate cold and bleak. The motto of the Virginia settlers became, "He who does not work shall not eat." "Busyness" and thrift became cardinal virtues with almost religious significance. Some of our church hymns express the same idea:

> Give every flying minute
>   Something to keep in store,
> Work for the night is coming
> When man works no more.

These ideals are strongly embedded in the American mind and still color much of our thinking. They have so pervaded society that the idle rich, as well as the idle poor, are considered a menace. The wandering hobo is considered to be little better than a criminal. Many men work hard, taking no time for relaxation, with the avowed purpose of making enough money to retire and enjoy their leisure. When the time for retirement comes, however, they find themselves either so broken in health that they cannot enjoy their free time or unable to enjoy it because they never have learned how.

PRESENT ATTITUDE TOWARD LEISURE

Into this atmosphere of struggle and strain, of external striving for wealth and power, of the exaltation of work and efficiency, there have recently come some disturbing elements. First, the conviction has come that, no matter how long and how effectively they work, many men can never, by their own efforts, accumulate enough wealth to live comfortably when retirement comes. Under our present system the distribution of wealth will always be uneven. A living income and a comfortable old age for everyone can be assured only by a social order that plans for them. The present tendency in state and federal laws seems to indicate that, wisely or unwisely, we are drifting toward a state where this ideal will be realized. Second, production has been so much speeded by labor-saving machinery and improved techniques that enough goods may soon be produced to provide a reasonably high standard of living with a work week of thirty hours or less. Men will no longer need to work long hours for there may not be enough work to keep them busy more than five hours a day. We may have thrust upon us five or six hours a day which cannot be spent in the activities of one's job. The old ideals of work and "busyness" are quite inadequate to deal with such a situation. As a result of these changed economic and social conditions, we are rapidly developing a leisure class, not like the old privileged wealthy class, but a class composed of the entire group of unskilled, semiskilled, and skilled workers who constitute the great majority of the population. We are indeed witnessing the movement of a whole society into a way of life which has hitherto been reserved for a special privileged class.

Whether the same shortening of the hours of labor will apply to professional workers remains to be seen. The problem of leisure time is quite possibly the greatest single problem for education today. This situation is both a challenge and an opportunity. As increased leisure becomes available for millions, there will be more time available for individuals to develop their talents to the greatest potential, thereby achieving new dimensions of happiness and satisfaction.

Social and Personal Functions of Leisure

The function of leisure is largely determined by the kind and amount of free time available and the ideals of the time. In different societies leisure assumes different functions—in one it provides an opportunity for conspicuous consumption, in another it enables science and literature to prosper. For different individuals leisure performs different functions also—some benefits are socially and personally desirable, some are not.

LEISURE TIME AS RELATED TO INCREASED PRODUCTION

When leisure time is merely a short breathing space between long periods of sustained labor, its function has been to increase production. This is accomplished by giving the worker a rest from time to time—the "coffee break"—so that he can recover from fatigue and accomplish more. Sometimes the employer helps his employees to get comfortable homes and provides better working conditions, rest rooms, or recreation facilities. This practice helps his business, for it creates good will and increases production. The Roman emperors provided holidays for the populace, great gladiatorial combats, thrilling spectacles, and sports of all kinds. These activities helped the common people to be satisfied with their lot and to produce more.

LEISURE TIME AS RELATED TO INCREASED CONSUMPTION

Leisure is also thought of as a means of increasing consumption. The more time an individual has free from work, the greater is his demand for goods that will help him make his leisure more satisfying. This fact is evidenced by the great demand for sporting goods of all kinds. Consumption of this kind also increases production, and so it is good for business. Both these points of view about the function of leisure are founded on a belief in the sacredness of work and the importance of increasing wealth as an end in itself.

LEISURE TIME AS RELATED TO CRIME AND DELINQUENCY

Crime and delinquency flourish when youth and adults have nothing worthwhile to do, when they have "time on their hands." It has been shown in many cities that, whenever interesting sports and other useful activities are provided, delinquency decreases. Productive people are less likely to engage in crime, but few would subscribe to the notion that we should keep people working simply in an attempt to keep them out of mischief.

LEISURE TIME AS RELATED TO HUMAN DEVELOPMENT

The functions of leisure time just mentioned fail to touch the most fundamental and important need of an individual—the need for his development as a human being.

If we are to meet the problem presented by our enforced leisure, if we are to set up the machinery by which to realize the "dream of America," we must put more emphasis upon the development of the individual himself.

Types of Leisure-time Activities

The choice of a leisure-time activity should be suited to the needs of the individual, and the basis for choice may well vary with the individual. In most cases, however, it should be sufficiently different from the activities in the regular occupation to afford recreation and real enjoyment. The required skills should be within the participant's capabilities. Before taking up a leisure-time activity, we may want to ask ourselves some questions: "Do I have time for it? Can I afford it? Will it meet my social needs?"

There is a great variety of leisure-time activities and a great overlapping in meaning and purpose. Each activity has within itself possibilities of different values or objectives. The value of an activity depends largely on the individual who participates in it. For this reason it is impossible to make any completely satisfactory classification of leisure activities.

RELAXATION

One of the principal meanings of leisure has always been relaxation. The activities engaged in for this purpose are varied and numerous.

Paradoxical as it may seem, there are those who relax in very systematic and even stylized fashions. Some Eastern religions and Western imitations of them make relaxation a very difficult and complex art.

More generally, however, relaxation may take the form of simply doing what comes naturally. To some this will consist of puttering around the house or garden. Others will take walks with no special aim in mind and no special effort involved.

Passive relaxation is probably the most frequent form. The docile television viewer, record or radio listener or sports viewer probably best exemplifies passive relaxation. While it is customary to be scornful of such activity, the fact that it is quite usual in our society suggests that it does, in some way, fulfill a necessary need.

ENTERTAINMENT

As usually understood, recreation, which is the commonest form of entertainment, may include practically all types of leisure-time activities, especially amateur sports and games—anything done just for fun. However, its original meaning has great significance. "Recreation" has the meaning indicated in "re-creation." It means to revive, to refresh, to renew. It presupposes that the individual once had something that he valued and has now lost it or is in danger of losing it because of exhaustion, ill health, neglect, or some other cause; through recreation he wants to get it back. "Re-creation" includes the need for rest or for types of exercise which will renew one's strength. It also includes renewal of happiness, faith, courage, trust in people; the meaning of life, of sorrow, of sickness, of death. It thus includes every type of human activity which helps in the renewal of human values.

A common type of recreation is a hobby. A hobby may be described as a nonvocational activity that involves more than a mere passing interest and one to which the amateur turns persistently when opportunity permits. Hobbies are recognized as being among the most valuable of the leisure-time activities. Some authorities say that every person should have some sort of hobby, but this certainly is an exaggeration because not infrequently a number of varied activities is more valuable to a particular individual. Hobbies may have a great prognostic value for the choice of an occupation.

Escape activities are those engaged in as a release from the daily round of labor or from situations that are unpleasant or disturbing. They are calculated to make one forget unhappiness, at least temporarily. They must, therefore, be absorbing activities and as different as possible from the experience that caused the unpleasant emotions. A large number of people employ their spare time in activities that are entirely of this kind. They read detective stories, romantic novels, the sports page, the comics. They go to second-rate movies that appeal entirely to the eye and ear or spend their time before the television set where conversation is taboo. They attend football, baseball, and hockey games that grip their attention and stir the emotions to a point of forgetfulness; they play bridge, tennis, golf and play as strenuously as they work. When they travel, in order to get the most for their money they join a planned tour which leaves them no time to themselves. On shipboard the steward thoughtfully plans their every minute in deck sports, dances, special parties, or bridge. At times we all need such forms of relaxation, but far too often they are the only ones in which we engage. Anyone who looks upon the usual vacation activities of the tourist may well say, "At work man is sublime; at leisure he is ridiculous."

Competitive activities are those in which one person or group seeks to surpass another person or group in the exercise of certain skills. Indoor and outdoor games and sports of all kinds come under this heading. These activities are among the most popular ways of spending leisure time and may have very great value for the participants. Some critics say, with a fair amount of truth, that with the great popularity of professional sports we are afflicted with "spectatoritis" and do not engage enough in sports directly. There are, however, some real recreational values in being a spectator with a large social group witnessing the same exercises and cheering for "our side."

PERSONAL DEVELOPMENT

Many thousands of youths and adults are using their leisure time to prepare themselves for college, for better positions in business and industry, and for different types of work. Evening schools, correspondence schools, and radio and television courses are utilized for these purposes.

These activities broaden our outlook and vision, and increase our appreciation of music, art, literature, and all that is high and noble. They help us keep in touch with the world and maintain and deepen our intellectual, moral, and spiritual nature. They involve cessation of haste and strenuous struggle and require us to take time to stretch, to think, to enjoy, to appreciate. Thoreau had this purpose in mind when he wrote, "I went to the woods because I wished to live deliberately, to front only the essential facts of life, and see if I could not learn what it has to teach, and not, when I came to die, discover that I had not lived."

Creative activities also contribute to personal development. These activities are those where one does not sit passively and enjoy the creation of others but participates in the creation. The field of such activities is very wide and offers opportunity for everyone. Under this category would come the composition of music, painting, sculpturing, dressmaking, cooking, working in wood, metal, or other material, writing, and any other activity in which one is not merely a spectator but actually produces something. Such activities give us satisfaction and a feeling of accomplishment.

Finally, service activities may play an important part in personal development.

These are the activities that are done to help others. They may take the form of a personal service to a member of the family or a friend or services to various groups and clubs. Many service activities may also become creative ones. Women who volunteer to help in hospitals and men who work with youth groups are performing service activities. Leisure time spent in such activities may give the feeling of satisfaction which comes from being engaged in a socially valuable task.

Responsibility of the School for Leisure-time Activities

The curriculum of the school is considered here as consisting of those educative experiences which are under school supervision. Such educative experiences may take the form of regularly scheduled classes or may consist of extracurricular activities.

CLASS INSTRUCTION AND LEISURE TIME

Through the curriculum are developed the fundamental skills in reading, writing, art, music, home economics, and industrial arts which are essential to effective participation in many of the leisure-time activities. We must rely on class instruction to develop an interest in such activities and a desire to participate in them. There needs to be a somewhat radical change in the attitudes of some superintendents, principals, and teachers before the school can become really effective in its contribution to the leisure-time activities of the students. Even more important is the change that needs to take place in the patrons of the school. The taxpaying public and school boards must be persuaded that activities preparing students for the wise use of leisure are not "fads and frills" to be eliminated when the financial situation becomes acute. More time and attention have to be given to the school's responsibility for assisting the students to develop the skills for effective leisure-time activities and for making wise choices among such activities.

The intelligent choice and wise planning of leisure-time activities are dependent upon knowledge of the different types involved, skill in their use, and real interest and desire to participate in them. Since this is the case, the curriculum of the elementary and secondary school has an important function in leisure-time guidance. Courses in civics, history, general science, English, and geography are now being organized in such a way as to help the pupil learn the facts of modern social, civic, and economic life which are important for him and to develop in him interests and attitudes that will function in his life both in the school and outside it in work and in leisure.

STUDENT ACTIVITIES AND LEISURE TIME

Although closely related to the organized classes, the various forms of student clubs and activities and the general school life contribute much toward preparing for wise choice of leisure-time activities. Student participation in the government of the school affords splendid opportunity for acquiring facts about forms of government and for developing right attitudes toward service activities, especially those related to citizenship. The best preparation for civic responsibility in later life is participation in the duties connected with the social group with which one is now connected. For the student, the most important group is the school. If students feel that the responsibility for the government of the school rests partly upon them, they will assume a very different attitude toward the life of the school and toward discipline. One of the reasons why so-called "student" government is not more helpful in civic guidance is that it is often student government in name only. Policies are really decided by the principal, and the officers of the organization are mere puppets moving at his behest. To be effective, real responsibility should be placed upon the officers of the student body. The government of the school should be a cooperative matter, with definite responsibility being delegated to the students for some decisions. Problems that arise in connection with the government of the school afford excellent material for group discussions, assembly talks, homeroom conferences, and individual conferences between students and principal or teacher.

The student activities program and the general school life are important factors in the acquisition of facts, in the development of skills and attitudes that are useful in adjustment to others, and in general social relationships. Such attainments are vital in appreciation and service activities. Most of one's life is concerned directly with other people, and individual success and happiness are dependent in large measure upon the way in which one gets along with others. Individuals differ by nature very greatly in their power to adapt themselves to social situations; for some, it is very easy; for others, it is extremely difficult; for all, it is largely a matter of training. Everyone needs guidance in social adjustments no matter what sort of home he may come from or how well he may be endowed by nature.

SOCIAL SKILLS AND LEISURE TIME

Manners are of very great importance, and manners can be learned. In our cosmopolitan high schools, students need special help because there are many social customs of which they are entirely ignorant. Since their homes do not give help, someone else must. Help is given in classes set apart for this special purpose, by the definite provision for social occasions in the school, by parliamentary activities in student assemblies, and in club and class meetings and private conferences. Some schools utilize the entire school life for purposes of social guidance. Formal and informal teas are given to accustom students to such occasions and to train them in conduct proper to the occasion. Parents' receptions are organized with the help of students. Formal and informal dances and parties are employed where invitations are issued and letters of acceptance or regret are sent. These activities are all organized and administered with the definite purpose of giving students the most practical help and training in methods of social conduct and forms of social usage. Such matters are often considered in homeroom discussions. Several very helpful manuals on manners have been written and are now being used in the schools.

Student clubs often serve to develop or to deepen interest in desirable activities that develop into hobbies or avocations in later life and function as leisure-time activities, cultural and appreciative, creative, and service.

SPORTS AND LEISURE TIME

The physical education program is directed partly toward the development of skills in certain games, group and individual, and partly toward the development of an interest and desire to continue such participation after one's school life is over. If this work is to become really effective, studies should be conducted which will show the effect that certain forms of recreation have upon the physical and mental life of the participants and the forms that are best suited to meet the needs of different types of people. We need to examine our school program of athletics and student clubs to determine which ones will be helpful in after-school life. We already know, for example, that the great majority of people, after they leave school, will not play football, baseball, hockey, or basketball. They are far more likely to play golf, tennis, or volleyball, or to swim, go hiking, or dance. Group play is valuable in many ways and should not be neglected, but directors of physical education are coming to feel that such games should not crowd out forms of recreation in which most people will engage after they leave school. Definite provision should be made in school for the development of an interest in these forms of sport which have carry-over value in later life.

The Counselor's Responsibility for Leisure

Whether working with children or adults, the counselor will have as his responsibility helping them integrate their leisure life with other aspects of their existence. The student who is getting in trouble because he has too much time on his hands might be guided into activities which will provide him socially desirable entertainment. He might be helped to join a club, go out for athletics, or develop an appropriate hobby. The adult who appears unduly driven or anxiety ridden may be encouraged to find ways to relax. Again, socially appropriate activities might be pointed out to him and he may be helped in getting started with these new behaviors. Either children or adults whose lives seem to lack meaning, who live at a shallow level and seem to be victims of ennui, may be encouraged and guided toward leisure activities resulting in personal development. Joining organizations which perform socially useful functions, taking courses to make them better and more alert citizens, developing deep interests or hobbies may all be ways in which the counselor can aid the client to develop better use of leisure time.

Tomorrow's counselor may find that his major problem is not helping people select vocations but is helping them integrate their work life with their leisure time for greater total personal development. Already, for many workers, the line between labor and leisure is thin and permeable. If America is able to make available creative leisure to its citizens, the distinction between work and leisure will continue to lessen. Certainly the counselor's role will be central in any such undertaking, for it is the counselor who particularly asks such questions as "How do I want to use my time?" "What activities and experiences will make me most aware of myself and my world?"

Summary

Leisure time is usually understood to mean time that is not needed for making a living or for activities concerned with eating, sleeping, and care of the body. Leisure is not the same as idleness, for idleness is only one way of employing leisure time. Throughout human history, the effective use of leisure time has been a serious problem, and the greater the amount of "time on our hands," the greater the problem becomes. Whenever people have no worthwhile ways of using leisure time, leisure becomes a menace to the idle adults or young people.

The problem is not merely that of keeping busy but of finding activities that will promote the welfare and satisfaction of the individual and be socially valuable. The use of leisure time is extremely varied in purpose and activity. It may be used to increase effectiveness on the daily job, to promote the comfort or convenience of home or community life, to develop some value that the job does not supply—aesthetic, spiritual, creative—or to recreate some value that has been lost.

There are many different ways of achieving these values, depending upon the particular abilities of the individual and his social surroundings. The school has a definite function to perform in developing useful leisure-time activities and in supplying guidance in their wise employment.

Exercises

1. Select three to five general criteria that would be useful in the choice of leisure-time activities. State the occupations in which you expect to be engaged for several years at least. On the basis of the criteria you have selected, state several types of leisure-time activities that would be useful and desirable to you.

2. Try to discover the leisure-time activities of three prominent persons now living.

3. What responsibility should the schools assume for guidance and training in leisure-time activities? Describe what one school is doing to prepare its students to use effectively the leisure they will have as adults.

References

Donahue, Wilma, et al. (eds.): *Free Time: Challenge to Later Maturity*, The University of Michigan Press, Ann Arbor, Mich., 1958.

Dumazedier, Joffre: *Toward a Society of Leisure*, The Free Press of Glencoe, New York, 1967.

Green, Thomas F.: *Work, Leisure, and the American Schools*, Random House, Inc., New York, 1968.

Kaplan, M.: *Leisure in America: A Social Inquiry*, John Wiley & Sons, Inc., New York, 1960.

Larrabee, Eric, and Rolf Meyerson (eds.): *Mass Leisure*, The Free Press of Glencoe, New York, 1960.

14

Guidance toward Life Goals

The wise choice of an occupation is of extreme importance. It should be one that is suited to the abilities of the individual and that will enable him to fulfill his basic needs, to develop his "self-image." The wise choice of leisure-time activities is also important not only to refresh and revive mind and body but also to minister to the aesthetic and spiritual side of life. But neither one nor both together are sufficient to give the highest meaning to life. An effective and satisfying life is not one that is made up of separate, unrelated parts; it is not like a patchwork quilt in which pieces of cloth of different materials, colors, shapes, and sizes are included without a discernible pattern; it is not merely a series of somewhat unrelated thoughts, feelings, and acts that are made in response to surrounding stimuli. Life is more than the sum of all its parts. Some unifying principle is needed which will bind together all the aspects and activities of one's life into one consistent whole. This is found in the concept of the life goal. This being the case, the choice of a life goal is, perhaps, the most important choice in one's life. The process of selecting a suitable life goal is one of the most essential and complex experiences in the area of guidance.

The Meaning and Implication of Life Goals

A goal is a dynamic concept. It is not merely an end to be reached so that some activity can cease. It is not an ideal which is to be worshiped but which will remain beyond one's reach. A goal involves something that the individual believes is valuable and a compulsion or effort to attain it. It is "a-something-of-value-that-I-am-trying-to-attain."

A life goal is one that permeates all the aspects of one's life at any given time. To attain it may involve all the areas in one's life. It may be reached in a short time or never. The important element is the effort to attain, not the attainment. A life goal is based upon and determined by a

211

set of values that govern, bind together, and give meaning to all the activities of a person's life. It provides a center for the gradual integration of all the physical, intellectual, and emotional factors in life.

A valid life goal must take into consideration the worth of the individual himself and his obligation to society. Such a goal is a rejection of the idea that a man's job is the most important thing in his life and that all his activities should be centered around it. A job is not an end in itself but merely a means to a larger and more important goal. This point of view, while generally accepted as an ideal, is often forgotten in practice. There is danger that the occupation will become an end in itself and that the really important end will be neglected. This does not mean that a job is not important or that one should do less than his best in work but, rather, that there should be a deeper meaning in life—an objective or goal that may serve to unify, integrate, and dignify all the activities of the individual. Any other position is likely to result in a lopsided, misshapen personality and general unhappiness.

The implication of this position is that the life of an individual should be considered as an organic whole, not as a mixture of more or less unrelated and often conflicting elements. Therefore, in considering the usefulness, effectiveness, or desirability of any job or any aspect of life, the entire pattern of life should be taken into account, not merely one segment of it. One should take into consideration how a given job will contribute to the attainment of one's life goal. While there are other elements of value that must be considered—working conditions, wages, chances for advancement, etc.—the life goal itself is the crucial element that ties together and serves to complement and give meaning to the job as a part of the life of the individual.

For many people vocational activities occupy a large part of life— in time, energy, and interest—and they often bring real satisfaction and joy to the worker; but they are not the whole of life, although they may furnish the chief avenue through which the life goal may be attained. Other aspects of life must also be considered, however: home life and recreational and civic activities. Many occupations are of such a nature that they cannot serve as the chief expression of the life goal. A man's central purpose or goal in some cases may be best seen in his home, his civic activities, or his church instead of in his occupation. In order to find whether his various activities are congruent with his real life goal, we must ask this question: Is the same central goal or purpose shown in all these activities? Guidance that relates only to the choice of an occupation can never be completely effective or satisfactory because it includes only one segment of life. Even joy in the activities of an occupation cannot be an entirely satisfactory element by itself because it furnishes no central, guiding principle for the selection of other activities that are nonoccupational.

There is, for most persons, no one best, predetermined avenue through which the life goal may be realized. Any one of a number of different avenues may be equally effective and satisfactory in getting an individual to his goal. The particular avenue that we take is influenced by many different elements in our environment.

One does not always need to change jobs in order to make his occupation more useful in achieving his goal. In most occupations there is some opportunity for a personal adjustment that may make it possible to use the job in such a way that it will be more helpful in the attainment of the life goal. Life is full of illustrations of men and women who have so interpreted their jobs and so governed their activities as to make them avenues through which they have attained their life goal. The lives of individuals we know—carpenters, plumbers, nurses, lawyers—constantly remind us that any job that is not in itself antisocial may be used in such a way as to contribute to human welfare when making such a contribution is the worker's life goal.

EXAMPLES OF LIFE GOALS

There are as many life goals possible as there are value systems and different social contexts in which the values can find expression. Some may devote themselves to working for the equality of opportunity for all Americans. Some may think that the highest goal is the achievement of peace and goodwill among nations. "To make two blades of grass grow where only one grew before" may be a life goal. Others wish to emulate Schweitzer, King, or Lincoln. These and other purposes can give meaning to life and help the individual make choices of all kinds as they are related to this goal.

DIFFICULTY OF CHOOSING LIFE GOALS

It is often very difficult to select a life goal that is suited to the abilities, needs, and interests of the individual and that has a reasonable promise of attainment. After the choice is made, it is sometimes difficult or impossible to reach the goal. Both choice and attainment often require assistance from others. The process of so clarifying our values that we know what we stand for is a lifelong task. Many live confused, shallow lives unable to differentiate the important from the trivial. While we should not expect most students to have clear and expressible life goals, we should assume some responsibility for helping them to learn the dimensions of this human problem and to have some acquaintance with the major tools useful in its solution.

A life goal is not a gift from the gods. It is not inherited but learned. Parents, teachers, and associates may do much to shape an individual's life goal as may his general social environment with its war, famine, disease, estrangement of parents, or death of close friends. A person develops his life goal slowly, often unconsciously, and may revise it from time to time. Sometimes a religious conversion or a personal tragedy may cause sudden dramatic changes. Although it is usually not fully developed until maturity and sometimes not even then, the important elements begin to appear in adolescence. It is clear, then, that the period represented by the secondary school and college is of maximum importance in the development of a life philosophy—in the formation of a life goal. The guidance needed for this phase of development lends itself especially well to group discussion, supplemented from time to time by individual counseling. Here, again, is where teachers can be of great help, especially teachers of English, history, science, music, and art. The lives of men and women who have made contributions in these fields can be studied and emphasis given to their special gifts, their purposes, and their motives.

The school will influence the life goals of its students whether it wishes to or not. The only question which remains is whether the influence is to be unconscious, disorganized, and negative or whether it will be conscious, systematic, and positive.

Major Life Goals

While, as has been explained, there may be many life goals, we may group them into three major categories—self-realization, service, and satisfaction. This grouping does not suggest that other possible life goals might not be of comparable merit and importance, but rather that these three divisions lend themselves to illustration and comparison and therefore seem most useful for our present explanatory purposes.

SELF-CONCEPT AS GUIDE TO LIFE GOAL

The importance of a life goal is forcibly demonstrated in the findings of Roe and Super in their investigations of the factors that are associated with the choice of an occupation. Among these factors is the "self-image," or the "self-concept." The self-concept may be described roughly as the elaboration of such statements as, "I am this sort of a person. These are my strengths and my weaknesses. These are the things I like to do." Although a self-concept is far from being a life goal, it is a very important factor in the choice of a life goal. Self-realization is becoming what one wants to be, and what one wants to be should take into consideration what one is—the present self-concept. A life goal, however, is far broader and more comprehensive than the image of what one is now. The selection of an impelling life goal often serves to eliminate weaknesses and to utilize strengths not apparent to the individual; in short, it provides motivation. In the two-way classification of occupations described by Roe, it can easily be seen how a clear life goal might help in the realistic choice of one of the occupational groups, but it would be of even greater significance in the choice of a level of work. The relationship of the self-concept to the life goal is an instrumental one because, while the life goal should underlie and be basic to any valid occupational choice, the self-concept governs the selection of the best avenue or channel for attaining it.

There is real danger that the use of the self-concept may be restricted to the selection of an occupation. To be of maximum value it should include a clarification of factors and traits which may not be closely related to what is called "success on the job" but which are definitely essential to a successful life. Guidance should help an individual relate his self-concept to his goals in such a way that he achieves "peace of mind" or "serenity of spirit." One of the best statements of this relationship was given by Paul: "I have learned in whatever state I am therein to be content." It is important to note that Paul did not say "therewith" to be content. Progress never results from contentment with one's state; discontent with one's state is an essential factor in progress. Paul was content in shipwreck, in prison, in hunger, and in thirst. Peace of mind, contentment, serenity in the midst of danger, of failure, of difficulties clear the mind of the fear and discouragement that interfere with sound judgment and valid decisions. Such peace of mind comes only from the understanding and acceptance of the fundamental values of life. Finally, there is some danger that the life goal itself may become an idol for worship, and, instead of losing himself in the service itself, the individual may become so enamored of the high value of the activity and of his own importance that he will neglect his work.

SERVICE AS A LIFE GOAL

Because a life goal brings together all the forces of the individual upon a single objective, it exerts a tremendous influence on the accomplishment of the objective chosen. The result may be useful or disastrous to the individual himself or to society. History is full of examples of both.

Without question the life goal that has had the greatest influence for good is that of service to others. Service is the keystone on which any stable and enduring government is built. In human history civilization after civilization has fallen because it has placed the selfish interest of the rulers above service to its people. Nearly every world religion is based on the concept of a supreme being and the obligation to serve one another. Service is the core of Jewish and Christian ethics. Democratic government, too, is founded on service. Sometimes the ideal of service has been too restricted to a particular country.

Certain occupations, such as medicine, nursing, law, teaching, social work, and the ministry, are based directly upon service to others. And all have been of great benefit to society.

There are many organizations like Rotary, Kiwanis, Lions, and Optimists which are distinctly service agencies devoted to high standards of professional, business, and civic life, to good citizenship, and to mutual assistance to fellow members. Many of these service clubs have direct connections with young people in school and college. Fraternal societies such as Masons, Elks, Odd Fellows are also organizations based on service, as are others related to church denominations. It can be seen that service is a powerful and widespread life goal and a useful force in our society.

SATISFACTION AS A LIFE GOAL

Satisfaction is a state of mind or an emotion that normally results from the successful attempt to reach a goal or satisfy a felt need. It is an essential element in a successful life and an invaluable asset in learning. It is imperative for every individual to have satisfaction somewhere in his life. Satisfaction may also come from the effort to attain the goal even when the goal is not reached or the need satisfied. The very difficulty of attaining the goal becomes a challenge which may have value. As James said, "Keep the quality of effort alive within you by doing some gratuitous exercises every day."

Satisfaction in itself, however, cannot be a safe guide to the choice of an occupation or any other goal. Unfortunately satisfaction may also come from the effort to attain a harmful or undesirable goal. Theft, rape, murder, oppression, cruelty give satisfaction to some people. It is the goal that is important, not the satisfaction in achieving it. But within the group of useful and desirable occupations that are suited to the needs and abilities of the individual, the possible satisfactions are very important in determining choice. Some occupations give opportunity for pride and satisfaction in the quality of the product and by the contribution that the worker makes to it. In some others, however, the worker never sees the finished product but merely feeds an automatic machine that makes only a small part of it. In such situations whatever satisfaction the worker gets is from the wages received and, possibly, from his friendly relations with other workers.

The present tendency is to increase the proportion of occupations that involve complicated machinery. Thus the professions now give the greatest opportunity for satisfaction in work. As already pointed out, although satisfaction alone is not a safe guide for the choice of an occupation, it may be a real help in such a choice. The types of activity which give satisfaction vary with different individuals. Some get their satisfaction in the production of articles made out of cloth, wood, metal, or plastic. Others get satisfaction from gardening, horticulture, farming, or forestry; and others, from working with people in such occupations as teaching, nursing, medicine, the law, and social work. The hope of satisfaction may serve as a guide in choosing an occupation by permitting a comparison of the activities that give the individual satisfaction with those that are involved in various occupations.

In some cases it may not be necessary or possible to choose an occupation that satisfies. The important objective, however, is to find satisfaction somewhere in one's life—in the job, the home, civic life, the church, or recreation. The ideal life is one in which each element supplements and enhances the value of the total in the attainment of a satisfactory life goal.

The selection of a life goal is often very difficult for youth. It is hard to choose one which is suited to the abilities, needs, and interests of the individual and which has a reasonable promise of attainment. Youth's limited experience does not provide sufficient background for a wise choice. Parents, teachers, and counselors can help by suggesting types of life goals for consideration.

Cooperation between the Public School and the Church in the Guidance of Youth

The principle of the separation of state and church is well established in this country. The public school, as an instrument of the state, is obligated to accept this. This principle, however, does not imply that there should be no cooperation between public schools and churches. In fact, it is essential that some sort of concord be provided if the best interests of the state and the church, as well as those of youth, are to be promoted. This need for cooperation is greatest in the guidance program which is designed to assist youth in the choice of a life goal and in the selection of occupational and other activities through which the goal may be attained.

If the church worker is to be of maximum assistance, he must understand the school life of the youth. He must know how the student is progressing in his schoolwork, how he behaves, what special interests he has developed, what points of strength and weakness are evident, and how he is liked by his teachers and his fellow students. This information, which is known by his teachers and his counselor, is usually available in the school records. Some of these records are confidential and cannot be given to out-of-school persons, but there is much valuable information that could be made available to the church worker.

SCHOOLS HELP DEVELOP LIFE GOALS

Although the schoolteacher and the counselor are barred from exerting any influence regarding the religious beliefs and activities of the youth, the very knowledge that the youth is active in the church may help them to understand his attitudes and conduct. It might aid the counselor in his attempt to give guidance toward life goals.

Especially in assistance in the selection of a life goal are the church and the school on common ground. In this country the basic ideals of character and conduct—honesty, integrity, obedience to authority, sincerity, industry, loyalty, and service to others—are evidences of good citizenship and are essential elements in Christian living. The special contribution of the church is to provide the religious incentive in the selection of a life goal and in the effort to attain the goal selected. Cooperation between school and church is often very difficult to develop, and great care must be taken that neither the public school nor the church assume the special rights and privileges of the other.

For many years there has been very effective cooperation between church and state in many areas of life. The church and church workers are basically committed to service of all kinds. In peace, in the ravages of war or epidemics, in destructive storms, in dealing with crime and delinquency, church workers of all denominations cooperate willingly to help those in need, with no consideration of their religious position. Cooperation between church and state is taken for granted. It seems strange that cooperation between church workers and the school for equally important ends should be considered undesirable.

CHURCH RESPONSIBILITY FOR GUIDANCE:
AN EXAMPLE

There have been, for many years, sporadic attempts at cooperation between churches and public schools, but they have been largely based on the initiative of individual schoolteachers, counselors, pastors, or church youth leaders. However, there have been some significant and interesting endeavors at more systematic cooperation. One of these attempts, initiated by the Department of Christian Vocations, the Board of Education, the Presbyterian Church in the U.S., in Richmond, Virginia, aims at providing vocational counseling in cooperation with public schools.

The name "Christian Vocations" might well lead one to think that this program was concerned primarily with the recruitment of young people for the ministry, missionary work, or other types of church work, but such is not the case. Without neglecting these vocations, the counselors include consideration of all kinds of honorable occupations, for they believe that any occupation can be a Christian vocation, since the goal of all occupations is service. Therefore, in counseling relating to choice of an occupation, they emphasize the opportunity for Christian service in all occupations. They also consider the usual elements such as kind of work, surroundings, ability needed, and chances for advancement. The reception given to this approach has been very encouraging. More than a thousand churches participate actively at various stages of the program's development. Seven colleges cooperated by providing counseling centers for instruction in the use of counseling techniques and in the giving and interpreting of tests of various kinds. In each church, the pastor and the director of Christian education give the actual counseling service. Helpful "counseling kits" are sent to each "vocational aide" of the church after he has been trained in their use. Local churches are urged to participate by (1) helping youth to acquire a Christian philosophy of life work; (2) assisting youth to plan intelligently for career decisions; (3) referring its youth to Presbyterian guidance centers, if available; (4) informing its youth about community guidance resources and how to use them; (5) encouraging its youth to follow up this guidance by community help; and (6) working to get its Presbyterian Synod to establish and support a Presbyterian guidance center.

Stimulated by the success of this project, the Presbyterian Church in the U.S.A. has inaugurated a similar project. A well-trained and experienced guidance specialist was appointed as general director of the project, and conferences were organized in which careful study was made of the responsibility of the church in the guidance of youth; methods of cooperation between the church and the public school were also discussed. The difficulties and dangers of such cooperation were clearly recognized, and plans were discussed for pilot projects in selected areas. Reports from these projects indicate definitely that such cooperation is not only possible but accepted eagerly by the school, the churches, and the community.

The basic purpose of the project is to help every youth to find a vocation which is right for him and through which he can express the values of a Christian vocation. In the course of working toward this goal, it is assumed that certain youth will accept church vocations. In fulfilling this purpose discussions among representatives from the churches, the schools, and the community centered on three questions. (1) What are the guidance needs of the young people of this community? (2) What is being done to meet these needs? (3) What yet needs to be done? Agreement was reached that both the church and the school have responsibilities in the area of vocational guidance.

The initial focus was on the relationship between the church and the public school and the points on which they might be able to serve one another. Up to the present time there seems to have been little difficulty in securing cooperation between them. Pastors and directors of young people in the churches do not think of themselves as trained counselors. They restrict their function for the most part to helping organize the program and making available information which will aid students in learning more about the vocations in which they are interested. The church worker does not exert pressure on the youth to become a minister but helps him choose an occupation that is suited to his ability and needs.

CHURCH RESPONSIBILITY FOR GUIDANCE:

A SECOND EXAMPLE

The following statement taken from a 1957 issue of the *Catholic Counselor* indicates the interest of the Roman Catholic Church in guidance for youth and the recognition of the importance of life goals that are centered upon and motivated by a religious belief that demands a life of service to others:

> The Catholic can impress upon the profession the need for helping individuals solve their problems, in terms of physical, mental, and spiritual phases, if the person is to live a full life and be able to give his utmost to job, family, and community. Here emphasis on the importance of the individual and his freedom to make choices can help to explain good guidance practices, as well as the Catholic viewpoint.

It is, of course, recognized that public schools cannot be concerned directly with choices related to church affiliations or religious beliefs. However, because both church and school share in a concern for the welfare of youth, there are many opportunities for them to cooperate in the field of guidance.

Summary

A life goal is not a gift from the gods; it is not inherited, although it is often strongly influenced, for good or bad, as pointed out previously, by parents, teachers, famine, disease, or the death of close friends. It develops slowly, often unconsciously, and it may be revised. It usually is not fully developed until maturity and sometimes not even then, but in adolescence the important elements begin to appear. Thus the period represented by the secondary school and college is of maximum importance in the development of a life philosophy. Guidance toward life goals lends itself especially well to group discussion, which may be supplemented from time to time by individual counseling. Here, again, teachers can be of great help.

In assisting a student in the selection of an occupation, we should help him to look beyond the occupation itself and to consider what sort of a person he wants to be. He needs to think of an occupation in terms of whether it will be helpful in satisfying his basic needs and enable him to move toward his ideal self. He must consider what sort of a life he wants to live. We should help him in defining his life goal. After this is done, he is ready to consider how the occupation under consideration will fulfill his needs.

Because a life goal has such great potential power for good or evil, it is also very important that it be one that is useful and constructive rather than one that is selfish, harmful, and destructive. One of the most powerful and constructive goals is that of service to others. This ideal has always been especially attractive to youth and should be stressed.

Both the school and the church have responsibilities in helping youth clarify their values and select occupations congruent with them. Many churches recognize their responsibility in this area and are actively working out ways to cooperate with the school in furthering the guidance of young people. Such cooperation, of course, needs to be done without violation of the American principle of separation of church and state.

Exercises

1. What do you see as the school's responsibility for guidance toward life goals? Are there differences between the proper roles of public and private schools in this matter?

2. Tell what churches in your community are doing to give guidance toward life goals. Discuss the meaning and techniques of pastoral counseling.

3. Select three public personalities whose reputations would be known to your classmates and decide what you think are their major life goals. Be prepared to elaborate and defend your decisions.

References

Barclay, James R.: *Counseling and Philosophy: A Theoretical Exposition*, Houghton Mifflin Company, Boston, 1968.

Hall, Robert King, and J. A. Lauwerys (eds.): *The Yearbook of Education, 1955: Guidance and Counseling*, Harcourt, Brace & World, Inc., New York, 1955.

Jones, Arthur J., and Harold C. Hand: "Guidance and Purposive Living," chap. 1 in *Guidance in Educational Institutions*, forty-seventh Yearbook, National Society for the Study of Education, part 1, Public School Publishing Company, Bloomington, Ill., 1938.

Kemp, C. Gratton: *Intangibles in Counseling*, Houghton Mifflin Company, Boston, 1967.

Miller, Carroll: *Foundations of Guidance*, Harper & Row, Publishers, Incorporated, New York, 1961.

15

Current Issues in Guidance

The past decade has witnessed some very important changes in the concept of guidance and in many of its techniques. The next decades will continue to change our world, our schools, and our guidance programs. What the morrow will bring we can but speculate, yet certain trends seem evident and certain changes predictable.

Changes in Guidance Programs

During the next decade our population will expand at an unprecedented rate. We will see a large increase in the age groups that are not economically self-supporting (the young and the old) and therefore a relative decrease of those of the middle-age group. There will be a continuation of the movement of Negroes into urban centers. Young workers will flood the labor market. Women workers already constitute more than one-third of the labor force. Most of these women are married, and many have children. School counselors therefore must take a girl's occupational planning as seriously as her marriage. A rapid increase in professional and technical workers and a decrease in farm workers is predicted. Automation will change the nature of and preparation for some occupations and reduce or even eliminate many present jobs. The family will continue to become less authoritarian. Marriage and birth rates as well as divorce rates seem to follow levels of prosperity, and the discipline of economics will be of more and more concern to the school counselor who is trying to understand his world and make occupational predictions. Finally, the relation of our nation and our culture to other nations is of supreme importance to youth today, and the school counselor cannot be ignorant of international trends and developments.

CHANGING PERCEPTIONS OF GUIDANCE PRACTICES

To be effective, the counselor must keep in touch with the frontiers of the science of human behavior. Among these are such divergent approaches as those expressed in psychoanalytic concepts and those of behaviorism. The neo-Freudian approach with its emphasis on the social as well as the biological elements may be particularly important to the future of guidance. The phenomenological explanation of behavior has already profoundly changed counseling techniques and may well influence guidance practices in still other ways.

Recent studies show that our older ideas of intelligence and aptitudes were far too simple. Our understanding of "talent" now goes far beyond performance in academic tasks, and we realize that the creative student is not necessarily the same as the talented student. Predictive appraisal by tests alone has been found to be far from sufficient, and new evaluative techniques must emerge.

CHANGES IN SCHOOLS WHICH WILL INFLUENCE
GUIDANCE

One of the important problems of the counselor is the relative attention he should give to developmental needs and how much to the crisis needs. In the future it is likely that he will spend more time on the psychological development of students and less on emotional first aid. The creative ability of students must receive as much attention as their handicaps. The counselor must be concerned both with intellectual development and vocational preparation and with a balance between socialization and individuality. Schools will be more concerned with helping students to solve problems with maximum competence and personal security, to grow in skill in evaluating evidence, and to develop their capacity for being mentally and culturally creative.

PROPOSED CHANGES IN GUIDANCE PRACTICES

At the present time elementary-school counselors are more likely to be assigned full-time guidance duties than are secondary-school counselors. These full-time counselors spend from one-fourth to one-third of their time in counseling individual students. Elementary-school counselors spend more time consulting with parents or teachers, and secondary-school counselors spend more in work with students. An overwhelming number of high-school counselors emphasize individual counseling with students, while elementary-school counselors see the clinical emphasis with children as being less important than working with teachers and parents and coordinating the counseling facilities in school and community.

In the future the confusing term "guidance services" should be abandoned and "pupil personnel services" used to designate the activities performed by a team of workers—school counselor, school psychologist, school social worker, school health worker, and school attendance worker. The counselor member of this team will (1) counsel a wide range of students using both individual and group approaches, (2) consult with parents and teachers as they have need for better understanding of individual pupils, (3) assume responsibility for continuing the study of the changing characteristics of the student population and interpreting this information to administrative and teaching staff for use in curriculum planning and in the development of administrative structure and regulations, and (4) serve as liaison among the various student personnel specialists and as coordinator of counseling resources within the school and community. (Pupil personnel services are discussed at greater length later.)

As is true of the members of many professions, the counselor will be both a generalist and a specialist—a generalist in the sense of knowing school resources thoroughly and being available to the total range of students and staff and a specialist in his specific knowledge of student behavior and in his understanding of the dynamics of human behavior generally.

At the elementary-school level there must also be a strong emphasis upon the early identification of both pupil talents and origins of nonsocial behavior. Elementary-school counselors must be particularly competent in diagnosis and in an understanding of play therapy, reading problems, and work with parents. Elementary-school and junior-high-school counselors are also responsible for the vocational counseling of students who may leave school at the end of the eighth or ninth grade.

PROPOSED CHANGES IN THE EDUCATION OF

COUNSELORS

Soon we must decide such major issues in the education of counselors as the amount and the kind of psychological preparation needed, the amount of attention given to an understanding of the changing nature of cultures, the means by which an understanding of school purposes and procedures is reached, and the development of research competencies together with counseling sensitivities.

The education of counselors must begin in the undergraduate program for no graduate program alone can provide the necessary cultural underpinning for the development of an educated as opposed to a "trained" counselor. It is proposed that the undergraduate program of some students be freed from the necessity of meeting the requirements of a teaching certificate as a prerequisite to the securing of teaching experience before becoming a counselor. The pattern might be (1) teaching experience of from one to four years, followed by graduate study and supervised counseling experience; (2) two years of graduate study directly following undergraduate work, one year of graduate work to be in full-time supervised internship, followed by one or two years in a paid position as a "junior counselor"; or (3) undergraduate education followed by several years' experience in any one of many life experiences which contribute to one's knowledge of human behavior and societal functioning, to be followed in turn by graduate study and supervised counseling experience in a school setting.

The following emphases in counselor education have been proposed:

1.   A minimal two-year graduate program for school counselors which would include one major core in psychology, emphasizing developmental and child psychology, personality growth and dynamics, and group psychology, and a second major core in the study of societal forces and culture changes involving the graduate areas of sociology, anthropology, economics, and international relations. This would also involve supervised experience in both individual counseling and planned group situations to the extent of not less than one-fourth of the total graduate program and provision for the essential applied or technique courses in counseling, measurement, educational and occupational information, etc., to the extent of not more than one-fourth of the total graduate program. There should also be training in elementary research methods, including an introductory understanding of electronic computer programming and the outcomes to be expected from computer use; an understanding of the basic educational philosophies and school curriculum patterns; and an introduction to the problems of ethical relationships and legal responsibilities in counseling.

2.   The graduate faculty in this field should give attention to the need for the graduate student in counselor education to understand himself through some form of personal counseling.

3.   There need to be professional associations in pupil personnel work to develop appropriate criteria of proficiency in counseling and to work with graduate schools on selection procedures.

4.   The state departments of education, in close collaboration with graduate schools, should modify state counselor certification requisites in order to require a block of graduate work in the social sciences and in the humanities and supervised experience as part of the graduate school program and to liberalize the experience requirements of state certification to permit the acceptance of various kinds of experience other than that of teaching, provided there is an adequate block of time as a supervised intern in a school situation.

Changes such as these may profoundly alter the training and duties of the school counselor over the next few years. As a consequence of such changes counselors should consider professional updating as a continuous process lest he become fixated at one level of understanding and practice while the world of psychological and sociological thought and practice moves on and leaves him behind. He should include in his continuing professional education graduate courses and public lectures in the social and behavioral sciences. He should travel widely as a planned part of his attempt to understand other cultures and peoples. He should study his own interviewing *habits and attitudes,* and secure professional assistance in this process whenever possible. He must attempt to understand himself better through counseling or other professional help. He should give thoughtful attention to his purposes and goals as a counselor. One crucial decision regarding counseling goals must be made by every school counselor: Is he a specialist for a few who are in trouble, or is he a specialist for many with normal growth problems? He should engage in self-study and in discussion with others to clarify his own deeply held convictions and ethical concepts so that greater personal insights and better counseling relationships will result. He should develop a program for living in a personally satisfying manner. He needs concerts, reading, travel, stimulating companionship, and a reservoir of deep emotional and spiritual experiences upon which to draw if he is to become, or remain, a person who is interesting to students and to colleagues. (The ideas in this section come largely from C. Gilbert Wrenn's *The Counselor in a Changing World.*)

Evaluation of Guidance

Evaluation is the process of finding the value of something. In evaluating a function like guidance, we attempt to find out to what degree the objective of the service has been attained. The objective of guidance is to assist individuals to develop the ability to be self-sufficient, to solve their own problems, and to make their adjustments. The following discussion will be divided into three parts: (1) evidences that are now often used to indicate the attainment of this goal, (2) methods used in evaluation, and (3) outline for a plan of evaluation in a school.

EVIDENCES OF SUCCESS

Many evidences of success in improving guidance have been described in the preceding pages. An increasing number of people are actively engaged in guidance, as can be seen by the membership in guidance associations, the success of journals devoted to guidance, and the attendance at annual conventions of guidance associations. The efforts to improve the training of guidance workers probably have resulted in better guidance programs.

More proof is seen in the efforts to increase the effectiveness of guidance instruments and techniques of counseling and in the reduction in the ratio of students to counselors. These and other examples of improvement permit us to have some optimism about the future of this movement.

METHODS OF EVALUATION

One approach to the evaluation of guidance is that used by the American Board on Professional Standards in Vocational Counseling. This organization has set up criteria for the approval of all agencies operating in the field of guidance. These criteria include professional and educational standards for the director of the agency and his staff, particularly as measured by membership in professional associations. Negative criteria include insistence that the agency have policies against serving its clients mainly or entirely by correspondence, assuming that adequate counseling can be completed in one interview, having a set number of interviews for every client, or basing counseling entirely on tests. Counselors in the agency must be prepared to use such tests as may be necessary, and the agency itself must have a program for professional development. The staff must be relatively stable, and systematic records of clients must be maintained. Any publicity must be dignified and in accordance with professional rather than commercial standards. If fees are charged, they must be in proportion to the service rendered; no fees may be given to others for referring clients or accepted for recommending that clients go to schools or other agencies. These standards, when applied by objective professional observers, guide the evaluation process and provide criteria by which success in establishing and maintaining a guidance agency may be judged.

The most frequent form of evaluation of guidance services consists in applying external criteria to the existing situation to determine whether the present program meets the standards that have been designated by experts as the mark of a satisfactory program. This application of external criteria may be made by the school staff, by outside experts, or by a combination of the two. This type of evaluation requires a survey of the present situation and provides direction for changes and improvements.

This method is not unlike that of the American Board on Professional Standards in Vocational Counseling except that the criteria deemed relevant are applied to a school rather than to an agency. Such criteria typically ask for judgments about the personnel involved, the physical facilities used, and the functioning of the several guidance services.

OUTLINE OF STEPS IN EVALUATION

The process of evaluation is the attempt to find the worth or value of any enterprise. The evaluation of the school guidance program is the attempt to find its value to the students. While evaluation is primarily concerned with the individual student, it also takes into account the school and society at large.

To evaluate a program of guidance we must take the following steps:

1. Clarify the objectives of the program. Are they valid, clearly stated, understood, and accepted by the guidance personnel, and are they attainable by the students concerned?

2. Consider the guidance personnel. Are they concerned with the guidance program; are they sufficient in number, adequate in training and personality to carry out the program? To what extent, if any, are classroom teachers included in the guidance program?

3. Consider the facilities. Are the facilities and time available for guidance work sufficient for an effective program?

4. Examine the available data about students to determine if they include tests and measurements, estimates and information by teachers, and information from outside the school supplied by family, employers, and others in the community.

5. Examine the records to determine if they are adequate, well kept, and available to all guidance personnel.

6. Consider the extent of cooperation with employers and college personnel. What opportunities are there for students to have conferences and personal contact with employers and college representatives for help in the selection of occupations and the choice of college?

7. The last step is to make judgments about the attainment of the objectives of guidance. Among the most common elements given by authorities for determining the success of a guidance program are the reduction in disciplinary cases in school, decrease in failures by individual students, better social adjustment, success in college or university, success in business and industry, salary, and job satisfaction.

By following these seven steps, we may arrive at a reasonable estimate of the extent to which the guidance program is achieving its objectives.

Pupil Personnel Services

There seems little doubt that guidance in the future will be thought of in a context of pupil personnel services. City-wide management of guidance will come under the direction of the superintendent or coordinator of pupil personnel services. This new conception of guidance services inevitably requires some definition and clarification of function. Otherwise, overlap, competition, and professional rivalry seem inevitable.

Although the organization of pupil personnel services has not been completely standardized, there are some generalizations which are frequent.

School psychology, nursing, school social work, and attendance workers are, perhaps, most frequently found in the pupil personnel bureau.

There is less uniformity with regard to educational researchers and special education teachers. In some cases, the director of special education may have control over all pupil personnel services. In other cases, special education is found under the direction of the coordinator of pupil personnel services. Perhaps the most frequent organization separates special education from pupil personnel work.

School psychology, since its inception in 1899 with the inauguration of a department of child study in Chicago, has grown rapidly. While the functions vary from district to district, in general they include child study, consultation with staff and parents, in-service education for staff, and research in the application of psychological principles to school learning. The focus of the school psychologist's concern is the relationship between the teacher and the child. While many school psychologists are presently limited to rather narrow assessment functions often related to special education, in the future they may perform broader functions. The professional relationship of the school psychologist to the school counselor is not always clearly defined. Because the school psychologist will typically have more training than the school counselor, a pecking order is sometimes established which puts the school psychologist ahead of the counselor. Such potential conflict leads to many questions. Should the school psychologist do psychotherapy? Should the school counselor ever give individual tests? Which one should be responsible for the education of parents and teachers regarding measurement?

School social work grew out of a concern with delinquency and the special problems of urban children around 1906 in the northeastern section of the United States. Early emphasis frequently was on problems of attendance. The number of school social workers doubled between 1950 and 1960, but there is still wide variation throughout the United States in the use of this pupil personnel specialist. Where he appears he is most apt to be concerned with casework on a supportive rather than on a long-term therapeutic basis. He makes referrals to community agencies and consults with parents and staff on such matters as child adjustment and growth and development. Through a series of historical accidents, the school social worker usually works with elementary-school children while school counseling is most prevalent at the secondary level; therefore there has been relatively little conflict between these two specialists until recently. Now that they have begun to invade each other's domains, questions do arise. Which students should be counseled by the social worker and which by the school counselor? Should the school counselor ever visit homes and work with parents or should this be left entirely to the social worker?

The school nurse has been a part of the American school since her introduction in 1892 into the New York City school system. Although the purpose of school nursing in the earlier days was to control contagious disease, the nurse is now more concerned with health appraisal, health counseling, and motivation for better health. One of the continuing concerns in the use of school nursing is the extent to which she is a school employee as opposed to a public health employee working for a county or similar governmental district. Too often in the past, she has been *in* but not *of* the schools. The newer trend sees her as an integral part of the school staff concerned with curriculum, pupil adjustment, etc. Obviously, as she becomes more central to the functioning of the school, possibility for conflict with other pupil personnel workers becomes greater.

Other pupil personnel workers may also find that their functions need greater clarification because of the greater complexity of pupil personnel services. Certainly the problem of who does what to whom becomes more difficult to answer as we increase the number, the levels of training, and the complexity of the pupil personnel staff.

The Emerging Technology of Guidance

The use of computers and other data processing machines may have a great influence on the work of the counselor in the future. Many tasks which have taken much of the counselor's time and kept him from using his professional skills may soon be performed by machines. When this happens, the counselor's role will be dramatically changed. No longer will he be a slave to routine work, but on the other hand, no longer will he be able to hide behind a paper curtain. He must then emerge into the professional spotlight where his skills can be evaluated without the excuse that he has no time to do what he has been trained to do.

Machines first made inroads into the counselor's clerical duties when they began to take over the job of scoring tests and providing such simple statistical results as medians, ranges, percentiles, and standard deviations. Before this time counselors spent hours handscoring tests. There is now no reason for them to continue such activities, except in those few cases where unusual tests are given or where the school itself is exceptionally isolated.

In many schools, machines are already making schedules. If you give a computer sufficient information about such matters as the staff, plant, courses that will be offered, and desired class size, the computer can design the schedule much more quickly and efficiently than can a human being. Beyond the making of the master schedule, which was sometimes a counselor's function although more generally that of an administrator, computers are also now doing the scheduling of individual students. A computer can determine more quickly and efficiently than can a counselor whether Johnny should have Algebra I second period or fifth period. Heretofore, scheduling the students into classes probably took more of the counselor's time than any one single activity. However, it has long been plain that this is a relatively routine task. Some schools have turned it over to secretaries, others have taught counselor aides to perform it, but the best current solution is to have this task performed by computers. Should the schools so desire, the computer can not only schedule, but provide class lists with whatever data about the individual student that are needed. Those who complain about the lack of personalization in such an activity need only to specify to the computer those personal elements which they want considered. The computer will take into account intelligence test scores, achievement scores, vocational goals, or any other matters which can be specified and fed into its memory.

Data processing machines can also be used for the storage and retrieval of personal data. The handwritten cumulative records can now be replaced by central data processing machines. The individual student is given a code number (sometimes the social security number is secured and used for this purpose), and information about him is fed periodically into the machine. Such information can include test scores, data about his home, school grades, school marks, tentative educational and vocational plans and, in short, all the information which is typically found in a cumulative record. When the counselor wants to retrieve this information, it can be done either by having the information appear on a screen where he can read it or by having it printed out so that he can have a summary of it. Counselors who have spent hours transferring test scores and other information to cumulative records, filing them, and finding them again can now have this time for the practice of counseling itself.

Another kind of information storage and retrieval lends itself to the dissemination of occupational information. The bulky occupational files may now be replaced by computers which may be at some central location, so that several schools can use them at the same time. A student who wishes information about a particular occupation can then retrieve it in the same manner as described above. In some cases, the computer may even "suggest" occupations that the student may want to think about in view of his school record or vocational plans.

Finally, a form of counseling has been taken over by computers in at least some experimental situations. Such counseling may more accurately be referred to as automated feedback of probabilities. But there is no suggestion here that this feedback is markedly different from what happens in many counseling interviews. For example, the student might indicate to the computer that he is planning to take third-year French next year and after high-school graduation go to the state university to major in chemistry. The computer, armed with much information about the university and about the student's background, may suggest to him that his chances of getting into the university are 1 in 3, and his chances for completing successfully a major in chemistry 1 in 50. Obviously, these predictions may be more precise and accurate than those typically made in the counseling interview. Furthermore, there is no implication here that the student must follow the probability pattern that gives him the best odds of success. The degree of risk taking that each student wishes is left to him, but the risk should be taken with some understanding of how great the risk is.

The intelligent use of computers for these and other activities should result in the human use of human beings. Counselors should be free for those exceptional situations in test scoring, scheduling, information discussion, and either personal or occupational counseling which merit the use of their valuable time. Routine activities which can be done by a machine should be left to the machine.

Some states are obviously far ahead of others in this new trend. In some cases, small districts have banded together to make the best use of computers. Sometimes a county organization provides computer help to many schools. In at least one case, the state has divided itself into regions with the thought that large regional data processing centers will provide coverage for the total state. When this electronic revolution is more completely developed, the counselor more than ever will be called upon to use his highest level of skills for counseling and those other activities which call for an understanding of individuals and of the school as a social system.

Counselor Aides

With increased need for the skills of professional educational workers, there has developed a movement toward allocating some of their less demanding duties to workers trained at subprofessional levels. Teacher aides were the model for this movement, and their work in the classroom was so successful that attempts are now being made to duplicate this differentiation of function in the guidance program.

These new workers are variously named as subprofessional guidance workers, paraprofessional guidance workers, counselor aides and assistant counselors. There is as yet no agreement with regard to the kind of person this should be or what duties he should perform. In some cases, the counselor aide may be someone with a college degree who has a few weeks of training in guidance. In other cases, they may have much less education and be trained only on the job. The federal government underwrote training in this area for the special needs of the "poverty programs." It requires no great imagination to separate from the counselor's duties a number which could be performed by counselor aides. The aide might be particularly valuable in the area of test administration, scoring, and recording and in the dissemination of occupational information. Some schools have trained secretaries to do the class scheduling which has absorbed so much of the counselor's time for so long. One advantage is that the counselor aide may provide a much better social model than the counselor himself, particularly if the social class distance between the counselor aide and the student is less than that between the counselor and the student.

Tomorrow's counselor may find himself in the position of a physician surrounded by many paraprofessional workers who will permit him to utilize his professional skills without spending a great deal of time on work which could be done by others. The physician with his laboratory technicians, nurses, nurses aides, etc., has been freed for strictly professional activities, and the counselor may soon join him in this professional freedom.

This movement, of course, has obvious implications for the selection and education of counselors who are going to supervise counselor aides and manage the guidance function so that they themselves will have time for such crucial activities as counseling. Tomorrow's counselors will need training in supervision, job analysis, and in-service training of aides. Ever more important, they must come to their jobs prepared to counsel.

Federal Support

Federal support of counseling and guidance programs through a number of national laws has provided a great impetus for the school counseling movement. Many counselors now in the schools received their professional training with the help of the National Defense Education Act Institutes which were designed to train or upgrade counselors while they received stipends making such education possible for them. Federal laws have also provided the basis for a number of demonstration and research projects dealing with the disadvantaged children or other special populations which have used the skills of school counselors. Sometimes these programs were run in conjunction with a regular school program; at other times they were in separate institutions which were supported by the federal government, such as the Job Corp and Neighborhood Youth Corps.

The future will disclose whether federal support will enable school counselors to demonstrate their value in such a way that schools will continue supporting counseling if and when federal support is withdrawn. Certainly, the philosophy behind categorical aid (that is, money given for specified purposes) has enabled the expansion and improvement of school counseling. However, it may at the same time have alienated certain bodies of the educational establishment who would prefer general aid (for the general improvement of education), which would permit the local school district or perhaps the state department of education to determine how the funds are to be used. Will federal aid result in teachers and administrators viewing the guidance program as an "extra" which has its place in the schools only to the extent that the federal government is willing to support it? If such a view prevails, federal aid may well prove to have been a most expensive innovation from the standpoint of the school counselor.

Professionalization of Counseling

The last few years have seen a strong movement toward the professionalization of school counseling. This movement has followed the pattern of that of most occupations when they strive to become more professional.

The functions of the counselor have been sorted out in a fashion which gives greater status to individual counseling and less to that which concerns itself with clerical and administrative duties. This aping of the independent professional is characteristic of increasing professionalization. In some cases, these "lesser" duties are now being assigned to counselor aides, and of course, in some cases they have been taken over by computers and other data processing machines.

Other characteristic marks of professionalization are increased membership in professional organizations, greater attention to ethics, and raising of entrance requirements. School counselors are encouraged to join the American School Counselors Association, which is a division of the American Personnel and Guidance Association. While at the present time it is probably true that less than half of the school counselors in America belong to this organization, they may express their professional aspirations through membership in comparable state or local organizations. The relevant professional journals are *The School Counselor* and the *Personnel and Guidance Journal.* The percentage of school counselors who regularly read these two journals is not known exactly, but research in the early sixties indicated that only about one-third did so.

Rehabilitation counselors join the American Rehabilitation Counselors Association, which is also a division of the American Personnel and Guidance Association. The seven other divisions of this parent organization are designed for still other guidance specialists, and each of the divisions has its professional journal.

Professionalization characteristically causes conflict, and the movement among school counselors is no exception. Simultaneous with the move toward greater specialization, toward higher ethical and professional standards, and toward raising of certification requirements, professional negotiations for guidance specialists have emerged, particularly in schools. Professional negotiations may be likened to the collective bargaining of unions and is a way by which the combined working staff of the school system join together to increase their salaries and improve their working conditions. Because the school counselor is a minority group in any such movement, his interests may not be well protected. At least in some cases, professional negotiations have spelled out in detail precisely what the counselor will and will not do. Sometimes these definitions enhance the professional level of the counselor, but in other cases they seem to have interfered with the movement toward professionalization. Because teachers are usually the strongest voice in such negotiations with school boards, the counselor may find it difficult to rid himself of such activities as discipline and attendance control because the teachers see these as institutionally valuable activities and believe that the school counselor is best placed to carry them out.

This dynamic tension between professionalization on the one hand and "unionization" on the other (even though it may not involve actual membership in or activity through labor unions) will continue to cause strife and conflict in the realm of school counseling. It is hoped that school counselors will find some way of integrating their desire for more professional behavior with their equally understandable desire for better working conditions and wages.

Summary

A variety of social forces have led to changes in the school guidance program. Numbered among these forces are social changes, changing perception of the counselor's role as well as of the school as an institution, and changes in the education of counselors.

Increasing attention is being given to the process of evaluating guidance programs, and the importance of the appropriate interaction between goals and techniques in evaluation is stressed.

Pupil personnel services are emerging as a new professional context in which the school counselor works, and it becomes necessary to separate his role from that of the other pupil personnel specialists.

The use of computers and other electronic devices as well as the introduction of counselor aides will free the counselor from clerical work. It is hypothesized that this second "industrial revolution" may do much to change the nature of school counseling in the future.

The consequences of federal support for guidance programs are not now clear, and the future will need to add up the balance sheet of such support.

Finally, the tension between drive for professionalization and drive for better working conditions and salary may place new strains on guidance workers. Whether one of these movements will cancel out the other or whether a higher integration of the two is possible is uncertain at this time.

Certainly, it is clear that the role expectation and status of the school counselor are in a process change. Each edition of this book has reported many changes, and the present guidance programs are not static but continually changing to reflect the dynamic nature of American society.

Exercises

1. Read an issue of one of the journals listed in this chapter and be prepared to discuss the extent to which the articles would be useful to a school counselor.

2. Talk to a student, a teacher, and an administrator at the same school and learn their ideas regarding the strong and weak points of the guidance program.

3. Interview a school psychologist, school nurse, school social worker, or other pupil personnel worker and report their activities and their relationship to school counselors.

References

Brewer, John M.: *History of Vocational Guidance*, The Macmillan Company, New York, 1942.

Landy, Edward, and Arthur M. Kroll (eds.): *Guidance in American Education III: Needs and Influencing Forces*, Harvard Graduate School of Education, Cambridge, Mass., 1966.

Miller, Carroll: *Foundations of Guidance*, Harper & Row, Publishers, Incorporated, New York, 1961.

Stone, Shelley C., and Bruce Shertzer (eds.): *Guidance Monograph Series* (see especially *The Function of Theory in the Guidance Program*, Merville C. Shaw; *The Function of Counseling Theory*, Buford Stefflre and Kenneth Matheny; and *Controversial Issues in Testing*, James R. Barclay), Houghton Mifflin Company, Boston, 1968.

Wrenn, C. Gilbert: *The Counselor and a Changing World*, The Commission on Guidance in American Schools, American Personnel and Guidance Association, Washington, D.C., 1961.

INDEX

This book was set in Fairfield by Monotype Composition Company, Inc., and printed on permanent paper and bound by The Maple Press Company. The designer was Paula E. Tuerk; the line drawing was done by Edward Malsberg. The editors were Steven J. Melmeck and Helen Greenberg. Les Kaplan supervised the production.

DATE DUE

APR 19 '71	APR 18 '71		
MAY 2 '71	MAY 2 '71		
JUN 30 '71			
GAYLORD			PRINTED IN U.S A.